BEYOND SIX SIGMA STATISTICS

LYLE DOCKENDORF

Beyond Six Sigma Statistics
Copyright © 2024 by Lyle Dockendorf

Published in the United States of America

Library of Congress Control Number: 2024900144
ISBN   Paperback: 979-8-89091-436-1
ISBN   eBook: 979-8-89091-437-8

All rights reserved. No part of this publication may be reproduced, stored in a retrieval system or transmitted in any way by any means, electronic, mechanical, photocopy, recording or otherwise without the prior permission of the author except as provided by USA copyright law.

The opinions expressed by the author are not necessarily those of ReadersMagnet, LLC.

ReadersMagnet, LLC
10620 Treena Street, Suite 230 | San Diego, California, 92131 USA
1.619. 354. 2643 | www.readersmagnet.com

Book design copyright © 2024 by ReadersMagnet, LLC. All rights reserved.

Cover design by Ericka Obando
Interior design by Daniel Lopez

Three major software suites were used in performing statistical analyses in support of this book:

- Minitab is a registered trademark of Minitab, Inc. Many of the formal graphs in this manuscript were created using Minitab software.
- Microsoft is a registered trademark of Microsoft Corporation. In this manuscript "MS" is sometimes used to indicate Microsoft. Some supporting analyses were performed using MS Excel.
- JMP and SAS JMP are registered trademarks of SAS Institute, Inc.

Within the book itself, these different software packages will not be specifically marked as trademarks.

TABLE OF CONTENTS

1. Introduction 1
   — Intent of this Book 3
2. Review of Basic Operational Six Sigma 6
   — DMAIC 7
   — Details of the Statistical Tools 8
3. Project Considerations 14
   — Project Selection 14
   — Conflicting Projects 15
   — Defect Definition 16
   — Non-Statistical Tools 17
4. Data Basics 19
   — Data 19
   — Distributions 20
   — Metrics 23
   — Outliers 25
5. Measurement Systems Analysis 29
   — Definitions 30
   — Statistical Considerations 33
   — Comprehensive Gage Study 35
   — Variance Component Analysis 37
   — Tester Correlation 40
   — Orthogonal Regression 42
   — A Few More Thoughts on Correlation 46
   — Metrics 47
   — Linearity 50

- — Part-Dependent, Systematic Measurement Error 51
- — Destructive Testing 55
- — Confidence Intervals and Gage Sigmas 56
- — Isolating Repeatability Error 57
- — Isolating Reproducibility Error 59
- — Stability 61
- — Short-Term and Long-Term Concerns 62
- — Composite Gage Errors 62
- — A General Word of Caution 65

6. Process Capability 67
   - — Short-Term versus Long-Term Capability 68
   - — Improvement Targets 69
   - — Non-normal Data 70
   - — Statistical Specifications 71
   - — The Taguchi Loss Function 76
   - — The Taguchi Loss Function Cost Metric 77

7. Probability 88
   - — Expected Values 91
   - — Bayes Theorem 93

8. Hypothesis Testing and Sample Size: 1 and 2 Populations 97
   - — Type I and Type II Risks 98
   - — Variables Cases: Means and Standard Deviations 101
   - — Special Cases: Tolerance Intervals and Cpk 103
   - — Attribute Cases: Proportions and Counts (or Rates) 104
   - — Sampling, a Special Case 108

9. Hypothesis Testing and Sample Size: Three or More Populations ... 111
   - — Variables Case: Means 111
   - — Variables Case: Standard Deviations 117
   - — Special Consideration: the Chi-Square Goodness of Fit Test . 117
   - — Attribute Case: Proportions 118
   - — Attribute Case: Counts or Rates 119
   - — Sample Sizes for Multiple Proportions, Rates and Goodness of Fit Tests 122

10. Batch Process Statistics 123
   — Hypothesis Testing with Batch Processes 131
   — Other Batch Process Scenarios 132

11. Regression 134
   — Linear One-Variable Regression 135
      Binned Regression 139
   — Linear Multiple-Variable Regression 140
      Pool of Potential Predictors 141
      Metrics 142
      Choosing the Best Models to Explore 144
      Collinearity and Multicollinearity 145
      Model Checking: Residual Analysis 147
      Model Verification 148
   — Common Mistakes Regarding Regression 150
   — Error in the Predictor Variables 153
   — Non-linear Regression 155
   — Conclusion 156

12. Non-Parametric Statistics 158

13. Experimentation 160
   — The Design of the Experiment 161
   — Highly Fractionated Designs 165
   — Alternative Designs 166
   — Design for Robustness 172
   — Analysis of Goodness 174
   — Design of Experiments for Standard Deviations 176
   — Optimizing Multiple Responses 178
   — Verification and Validation 179
   — Taguchi Designs 182

14. Statistical Process Control 184
   — Common Errors 185
   — Proper Subgroup Size and Sampling Frequency 189
   — SPC for Gages 196
   — Alternative Charting Methods 202
      Pre-Control 203

  Process Control Charts 203
  Weighted Charts 205
  Low Occurrence Attribute Chart 206
  Other Charting Methods 207
 — Appendix: Short Run SPC 209

15. Critical Thinking 214

16. Advanced Topics 222
 — Acceptance Sampling 223
 — Reliability 228
 — Binary Logistic Regression 233
 — Monte Carlo Simulation 234
 — Time Series Analysis 237
 — Other Advanced Methods 238

17. References 239

18. Index 241

CHAPTER 1

INTRODUCTION

Six Sigma is more than a slogan. It's the real thing.

In the late 1990's, Six Sigma was becoming a major force in the practice of quality in the United States and elsewhere. The founders, starting with Mikel Harry and Motorola, were able to merge a strategy with multiple tools and created an effective method to solve chronic production problems. The majority of these tools were statistical in nature, and nothing about them was novel. But the emphasis on their use in a specific structured manner *was* new.

Perhaps the most important development in the proliferation of these statistical tools was the easy access to Windows-based computer programs that allowed the investigators to easily choose among a large variety of analytic options. These programs could then be run, producing useful tabular results or relevant graphs. The user no longer needed to toil through the calculations—or even understand them!

I was lucky to be involved in the initial stages of the implementation of Six Sigma at Seagate Technology. In a previous job at IBM I had been a physicist-turned-statistician, and had a consulting role there for over eleven years as a member of what was called the Statistical Competency Center. Although the main charter of this group was to act as an on-call resource for statistical help, we also tried to increase the use of statistical tools by offering classes in general statistics, SPC, hypothesis testing, and Design of Experiments. Unfortunately, our efforts only had limited success. For the most part engineers preferred to use their knowledge of the physical world as well as intuition in a trial-and-error approach.

At Seagate at their Normandale facility (which straddled Edina and Bloomington, both suburbs of Minneapolis, MN) I had come in as a Quality Engineer with knowledge in thin-film processing. But when the decision came to implement Six Sigma it quickly became clear that a statistician would be needed both as a resource in facilitating the proper use of the statistical tools and also as an instructor. The original Six Sigma charter called for Master Black Belts (MBBs) who could do effectively all the important tasks: mentor, work complicated projects, be liaisons to management (at all levels), develop new tools appropriate to the business, and teach. But Seagate wisely rejected this paradigm of the MBB who could walk on water. And so they created the specialized MBB position whose main task was to instruct new Black Belts and Green Belts, and develop and present relevant "deep dive" (i.e. advanced topic) classes. Following completion of Black Belt and Master Black Belt training provided by the Six Sigma Academy, I became one of these MBB trainers.

The earliest set of tasks that I had in this new position was to collaborate with others in creating Seagate's own teaching material, since specific teaching aids for this hadn't been provided. Thus I was intensely involved in writing out MS PowerPoint slides, creating practice data sets, and producing Minitab output with the purpose of showing engineers how the different statistical tools worked and when they should be applied. From the Black Belt material which comprised about 18 days of training (including project reviews), we then created a 10-day class for Green Belts.

Besides teaching this material, I provided consultation on Six Sigma, primarily with regard to statistical applications. I would often get the questions that the mentoring MBBs couldn't adequately answer. But I also began developing new statistical tools, often in the form of MS Excel spreadsheets. One of the first involved calculating sample sizes for hypothesis testing. The earliest commercial software programs had not included Poisson rates nor the comparison of two standard deviations; I was able to provide software tools to easily calculate these. And even the calculations for proportions were questionable, which I tried to improve on.

As time went on, my work involved significantly helping develop and then exclusively teaching a 3-day class for technicians which we called Orange Belt training. By this time others at Seagate had created a transactional version of Black Belt and Green Belt training, and I used some of that material along with my own examples to develop a 2-day Orange Belt version for administrative assistants.

Through the next ten years I enjoyed solving the practical problems that the engineers brought to me. Besides applying common statistical methods, I often developed techniques and created calculating tools that further facilitated achieving more optimal solutions. Many of these techniques and tools make up a substantial portion of this book.

As demand grew from the engineers for learning more about statistics, I became a principal contributor in the creation of a new 9-day class called "Advanced Statistics." This class involved deeper investigation into standard statistical methods as well as an introduction into new topics such as reliability. But I also used this class to include the knowledge of many of those new ideas and techniques I had developed. I also co-developed a 16-hour "Advanced Measurement Systems Analysis" class and created a 6-hour "Reliability Using Minitab" class, both of which used some of my tools.

Intent of this Book

In a sense, I am a "renegade" statistician. Although I had a very strong mathematical education in college, I've had very little formal training in statistics. Most of what I've learned came from self study, which was often driven by trying to find solutions to practical problems posed by the engineers with whom I worked. Thus, much of my education involved learning about and implementing practical applied statistical methods. One thing I tended to avoid in my interactions with engineers was pushing the theory underlying the techniques. Even though exact solutions might be attainable through the application of more complex (and time-consuming) methods, I understood that for all practical purposes, most engineers needed only something fairly quick and relatively easy to apply, even if it wasn't exact.

I also learned that despite all the warnings about the "proper" use of the statistical technique being used, such as making sure that the variance is homogeneous when dealing with ANOVA or regression, engineers were still getting workable, although not perfect solutions to their problems by not strictly adhering to these rules. Typically, Six Sigma was getting them 80% of the way to a perfect solution, even when the tools were being somewhat misused. This was a substantial improvement over the quick-fix mentality that had been prevalent. The lesson here is that although there may be optimal ways to solve a statistical problem, that doesn't mean that it's the best practical way to solve an engineering problem. And it is extremely important to realize that engineers favor easy-to-use tools without necessarily having to understand what makes them work. (In a way, this is how they approach much of their equipment! Just as a TV viewer doesn't care how a TV works, most engineers don't care how an RF tube facilitates the creation of a plasma so that a thin film can be deposited. But if certain conditions must be met for this to happen, the engineer is vitally interested in those conditions.) Therefore, in teaching engineers I usually avoided all but the most essential theory.

Now I want to share this accumulated knowledge to a broader audience. But rather than repeat what is commonly known about Six Sigma statistics, I want to go beyond the standard methods and show many new ideas and techniques, along with lessons learned through over 20 years of practical statistical consulting. So this book will contain:

- Helpful ideas in solving problems
- Useful techniques to improve one's analysis
- Novel ways of looking at old problems
- New techniques that are not commonly known
- Warnings of disastrous assumptions that ruin an analysis

This book is intended for those who have already completed the equivalent of the statistics portion of Black Belt training. In the next chapter I will outline this basic knowledge so that I can assume a common background and language, and not get bogged down in explanations of what should be already known.

The target audience is engineers who want to enhance their problem solving skills—without becoming statisticians themselves. Master Black Belts in particular will benefit greatly from learning about new approaches to problems, or even methods that they didn't know existed. I ask the reader to take what is useful to him or her at present, and try to remember the basics of the rest of the book.

Within this book I will attempt to write somewhat informally, sometimes as if I were actually in a consulting situation. In many instances I will have to provide the statistical theory behind the technique or tool so as to give greater credibility to its use, but I do not intend this to be a work with so much rigor that portions could be published in professional journals such as the *Journal of Quality Technology* or *Quality Engineering*. In many applications close approximations are advocated rather than potentially non-existent exact solutions, again following the principle that getting somewhat close to a solution is better than none at all, especially in the engineering world where each one percent improvement in a process can mean millions of dollars.

Typically I will only cite other statisticians and writers where I know they had a major impact on the tool I am advocating. In most of my work I have used the basic knowledge of statistics, probability and numerical analysis to develop what I considered to be new solutions to existing problems. It is very possible that others have discovered the same solution or a variant of it, and have even published their findings. Certainly in some cases I've "reinvented the wheel." But I do not consider whatever duplication I may be doing to be plagiarism; in all honesty I often just saw a problem and found a solution.

Every statistician owes a debt of gratitude to all those men and women who have made both major and minor contributions to statistics and quality. For me, these include Ronald Fisher, George Snedecor, George Box, Søren Bisgaard, W. Edwards Deming, Joseph Juran, and Doug Montgomery. Hundreds of others made smaller impacts in one way or another. But it was Bill Diamond and his class in DOE who first demonstrated for me the real value of using correct hypothesis testing and efficient experiment designs. He opened the door to a field that I've enjoyed ever since.

CHAPTER 2

REVIEW OF BASIC OPERATIONAL SIX SIGMA

*Without first understanding and implementing the
basics, no advanced methods will be effective.*

Before I can go into the statistics *beyond* Six Sigma, it is necessary to first cover what Six Sigma basically covers. Essentially this defines the knowledge and exposure the reader is already assumed to have, and provides a framework from which to proceed. Otherwise too much of this book will be spent in review. In some cases review will be necessary, because the new methods or techniques will be an expansion or even a correction of the standard procedure.

Also, at most companies Six Sigma is somewhat personalized. So some tools may be deemphasized or perhaps given more emphasis. The American Society for Quality (ASQ) has published its version of the body of knowledge it expects within Six Sigma. I will cover a mildly abbreviated version, and provide much more focus on the statistical tools—not that they are more important, but because they most directly affect the assumptions I am making about reader's statistical knowledge.

Six Sigma begins with the DMAIC strategy:

Define

- Understand the Customer requirements
- Map Key Process Output Variables (KPOVs) to these requirements
- Select specific KPOVs for improvement
- Create a Project by scoping its size and writing a problem definition
- Assign resources to the Project

Measure

- Basic uses of statistics: descriptors, graphics, normality
- Understand the KPOV
    - Collect data on the KPOV; determine its capability to meet specifications; determine baseline
    - Map out the process that creates the KPOV
    - Assess the capability of the KPOV measurement system
- Begin the search for the Key Process Input Variables (KPIVs) [some consider this to be part of Analyze Phase]
    - Pareto Analysis
    - FMEA
    - Cause & Effect analysis: Fishbones and Matrices, Root Cause Analysis, Affinity Diagrams

Analyze

- Test the potential KPIVs to see their effect on the KPOV
    - Confidence Intervals
    - Hypothesis Testing
    - Sample Size Determination
    - ANOVA
    - Regression
    - Contingency Tables
    - Non-parametric analyses
- Narrow down the list to likely important KPIVs

Improve

- Narrow down the list to critical KPIVs
  - Experiments: design and analysis
- Choose and verify a solution
- Pilot the solution

Control

- Implement a large-scale solution
  - Set up procedures for integrating the solution into the process
- Set up procedures to maintain the improvement
  - Control Plans
  - Error Proofing / 5S
  - Statistical Process Control (SPC)
- Document the lessons learned

There is also generally a financial aspect that occurs during the execution of the project, and that involves tracking savings resulting first through intermediate process changes and then projecting, perhaps out to a year, what the implementation of the solution is expected to save. At this point the Black Belt has completed "Realization," and can walk away from the project.

Details of the Statistical Tools

Generally, each Operational Black Belt is expected to understand the following statistical tools in particular ways, including performing calculations to estimate various metrics or at least to apply a statistical computer program to perform the calculations.

Basic Statistics

- Types of data: continuous, discrete (counts or proportions)
- Descriptors: mean, median, mode, range, standard deviation
- Population parameters versus sample statistics
- Basic probability calculations: Z score, Poisson, Binomial, "dice"
- Graphics: histograms, scatter plots, boxplots, outliers

- Distributions: normal, uniform, skewed, normality test (such as Anderson-Darling or normal probability plotting), probability distributions
- Pareto Analysis

Process Capability

- Types: long-term versus short-term
- Processes distributed normally
- Metrics: Cp, Cpk, Pp, Ppk, Z score, σ score, % nonconforming
  · Conversions from one to another (when possible)
- Time-based performance: basic X-bar/R charts
- Non-normal continuous distributions: lognormal, exponential, Weibull (perhaps), batch processes (between/within)
- Discrete distributions: Binomial and Poisson

Measurement Systems Analysis

- Effect of measurement error on process capability estimates
- Sources of error from the measurement system
  · Accuracy: bias and mis-calibration
  · Precision: repeatability and reproducibility
  · Resolution (e.g. # of decimal places)
- Metrics: σ_{Gage}, P/T, P/TV, %R&R, Discrimination Ratio
- Standard gage study and its analysis
  · Procedure: 10 parts measured by 2-4 operators, 2 or 3 times
  · Understanding computer output

Standard Testing of Basic Statistical Measures

- Concept of a Confidence Interval (CI): probability and range
  · Population parameters versus sample parameters
- Concept of Hypothesis Testing
  · Null and alternative hypotheses
  · Type I (α) and Type II (β) errors
  · One-sided (> or <) and two-sided ($\neq$) tests
- Calculations and conclusions: CI and hypothesis tests

- p-values
- Means: μ and $\mu_1-\mu_2$ with σ known and unknown, paired means; normal and t-distributions
- Standard deviations: σ, σ_1/σ_2; Chi-square and F distribution; three or more σ's; Bartlett's test
- Proportions: π and $\pi_1-\pi_2$; Binomial and approximations
- Rates: R and R_1/R_2; Poisson and approximations

Analysis of Variance (ANOVA)

- Concept of ANOVA: testing the means of different levels by comparing mean-to-mean variation to within-mean variation
  - Assumptions: homoscedasticity (equality of variances), independence of observations, independence and normality of errors
- ANOVA model and table
- One-way ANOVA
  - Residual plots: histograms, normal plot, residuals vs. fitted, residuals vs. run order, outliers
- Two-way ANOVA
  - Balanced versus unbalanced designs
  - Method of General Linear Models applied to ANOVA
  - Interaction terms
  - Blocking
  - Main-effects plots and interaction plots
  - Multi-vari charts
  - Comparison of means for significant differences
- N-way ANOVA

Regression

- Concept of *Linear* Regression (vs. Nonlinear)
  - Purpose: prediction, variable screening, system explanation, and parameter estimation
  - Response as a function of predictor variables
  - Method of least squares

- Assumptions: homoscedasticity, independence of observations, no error in predictors, independence and normality of errors
- Single variable predictor
  - Linear, quadratic and cubic equations
  - Graphical output
    - Confidence and predictor intervals
  - R^2 and R^2-adjusted
  - Residual plots: histograms, normal plot, residuals vs. fitted, residuals vs. run order, residuals vs. predictor or other variables
  - Influential observations: outliers and leverage points
- Multiple variable regression
  - Selection strategies
    - Best subsets; forward, backward and stepwise selection
    - Using R^2-adjusted
    - Parsimony (i.e. favoring models with fewer predictors)
  - Collinearity and multicollinearity: VIFs
    - Handling collinearity due to polynomial terms
    - Standardizing or normalizing predictors
  - Diagnostics: residual plots, patterns, checking prediction capability, influential observations
  - Indicator variables for qualitative variables

Non-parametric statistics

- Concept of non-parametric tests: small samples or non-normal
- Assuring non-normal distribution is not a known distribution nor is caused by extra factors
- Box-Cox transformations
- One-way testing: sign test, Wilcoxon signed-rank test
- Two-way testing: Kruskal-Wallis test, Mood's median test
- Standard deviation testing: Levene's test

Design of Experiments

- Strategy of experimentation
- One Factor at a time versus *designed* experiments

- Full factorial designs: 2^2, 2^3, 2^n, generalized designs
  - Factors, levels and coded values
  - Center points and blocking
  - Main effects and interactions
  - Sample size
  - Graphics: Pareto, main effects, interaction and cube plot
  - Replicates versus repeats
  - Randomization of runs
  - Diagnostics: residuals
- Fractional factorial
  - 2^{k-p}
  - Confounding, defining relations, aliasing
  - Design resolution: III, IV, V
  - Foldover designs
  - Screening and saturated designs: Plackett-Burman
- Response surface methodology (not all BBs are exposed to this)
  - Central composite rotatable designs
    - Augmenting full or fractional designs
    - Reduction of model
    - Path of steepest ascent (descent); gradient
    - Contour plots
    - Optimum
  - 3^k, 3^{k-p} and Box-Behnken designs

Statistical Process Control (SPC)

- Natural versus special-cause variation
- Control limits as a 3σ confidence interval on a mean
- Types of charts: $\bar{x}$, R, s, I-mR, batch-process (I-MR-R/s), p, np, c, u
- Calculation of control limits
  - Rational subgroups
- Eight tests for special causes
  - Out-of-control action plans
- Alternative charting methods: MA (moving average), EWMA, CUSUM (this subset is often taught optionally)

Give or take a few tools or methods, these represent the main body of the statistical knowledge that a Six Sigma practitioner (e.g. operational Black Belts and some Green Belts) are expected to be exposed to and hopefully use depending on the project. A good training course will show what the method is, demonstrate how it is to be used, describe limitations, provide examples, and give the students the opportunity to practice the tool with an exercise or two (often combined with the application of previous knowledge). As the student works a first project in conjunction with the training, the hope is that the student will apply the tools shortly after he/she has learned them, giving still another opportunity for the absorption of the training material—especially as it applies to the real world.

CHAPTER 3

PROJECT CONSIDERATIONS

A good first project is not one that will result in substantial savings. It's one in which the Black Belt learns the tools and strategy thoroughly so that he can apply that knowledge later to achieve even bigger savings.

Project Selection

Fundamental to the success of a Six Sigma project is the proper selection of the project itself. Although it is not commonly considered a phase, the preliminary activity of project selection is extremely important, and should have its own set of tools and techniques for optimizing the choice of projects being worked on. The lack of a template for proper project selection severely handicapped Seagate in the initial stages of its Six Sigma implementation. Early projects were chosen because of their high financial impact, but the basic infrastructure necessary for completing the projects in a reasonable amount of time was missing. There were no Green Belts to provide support, many KPIVs had no means of measuring them, KPOV measurements were often inadequate, and the projects themselves were often very large.

    I believe that choosing a big project for a new Black Belt's first project is a major mistake. It is best that this earliest of projects for a new Black Belt actually be fairly simple, since this should be considered a learning experience rather than a resource-saving endeavor. (Unfortunately, when a company first starts Six Sigma they often feel compelled to get rapid financial savings so as to justify the program. In the long run I believe this attitude works against them.) Furthermore, it is far more optimal if the training follows more closely a just-in-time schedule. That is, the student should be able to get through most of the Measure Phase activities before starting the Analyze Phase training; get through most of the Analyze Phase activities before the Improve Phase training; etc. If the timing is right, the new Black Belt's activities are able to reinforce the training. Otherwise they have to go back and try to figure out a tool when much of the training regarding that tool has been forgotten. It is far better if the mentoring at this stage involves supporting the application of a tool in a real world application rather than a review of how to exercise the tool.

Unfortunately, the scheduling of the training and the complexity of the project seldom allow for this "luxury." The originally proposed scheduling by the earliest trainers involved only a 3-week period between training phases. This can work only if the project is very simple. Choosing, organizing and meeting with a team which already has many other commitments is itself calendar-time consuming. And so are all the other activities—particularly in Measure Phase. Too often the new Black Belt immediately falls behind and can never catch up to the training. Thus, it is probably best to extend the interim period between Measure and Analyze training to five or six weeks.

For subsequent projects, completing them in a reasonable amount of time is an important goal.

Conflicting Projects

There is another caution that may be applicable when first starting a Six Sigma initiative. Often critical processes logically get a lot of attention, and there is a tendency to start multiple projects that focus on different aspects of a specific process. Unfortunately, two negative things happen. The first is that the several Black Belts may call on the same people to help on their team. These new team members are often critical to running the everyday operations, and this multiple demand on their time can either have a deleterious effect on the process or create in the members a negative attitude against Six Sigma. The second problem results from several Black Belts making changes to the process simultaneously, which can result in suboptimization, the canceling out of the gains, or even the deterioration of the entire process because of unforeseen consequences. It is essential that these Black Belts have frequent meetings with each other to share lessons learned and to coordinate their strategies.

Defect Definition

The goal of most Operational Six Sigma projects is to reduce defects. When the defect has a clear pass/fail criterion, such as a circuit being open or shorted, or a machined part has a burr, the designation of a defective item is fairly straightforward. However, the quality of most manufactured parts is based on specifications relating to the measurement of the item: a part measuring inside specifications is good, whereas a part outside specs is considered a defect. Judgment of quality based on specifications has two flaws. The first involves how an out-of-spec part is handled. Because Production is rated on volume, I have seen that in many instances such "defective" parts are re-measured and passed if they now fall within specs (sometimes the parts are re-routed to a gage which has a higher pass probability—without checking why the gages are different). Of course, any part that had measured just inside specifications is never re-measured.

The second flaw becomes obvious from the literal interpretation of a specification: a part inside specs *always* works and a part outside specs *always* fails. All good engineers know this is nonsense, but they believe these types of specifications are necessary so that Production can make black & white decisions on a part-by-part basis. The reality is as parts fall further from the nominal they have an increasing probability of failure, and there is rarely anything truly accurate about a specification's pass/fail criteria. Perhaps some designers set the specs at those points where the probability becomes undesirable, but this is a rarity.

A better goal for the Black Belt would be to reduce the standard deviation of the part. In a sense, this should reduce the out-of-spec count as well, but it permits the error of potentially allowing for a tight distribution whose center is displaced near the spec, with the result that even in-spec parts could fail in actual use. The optimum goal is to both reduce the process σ and have the process centered at the nominal. But this requires a major paradigm shift away from the concept of specifications—a topic that will be addressed in the section on Process Capability.

Non-Statistical Tools

There are multiple non-statistical tools that a Black Belt should use, especially at the beginning of the project. Perhaps the most poorly done of these tools is the Process Map. As an instructor of Black Belt classes I have seen hundreds of project reviews through their early stages of implementation. Despite all the admonitions to the contrary, most candidates would create a simple Process Map in a flow chart style, without ever asking themselves, "What did I learn?" The intent of the Process Map is to determine what Production does in actuality, especially as compared to what it is supposed to do, and also to uncover the "hidden factories," those operations that wouldn't or shouldn't exist if everything is done correctly. This means looking at the operations of all shifts, and getting the feedback of those people who are most intimately connected with the operation—the operators.

Nick Pontikos, a Seagate Black Belt who did perform a diligent Process Map, discovered that during a cleaning operation two of the shifts performed it according to the manufacturing process instructions (MPI) while the remaining two shifts processed the parts following an older MPI. When the Black Belt also investigated how the process defects were distributed among the four shifts, he found that they overwhelmingly were being produced by the shifts which followed the current MPI! This discovery greatly facilitated both a solution and an important insight on what could go wrong.

Another tool that is frequently used, but whose result is often misused is the Pareto Chart. Here the trend is to categorize the defects and then perform a count. Those defects with the highest counts are the ones that get assigned to be worked on. What might get ignored is the fact that defects are not all equal. A defect that *will* cause a failure is worse than one that *could* cause a failure, which in turn is worse than a cosmetic blemish. And not all failures are equal either. Some are easily fixable, but others can create havoc to a customer, and still others might be safety hazards. These factors should all be considerations in directing which failures to address rather than simply their frequency. Thus, perhaps the best way is to assign a cost to each failure, and Pareto by that cost.

Some other subtle considerations about using cost for the Pareto Chart involve the probability and cost of fixing a problem and the time value of money. In its most simple expression, the Priority on the Pareto Chart can be designated:

$$\text{Priority} = \frac{(\text{Time value of projected savings}) \times (\text{Probability of success})}{\text{Time value of \$ to fix the problem}}$$

In practice, this may seem fairly difficult to implement, but some consideration to these time-based factors should be given when trying to estimate the true cost of fixing a particular process problem.

Another vital consideration in prioritizing a defect involves fully knowing what is important to the customer. In Six Sigma we often like to talk about what is "critical to x" (CTx) where x is cost, delivery, quality, or simply the customer. (A company simply cannot provide a product that always works perfectly, costs nothing and can be delivered yesterday.) In practice, I think that too little time is spent to really get the "voice of the customer," instead relying on what is thought to be important or what had been important in the past. Of course, with multiple customers, the CTx's might even vary, which compounds the problem. But at least some effort should be expended to better understand the customer's true priorities.

CHAPTER 4

DATA BASICS

Although data are the building blocks for analyses, they must be assembled carefully to see just what kind of building they came from.

Data

"An anecdote is not data." This is true not only because the word "data" is supposed to be plural, but also because a single observation particularly chosen—usually because it was uncommon—does not represent well what the Black Belt is trying to study. Unfortunately, there is often excess pressure by Management to explain this unusual observation, but in the scheme of a project, overall performance should be the focus.

Thus, as the Black Belt begins to look at data and wants to make inferences about them (whether it involves process capability, hypothesis tests, or some other conclusion) there are two major considerations. First, the data needs to be *representative*. That is, if the Black Belt is looking at fixing production, then whatever data is taken needs to reflect production, which in turn means that the data needs to be taken over a fairly long period. Past records can often provide this type of data for the KPOV.

But care needs to be taken in that sometimes the data has been altered. For example, if second measurements are taken when the part falls out of spec, it may be that only that second measurement is recorded. This would be even more misleading if there are multiple gages and the part was routed to a more forgiving gage. And what about rework? Is this entered as if the part was different, or is the original data overwritten?

Sometimes it occurs that certain machines are taken off line for repair or maintenance, or that a certain shift's production is curtailed for some reason. Then the production data may reflect a greater proportion of the data coming from select machines or shifts, whereas representative data would reflect an approximately even proportion amongst the shifts or machines. Possibly rework is performed only on a given machine or during a particular shift, which also would violate the data being representative.

The best policy is to get the raw first-pass data and look carefully at it by shift, machine, process line and gage, so as to have the best chance of getting data that will be truly representative of what will be produced in the future.

The second important feature of data taken for samples is that it be *random*. If all production is being inspected, then the idea of random essentially defaults to being representative. However, when samples are taken, great care is necessary to achieve randomness—where each part has the same chance of being selected. Generally, it is still better to segment the sample so that each possible grouping is equally represented. Thus, if I have 4 machines producing a product (and intend to pool the data), one-fourth of the total sample should come from each machine. Further, if there are three shifts, it would be best if one-twelfth of the total sample comes from each machine-shift combination. But within each segmentation the parts should be chosen randomly. Typically, a large sample will allow this.

Unfortunately, this segmentation has limits. Each part could possibly be categorized by process line, machine, shift, gage, tooling part, and ultimately pre- and post-operation handling. But this is where randomization at least provides the likelihood that any specific effects will be averaged out. It will later become the task of the Black Belt to determine if any of these are KPIVs.

Distributions

The study of distributions is crucial to a Black Belt's education. As much as we'd like to have all our distributions be normal (Gaussian), this does not happen frequently. [This stress on getting a normal distribution comes from the ease with which the analyst has been able to describe its physical attributes: the median and the mode are centered at the mean; the shape is symmetric; the values of the area under the curve are well tabulated, which then leads to an easy estimate of process capability. This, however, is an historical bias. With today's computers, virtually anything we had been able to do with the normal distribution we can now do with a huge variety of other distributions.] In a sense, the Black Belt is trying to find an empirical model (that is, a function that doesn't necessarily have a physical meaning) that best describes the data, since it is rare that physical reasons dictate a particular distribution for continuous data. It is true that there may be a practical lower limit (upper limits are extremely rare), which then implies a distribution that also has a lower limit, but the actual distribution still often must be approximated.

Having a good model then allows for a reasonable estimation of the tails, which can be crucial in assessing process capability. For long-tailed distributions, the presence of apparent outliers can also be more easily explained. Presently, excellent common software facilitates the finding of a fitting distribution. Unfortunately, finding the best empirical distribution can be difficult, since the criteria statistics, such as the Anderson-Darling value, often are close for different distributions; or diagnostics, like the probability plot, are enigmatic in their interpretation. The presence of outlier data which also may seem to fit the distribution can also affect the choice of a final model. Thus, it may be necessary to "play around" with the data, perhaps deleting one or two questionable observations, to see if the proposed distribution changes much.

One tool I have used to help judge between distributions is a chart originally created by Professor E. S. Pearson which appears in Hahn and Shapiro's *Statistical Models in Engineering*[1]. This chart maps out the various continuous distributions based on their third and fourth moments (in modified form). [Aside: the first moment is the mean $\bar{x}$; the nth moment is based on $\Sigma(x_k - \bar{x})^n$. The standard deviation is derived from the second moment, the skew from the third moment, and the kurtosis from the fourth moment.] On this graph some distributions lie on a curve, like the gamma and log-normal; some are points, like the uniform, normal and exponential (with the third and fourth moment values fixed); still others can be found in regions of space, like the beta. Mapping your own data's third and fourth moments on this graph allows you to better choose between competing distributions. Again, caution is advised since these higher moments are strongly affected by outliers.

As a check, always perform an "eyeball test." Overlay the proposed distribution onto the histogram to see if it really does describe the data—especially at the two ends. A poor practical fit means that making any conclusion based on an extrapolation, such as a process capability estimate, is inadvisable. It is a very interesting exercise to do simulations by generating about 200 random points from various defined distributions to see what a distribution analysis provides. Often, the empirically derived distribution values will be quite different from the values used for the simulation. One can also see how the empirical distribution curves approximate the histograms, thereby getting experience in doing the eyeball test.

With statistical computer programs now offering even greater analytic power, there is now an option to generate special empirical distributions, such as the Johnson or Pearson distributions. These are created by calculating the first through fourth moments of the data, and then creating an artificial distribution that possesses these four values. These have the disadvantage that they give no physical meaning to the data, which some known distributions can provide. But on the other hand, they aren't that much worse than choosing a known distribution just because it fits the data better than others. These empirical fits are still fairly new and might be difficult to explain to management. But they have value in predicting tails and process capability. As always with any empirically derived distribution, do an eyeball check of the smoothed distribution over the histogram, and be very reluctant to put too much faith in your conclusions if you have fewer than 200 random and representative points.

Finally, realize that many distributions may be composites. For example, two machines may both create log-normal distribution data, but the start point, scale and/or width may be different. Always look for multi-peak data. Even though the data may show only a single mode, an unusual flatness in the shape may signal the presence of the overlay of two or more independent distributions. In a sense, all product distributions are composite, being made up of perhaps hundreds of contributing distributions due to all the process variations that operate. Many are common-cause contributors whose variations are small but real, while some are larger. Typically, the Black Belt is searching for these special causes, and good project management will use the product distribution to help understand their effect. Unfortunately, there aren't good computer programs (at least that I am aware of) that can de-convolute a distribution just by looking at the output data. However, better programs are being developed that will use KPIV data along with the KPOV to find clusters of commonality. This arena is one of the most important developments in data analysis.

Metrics

The standard metrics for a distribution or a sample are the mean, median, standard deviation and range (the mode is rarely used, and the range should only be considered for very small samples). Usually, these are interpreted as if the parent distribution was normal. But this assumption must be verified. In fact, it is always important to try to coordinate the metric with the distribution in such a way that any reporting is not deceptive. For example, if the distribution is highly skewed, reporting the mean without the median might give a false impression, since management often assumes a symmetric distribution. Similarly, the standard deviation of a skewed distribution also does not provide a good descriptor. Generally, when the distribution is not normal, a report should always provide a histogram of the data so as to give the most honest general view of the data.

In some cases, boxplots provide a succinct picture of the data as well. But management may not be that familiar with these charts. Usually, boxplots are best used when there are different categories into which the data can be separated (shifts, lines, machines, etc.). If several categories exist, multi-vari charts might be appropriate.

Sometimes the Black Belt wants to obtain a reasonable estimate of a metric or take a look at a distribution in some way. Here is a set of "rules of thumb" I've made for establishing a <u>minimum</u> sample size to get such reasonable initial estimates:

Sample Size	Metric
30	Mean
60	Standard Deviation
120	Distribution that is close to Normal
200	Distribution (skewed or long tailed)
125	Initial X-bar/s Control Chart (25 groups of 5)
340	Proportion

For processes which don't have a continuous variable, the common metric is defects per parts per million (dppm). This is sometimes a questionable metric when the defect level is high. Which is easier to comprehend, 32,000 dppm or 3.2% defective? You should always use whichever metric is most easily understood and not insist on the Six Sigma convention in the hopes that a high reported number will get more attention.

There is one other conventional Six Sigma metric that also should be avoided in most cases: defects per million opportunities (DPMO). This metric causes undue confusion in its application! Perhaps it makes sense when the activity is based on a single operation, but this is uncommon. One hotel chain required that each potential guest entering the building be greeted before he got to the front desk. But how many employees encountered that person? If it was just a single doorman, then the DPMO metric might be acceptable. But what if there were several people who encountered that person. Should each encounter be counted as an opportunity? If a customer experiences a lost bag 2% of the time, does that represent a 20,000 DPMO? But suppose that each bag is handled by 10 separate people. Does the 2% occurrence now relate to about a 2000 DPMO because each person could cause the mix up? And let us suppose that each bag is handled twice in some way, such as reading the tag (correctly or not) and then routing the bag (correctly or not). Is the process now down to 1000 DPMO?

The DPMO metric becomes even more absurd in technology industries. In a disk drive, reading or writing of a bit occurs at over 100 million per second. Each operation represents the chance for an error. Should one uncorrected error every second, at a rate of .01 DPMO be considered exemplary or disastrous? And doesn't the application matter? One mis-assigned pixel on a photograph is virtually invisible, but the change occurring on a numerical digit in a banking operation is critical.

Another conventional Six Sigma metric is Rolled Throughput Yield (RTY). Here the first-pass yield for each step in a process is multiplied all together with the final value being the RTY. Although this can be a useful metric, it is misused when the RTYs of multiple processes are compared to prioritize action or to grade the health of a process. Which is better, a 3-step process with an RTY = 85% or a 30-step process with an RTY = 50%? The true value of the RTY is uncovering the hidden factories of rework. But even rework should not always be condemned. One project I know about saved over $20 million—over three times that of the next best project in the company. And it achieved this by introducing a rework operation. (Incidentally, that second best cost-saving project resulted when the Black Belt reversed an engineering change that he himself had implemented while being the responsible engineer on the process! There are lots of surprises in Six Sigma.)

The simple conclusion to all of this is to use the metrics that are the clearest and least ambiguous, and which will help drive the proper behavior. Requiring a common metric will almost always lead to misaligned priorities. Much more will be said about this in the chapter on Process Capability.

Outliers

One of the most difficult data situations to deal with involves outliers. These are points that fall outside the normal range of the distribution that best fits the majority of the data (what I term the "regular distribution"), and whose unusual values are often attributed to some kind of mishandling. Inclusion of these points in the analysis most affects the standard deviation, but can also influence the mean. This, in turn, might also give the impression of a poorer process capability than what actually exists.

The first action should be to determine if the outlier has an assignable cause. Explanations might range from being a misreading of the measurement to a part that has evidently been mishandled. Any mis-measurement can either be corrected in the data base, or at the very least be ignored and deleted from the analyses. Mishandling requires a different approach which will be discussed shortly. Unfortunately, in most cases the part is long gone and cannot be traced. Instead, there appear to be readings that just don't fit the primary distribution. How can the Black Belt handle these?

Another source of apparent outliers is the possibility that the distribution being looked at is actually a composite of multiple distributions, at least one of which has a long tail or whose mean is offset from the others. The separate tail then extends outside the range of the rest of the data and its furthest points look like outliers.

For example, consider the following observed distribution:

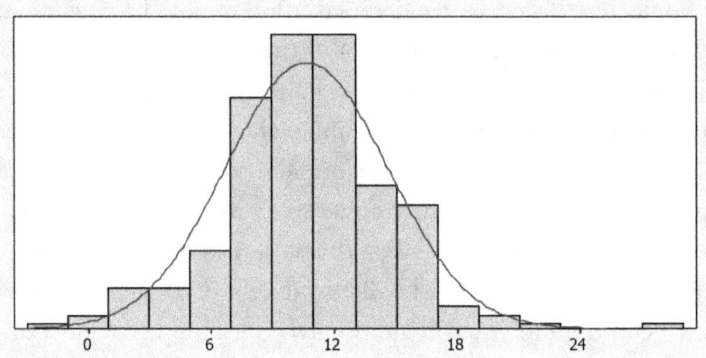

However, if the distribution is actually divided into its component contributors, here represented by the groups G1 through G6, it is seen to be a composite of several, disparate distributions, one of which has very long tails, as shown in the following dot plot.

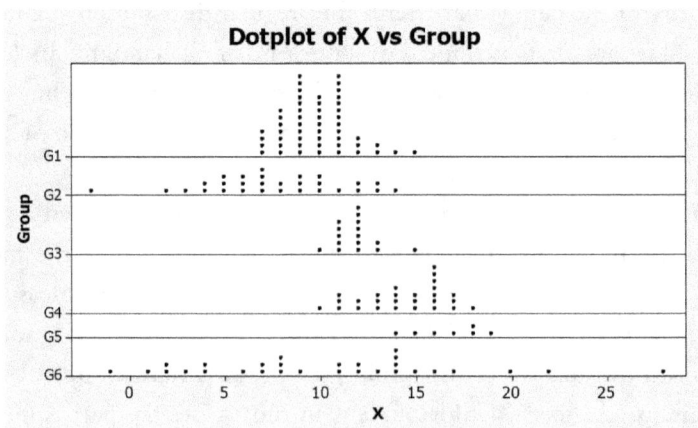

As with distribution analysis, it is always prudent for the Black Belt to sort through the data to determine if there are any sources which could create these long tails.

Assuming that no reasonable explanation can be found for some outliers and the intention is just to get back to what one would expect as the regular distribution, then a method for separating the outliers from that regular distribution is required. First, let us look at the probability of getting points at various distances from the mean (in standard deviation units), assuming a normal distribution:

2.00σ	1 in 22
2.50σ	1 in 81
3.00σ	1 in 370
3.25σ	1 in 857
3.50σ	1 in 2149
3.75σ	1 in 5655
4.00σ	1 in 15,787
4.25σ	1 in 46,779
4.50σ	1 in 147,160

Although a point falling at 3.5σ could be part of the parent distribution, unless the sample from the population is large (over 200), this would be unlikely. Furthermore, by inclusion of points over 3.5σ away from the mean, the calculated standard deviation is further inflated. Thus, it is probably prudent for the Black Belt to create "outlier limits" which will allow an objective criterion to be established for the data for removal of outlier points from inclusion in the regular distribution. This can be achieved in the following way:

1. From the initial distribution, calculate the mean (m_0) and standard deviation (s_0). Then calculate the values that correspond to $m_0 \pm 3.5 s_0$. "Filter" out any values that fall outside these limits and set them aside as outlier values.
2. Recalculate the mean and standard deviation (m_1 and s_1) of this first filtered distribution. Then repeat step 1 with the limits at $m_1 \pm 3.5 s_1$.
3. Repeat step 2 with the new limits at $m_2 \pm 3.5 s_2$.

4. Recalculate the mean and standard deviation a fourth time with the re-filtered distribution (m_3 and s_3). If this last distribution still produces multiple points outside $m_3 \pm 3.5s_3$, then it is likely that the original distribution is a composite distribution with at least one of the contributors having a substantially larger standard deviation than the other contributors.

In some instances when a very large data set exists with perhaps dozens of outliers, the first two steps should be done using limits at m ± 3s limits. And sometimes the process has to be repeated more than three times. For normal distributions the eyeball test can easily be implemented to identify a first set of outliers, reserving the more mathematical criteria for tails that are more questionable or if one wants to set up a program to do this automatically. If such a program is created, there should always be a check to see how many points finally fall outside of 3σ limits, since such points should occur fairly infrequently.

For non-normal distributions, the removal of outliers follows a similar path, except that instead of using m ± 3.5s as the criteria, the actual probability points must be established. Since the distribution is very likely to be skewed to the right, the removal will follow a truncation limit at the 0.00023 probability of occurrence.

In reporting the results for the distribution it is absolutely essential to declare information about both the regular distribution and the fraction of outliers. That is, the report might follow something like, "The data follows a normal distribution with a mean of 13.2 mm and a standard deviation of 1.2 mm. However, 1.6% of the data points appear to be outliers and are not included in the summary statistics. We don't know whether these outliers are occurring because of mis-measurement, mishandling, or are true outliers which result from normal processing." The reason it is important to include information about the outliers is that if these points are real, then they might be the sole source of the problem the Black Belt is trying to fix. If the regular distribution has good process capability, this may indeed be the case.

---

[1] Hahn, Gerald J. and Shapiro, Samuel S., *Statistical Models in Engineering*, John Wiley & Sons, 1967, p. 197.

CHAPTER 5

MEASUREMENT SYSTEMS ANALYSIS

The magnitude of the measurement error is usually underestimated, but its impact really depends on the capability of the process.

A good evaluation of the measurement system is an essential element of any operational project. How else can the Black Belt know whether the data that is being interpreted is even valid? I've seen two examples (in a leading-edge technology environment) where an evaluation of the gage showed that the gage error encompassed most of the variation seen in the data! Furthermore, gage evaluation is also quite important regarding the critical KPIVs, for the goal of the project is to control the KPOV by controlling the KPIVs.

Tragically, the traditional way of performing and interpreting a gage study often provides little understanding or estimation of the true gage error. First, consider how the standardized gage study is performed. Perhaps 10 parts are chosen (how? randomly?), and 3 inspectors measure the parts three times each. There are variations, but the numbers are representative. This might result in 90 or so measurements. Sixty of the available degrees of freedom (df) go to estimating the repeatability (which provides a good estimate), while 2 df go to estimating the reproducible effect of inspector (an abysmally bad estimate). Some (part × inspector) df's help spot outlier data. These estimates of gage error are then erroneously added together to provide a final

σ_{gage}. One then computes a semi-meaningless metric like P/T, compares it to a criterion—usually 30%--and then declares the gage "good" or "bad."

Where did this procedure come from? It originated from "long ago," when all evaluations had to be done by hand, and getting fast data was considered important. The 10×3×3 Gage Study procedure seemed simple enough. The easy-to-apply Range Method was used to get all the estimates for variation, and proper correction factors were applied to calculate the standard deviations. As computers became available, the procedure for getting the data remained the same, although the programs were revised to analyze the standard deviations rather than the ranges.

Unfortunately, during the transition time from the 1940's to the Twenty-First Century, measurements became much more complicated. They progressed from measures with rulers, verniers and micrometers (all of which measurements are quite affected by the skill/repeatability of the inspector, and whose errors might be in the 0.1 mm or even 0.01 mm range) to discerning microscopic diffraction patterns, evaluating reflection of laser beams, measuring nanovolts, or optically evaluating where an edge might exist in a photoresist location (measuring in fractions of a µm). These latter types, which are common in the technology industries, all are strongly affected by temperature or humidity, and the condition of the measurement equipment itself. Even for less technically challenging measurements, the requirements have often been tightened by factors of a 100 or more. Thus, an evaluation of reproducibility has become essential to capture the full gage error. But the standard procedure fails completely in this regard.

Definitions

To proceed, it is necessary to provide some definitions of terms to avoid future confusion.

Repeatability. Historically, this term has meant the variation due to taking measurements one right after the other. Thus, if there had been an automatic measuring device, it could have meant the error occurring in the electronics just by pushing the buttons. I believe that for greater clarity it is better to define it so that it includes the loading and unloading of the part, which would also include the loading and unloading into any fixture that holds the part for measurement. This should also include the time and care expended to take the measurement when there is manual adjustment. Thus, if Black Belts want to get a pure estimate of repeatability, they would remove the part from its storage container, load the part into the fixture, put the fixture into the gage, adjust, take the measurement, remove the fixture from the gage, and then unload the part from the fixture and replace it in its storage container; this multiple-step activity would then be immediately repeated. After doing this several (5 or 6) times, the Black Belts would repeat the procedure on additional parts.

Reproducibility. This term should represent the variation in the measurement system that is due to all the rest of the potential influences: different inspectors, gages (if not evaluated separately), fixtures, days, time of day, temperature, humidity, handling, condition of the gages (e.g. warm-up, deterioration of instrumentation, calibration variation), and probably many more sources of influence that may be unique to a particular gage or set of circumstances. [One particular example of this occurred for SEM (Scanning Electron Microscope) measurements in which I was involved. The night shift had significantly poorer measurement capability, which was traced to the fact that fork-lift trucks moving parts for the next day were running along a nearby corridor, creating vibrations that blurred the SEM images.] Furthermore, all interactions of any kind also contribute to the reproducibility. The standard procedure typically allows for only one of these reproducible factors which is usually the inspector, although any other factor could be substituted. And one valuable interaction is allowed: part by inspector. In some cases, by looking separately at the Trial variable, time effects might also be uncovered. But everything else is ignored.

Gage Error. Also designated σ_{Gage} or σ_{Meas}, this is just the calculated value of the overall measurement error as designated as a standard deviation. Although it is usually calculated (by the computer) through a relatively complex formula, it is essentially defined as:

$$\sigma_{Gage} = \sqrt{\sigma^2_{Reproducibility} + \sigma^2_{Repeatability}}$$

Accuracy. A measure of how close the average of multiple measurements of a part would come to the true value of the part. The use of standards and calibration are intended to optimize accuracy.

Precision. Most simply, this just represents how close multiple measurements of a part are clustered about their mean value. Essentially, it is just the standard deviation of the measurement error.

Correlation. There are really two different types of correlation with regard to the measurement system. The first involves how well the measurements relate to the true value of the part (something that can't usually be done easily and is therefore ignored). The second involves establishing a linear (straight line) relationship between two testers, so that one can estimate the measurements of one tester given the other. The format is usually a straight-line equation like: $X_{Tester\ 1} = a + bX_{Tester\ 2}$, where X is the measurement and a and b are constants.

Linearity. This is an ambiguous term, since it has been used for two different phenomena in the measurement system. In the first definition it refers to assessing how much the relationship of the measured values to the true values varies from the expected slope equal to 1 (and to some extent an intercept of 0). The second definition assesses how much the measurement error is constant over the range of measurements. The following graphs provide a picture of these two types of definitions of linearity, although they are not conventionally given a Type 1 or Type 2 designations.

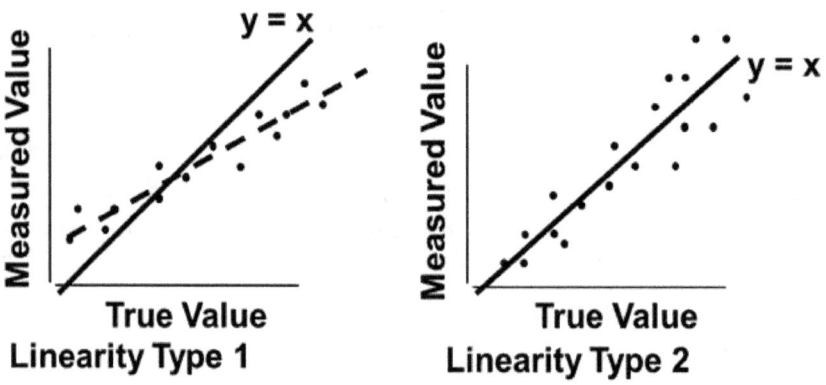

Stability. Ordinarily the capability of a gage is assessed only during a short span of time. With time, the accuracy of the gage can shift. More rarely, the precision can also change. A gage is considered stable if these changes are considerably smaller than what is witnessed through a gage study.

Metrics. In most cases the definitions of the metrics have been established. They are repeated here for clarity.

$$P/T = \frac{5.15 * \sigma_{meas}}{USL - LSL} \quad \text{(two-sided specifications; 99\% of measurement width)}$$

$$P/T = \frac{5.15 * \sigma_{meas}}{|SL - \text{Target Mean}|} \quad \text{(one-sided specification)}$$

$$P/TV \equiv P/P = \frac{\sigma_{meas}}{\sigma_{Total}} \quad (\sigma_{Total} \text{ is what the system sees: parts and measurement})$$

$$\%R\&R = \frac{\sigma^2_{meas}}{\sigma^2_{Total}} \times 100$$

There is also a "Discrimination Index" that indicates the number of distinct categories a measurement of a part could fall in to, but this metric has limited value.

Statistical Considerations

Remember that the goal of a gage study is to assess the precision of the gage, which means getting a good estimate of σ_{Gage}. But the estimated standard deviation as calculated is affected by how many measurements actually go into the examined factor, and these are then related to the degrees of freedom used. In the standardized gage study of 10 parts measured by 3 inspectors, 3 times each (10×3×3), there are 60 df used to estimate repeatability, but only 2 df (one less than the number involved) for the inspector. It's important to understand the errors in the estimates by looking at the 90% 2-sided confidence intervals on sigma for various values of df (as expressed in multipliers of the estimated sigma value):

DF	Lower CI	Upper CI
1	.510	15.95
2	.578	4.41
3	.620	2.92
4	.649	2.37
5	.672	2.09
7	.705	1.80
10	.739	1.59
15	.775	1.44
20	.798	1.36
30	.828	1.27
60	.871	1.18
120	.905	1.12

What this means is that in our standardized gage study using 3 inspectors, there is a 5% chance that the measurement error due to inspector is actually 4.4 times bigger than what we calculate for the estimate. Yet we can estimate the repeatability to within about 15%. This unbalanced view of the gage can potentially give an extremely erroneous result.

Another consideration for any gage study is that it is far better if the study parts are approximately uniformly distributed, doing what one can to get parts that measure outside the specifications. This may require assessing hundreds of parts just to get an appropriate study group. There is a very important reason for this precaution. A random sample would provide a fairly large group of parts near the nominal (there's about a 68% chance of getting a single part within 1 sigma of the mean). Yet what is the measurement used for? It is typically to assess whether the part is meeting specifications, so that the critical measurements of interest are at those specifications. Furthermore, the standard deviation of the gage error has been known to vary across the range of measurements, and so the uniform distribution of parts helps validate the consistency of the gage across its measurement range—essentially validating its Type 2 linearity. If a large proportion of parts are being dispositioned for being out of spec, it might be even more optimal to choose four parts each at the two specifications and two more points near the nominal. But be careful! Some computer programs use the standard deviation of the study parts in their calculation of P/TV or %R&R. Never allow that to happen if you can input the as-measured process standard deviation (which you should have available from a simple look at the process!). The uniform distribution will inflate the observed standard deviation of the parts so that those two metrics calculated from the sample data will look to be much smaller than they are. And if you have used a random selection for the study parts, realize that the true process sigma is estimated with only 9 degrees of freedom, meaning that there is a 10% chance it actually is 27% less or 65% higher than what is calculated.

Comprehensive Gage Study

In some cases, such as with measurements that are intensively associated with the skill of the person making the measurement, repeatability and simple inspector-to-inspector variation may be the primary contributors to the gage error, and they can be assessed—although inadequately—using the standardized gage study. But as measurements have become more technical and more exacting, other reproducibility factors can become the primary causes of a gage error—and these are not uncovered during the standardized gage study.

There are two problems in uncovering these troublesome reproducibility factors. The first is in identifying them. Typically there are multiple possibilities: fixtures, gage variation, ambient conditions of temperature and humidity, time of day, number and physical condition of the inspectors (are they at the end of a 10-hour shift?), etc. Certainly a Six Sigma project can use brainstorming tools and process mapping to provide an educated guess, but this is far from fool proof. The second problem is designing a gage study so that there are enough degrees of freedom to have confidence in the estimate of the standard deviation due to that factor. But even if such a possible factor turns up to have little effect on the gage error, might there not be other ignored factors that increase σ_{Gage} and which aren't being evaluated for their effect? And how do we even know that there is a problem with the capability of the gage?

Through my study of this problem I devised a novel method which has the potential capability of capturing the effects of all the reproducibility factors and providing a valid estimate of the overall gage error. With that method, if the gage truly provides too much variation, a detailed study of the resulting data (along with the project team's insight) can lead to an identification of the most likely culprits, which can then be later studied in detail. I call this a "Comprehensive Gage Study." The concept is simple.

Start by choosing about 20 parts, approximately uniformly distributed, over a 3-day period of manufacture. This last action is to give a better probability of getting a group of parts that demonstrate a representative range of characteristics the parts might exhibit. For example, some parts which require an optical measurement may have sharper boundaries or better reflective surfaces than others manufactured at a different time. To get a good group for the study may require gleaning through over 200 manufactured parts. This activity will provide the first set of measurements on these parts.

Then, over a period of at least two weeks (longer is better), measure these parts at random times (using all shifts, and never more than 4 of them in a two-hour period). Continue doing this until each part has been measured a total of four times. Do not, for example, have the second shift measure the 20 parts next, followed by the third shift making the third set of measurements, etc. This caution with randomness will help assure that most reproducible factors will be included in the measurements in a random fashion, so that any measurement helps represent the overall gage error.

By performing a one-way ANOVA on these measurements using "parts" as the fixed factor, the Black Belt will obtain an estimate of the residual error, which becomes an excellent estimate of σ_{Gage}, determined with 60 degrees of freedom, and which includes all the (unknown) reproducibility factors. It is this value that the Black Belt should use to determine if the gage is capable.

Perhaps the biggest drawback to the Comprehensive Gage Study is the extra amount of attention that must be made in order to make the study measurements in such piecemeal fashion. Single parts must be brought in and taken out without losing track of them. In a manufacturing environment it might be virtually impossible to interrupt the normal flow of parts, or to be able to retrieve a part once it is placed for measurement. But if the capability of the gage is suspect, and a large proportion of parts are potentially misclassified (parts that are truly in spec are determined to be out of spec and vice versa), this more complex study should be seriously considered.

If this study reveals inadequacy of the gage, further investigation is required. In some cases, the Black Belt will already have an estimate of the repeatability from a previous standardized gage study. Then a simple, slightly inexact, reverse calculation can be made to determine the overall contribution of reproducibility:

$$\sigma_{Reproducibility} \approx \sqrt{\sigma^2_{Gage} - \sigma^2_{Repeatability}}$$

If instead there will be no estimates for repeatability before running the Comprehensive Gage Study, it is possible to run that study with additional repeatability trials. This can be easily done by requesting that a second, repeat measurement be done occasionally on specific parts during different reproducibility trials. For example, during the second time that parts are measured, six or seven of them could have repeated measures done. Cycling through all 20 parts (one repeat each), would then potentially provide 20 degrees of freedom for repeatability error. (If more df are desired, a repeated measurement could be made for all of the subsequent measurements, and this would result in 60 df in estimating repeatability. Another alternative would involve not taking a third replicated measurement, allowing only 40 df; this would be very desirable when measurements are relatively expensive, and would have only a limited impact on the confidence interval of the gage sigma.) To obtain the estimate for repeatability would simply involve doing a paired t-test on the 20 paired measurements, using the residual error standard deviation, σ_ε, to derive the $\sigma_{Repeatability}$ using the following:

$$\sigma_{Repeatability} = \sigma_\varepsilon / \sqrt{2}$$

Variance Component Analysis

There is a an efficient and mathematically correct way of obtaining both reproducibility and repeatability estimates using what is called "Variance Component Analysis," which is an essential tool for being able to go beyond simple gage analyses.

When the standardized gage study is performed, the model that is being investigated can be written as:

$$\sigma^2_{Gage} = \sigma^2_{Parts} + \sigma^2_{Inspectors} + \sigma^2_{Parts \times Inspectors} + \sigma^2_{Repeatability}$$

That is, the variance of the gage equals the sum of several different related variances; these individual contributing variances are called "variance components." And the standard computer analyses produce estimates of all these variance components.

Variance component analysis is an offshoot of ANOVA. Ironically, ANOVA is called an "Analysis of Variance," yet is used to determine if the *means* of different levels of a factor are different; in a sense, it is an analysis of means (although there is actually another tool called "Analysis of Means" that works somewhat similar to a control chart). ANOVA provides significance testing by comparing the variance of the means of the levels to the variance of a lower order influence, such as the repeatability. Thus it actually computes the variances so that comparisons can be made.

These variances can be output merely by requesting them! However, there is one stipulation. Ordinarily ANOVA is used to determine if the means of different pre-established levels are different. These, then, are called "fixed" factors, and, generally speaking, it is meaningless to care about the standard deviation of these different means in comparison to some other standard deviation because we won't use that information except to claim that at least one mean is different. However, if we take a representative sample that is random, then an inference about the factor level's standard deviation can be important. Thus, in our analysis we usually will have to designate that the factor is "random" in order to request variance components—otherwise the software assumes the levels are fixed. In a gage study it is even legitimate to label Parts as "random" even if they have been specially chosen since the variance of the parts will later be ignored.

To perform a variance component analysis of gage study data that provides a breakdown of the variances in the same way that the gage study software does can be demonstrated in Minitab. Presume that we have performed the standardized gage study with 10 parts and 3 inspectors. Then, with balanced data (meaning no data is missing), call up the macro: Stat > ANOVA

> Balanced ANOVA. For the Model choose: Part Inspector Part*Inspector. Under "Random Factors" designate Inspector. The output will look like:

	Source	Variance component
1	Part	
2	Inspector	4.866
3	Part*Inspector	2.351
4	Error	6.722

To convert this to useful numbers, take the square root of each:

	Source	Var. comp.	Std. Dev.	
1	Part			
2	Inspector	4.866	2.206	← $\sigma_{Inspector}$
3	Part*Inspector	2.351	1.533	← $\sigma_{Part*Inspector}$
4	Error	6.722	2.593	← $\sigma_{Repeatability}$

Additional terms could be added, such as Trial and Inspector*Trial. The Black Belt can judge the statistical significance of factors, but further investigation requires specific requests of the program: outputting the residuals for further study; determining the values of the levels (using Least Square (LS) Means); graphing. These are a bit more time consuming, and generally it is better to use this analysis for specialized cases. In fact, recently software companies are better addressing more complex gage studies. For example, Minitab has allowed additional factors by creating an "extended" crossed gage study, and which produces better, immediate diagnostics. There is also another related tool that can be used, called "General Linear Models" (GLM), which has superior flexibility; it is particularly useful because it allows analysis when data is missing, and this can happen when data must be discarded because of a mismeasurement. It will be discussed in more detail in the chapter *Hypothesis Testing*.

Tester Correlation

It is rare that only a single tester is used to judge parts. Thus, a necessary activity is the establishment and maintenance of additional testers. This can be done fairly easily if there exists a set of parts with known values. These parts are measured on the new tester, and a regression equation can validly be produced. Typically the resultant equation is $X_{New\ Tester} = a + bX_{True}$. If the relationship turns out to be more complex (e.g. quadratic), then works needs to be done on the new tester to determine why.

However, what usually happens is that one tester has been deemed to be the "master" tester (oftentimes designated the "gold tester"). Then subsequent testers measure a set of parts that have been measured on the master tester, with a regression analysis providing a linear relationship between the two: $X_{New\ Tester} = a + bX_{Master}$. This analysis is <u>wrong</u>, and almost always provides an erroneous result!

To use regression properly, there must be no error in the predictor variable. Thus, if we are trying to establish a linear relationship between X and Y of the nature $Y = a + bX$, the equation will be valid only if there is no error in the X values that are used in the data. When correlating two gages, there is almost always error in the gage labeled X, and the larger this error, the more incorrect will be the slope, b, that results from using regression. The error that results can be devastating to the manufacturing line using the new tester, for the slope is almost always reduced, so that the true range between the given specifications (as measured on the master tester) translates to a narrower range on the new tester.

A simple example will suffice. Suppose that the true relationship between the new tester and the master tester is one of identity. That is, $X_{New\ Tester} = X_{Master}$. The only reason we may obtain different measurements on each tester is because of the inherent measurement error. But if we were to take hundreds of measurements on each of many parts on each tester and find the average of the parts by tester, the values would essentially be the same. Let the gage error of each be equal and not inconsequential. Now also suppose that instead we take 100 parts, approximately uniformly distributed, measure the parts once per tester, and perform a standard ordinary least squares (OLS) on the paired data. The result could look like the following graph:

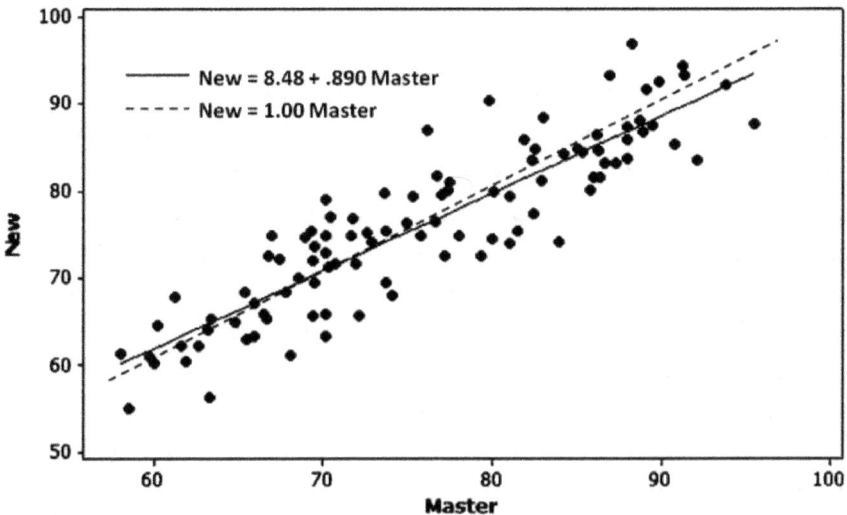

Admittedly this is a more extreme case, but it illustrates the principle. Suppose the specifications on the master gage are [60, 90]. Using OLS regression, these map to the coordinates on the New Tester [61.88, 88.58]; that is, these are where the specifications are to be when measured on the new tester. In actuality, the specifications on the New Tester should be the same as the master, but by using OLS regression, we have erroneously shrunk the acceptable range by .89—the slope of the regression line, and lost 11% of the original specification range. If anyone wants spec relief, the first thing to do is <u>not</u> use regression for correlating testers!

In this example, if we were to reverse the regression and regress the Master data as a function of the New Tester we would get: $X_{Master} = 7.91 + .895\ X_{New\ Tester}$. This is also nonsense considering that we know the two testers measure the same, but it brings up an interesting point about regression. If we try to establish a linear relationship between Y data and X data, we could come up with two different equations: $Y = a_1 + b_1 X$ and $X = a_2 + b_2 Y$. It is a mathematical identity that $b_1 b_2 = R^2$ (the R^2 of the regression which is identical for both regressions). If the "errors" in both X and Y are approximately equal, then we can anticipate that the regression slope will be lowered by a factor of about sqrt(R^2). The poorer the fit, the more in error is the relationship.

The solution is an old statistical tool first uncovered by W E Deming[1], but only recently "rediscovered" since 2000: *Orthogonal Regression*.

Orthogonal Regression

When both the X and Y variables of a linear equation have error, the assumption inherent in OLS regression is violated. But orthogonal regression takes into account that X error to create a more correct equation relating X and Y. John Mandel[2] elaborated on this method when the errors are correlated (that is, subsequent measurements are affected by previous measurements), but this complication needn't concern us in most cases. Both Minitab and JMP have routines for doing orthogonal regression, and the only extra information that the Black Belt needs to input is the ratio of the two error variances (it's best to avoid the "Principal Components" option when it is available). However, I want to go into depth on how the solution is mathematically set up because it will be important when in the Regression chapter I discuss regression when the predictor variables have error.

First assume that we start with a set of X:Y pairs that are matched: $[x_k, y_k]$. Next, assume that we also know the magnitude of the measurement error: σ_X and σ_Y. These might be available from gage studies. Actually, to get the correct equation we only need the ratio of the variances, λ, but if we want to see if the orthogonal regression agrees appropriately, we may also want the individual errors. Then we need to make a few, familiar-to-statisticians definitions (based on $\bar{x}$ and $\bar{y}$ being the average of all the x_k and y_k values respectively):

$$\lambda \equiv \frac{\sigma_y^2}{\sigma_x^2}$$

$$S_x \equiv \sum_{k=1}^{N} (x_k - \bar{x})^2$$

$$S_y \equiv \sum_{k=1}^{N} (y_k - \bar{y})^2$$

$$S_{xy} \equiv \sum_{k=1}^{N} (x_k - \bar{x})(y_k - \bar{y})$$

Then our best estimates for the slope and offset are:

$$b = \frac{S_{yy} - \lambda S_{xx} + \sqrt{(S_{yy} - \lambda S_{xx})^2 + 4\lambda S_{xy}^2}}{2S_{xy}}$$

$$a = \bar{y} - b\bar{x}$$

From the correlation fit, estimates of σ_X and σ_Y (s_X and s_Y) can be obtained.

Define: $$S_e = \sqrt{\frac{S_{yy} - 2bS_{xy} + b^2 S_{xx}}{N-2}}$$

Then $$s_X = \frac{S_e}{\sqrt{b^2 + \lambda}}$$

$$s_Y = s_X \sqrt{\lambda}$$

What is particularly appealing about the results of orthogonal regression is that unlike OLS regression, the equation is completely invertible! That is, if one obtains the equation y = a + bx, then when the x and y data are switched to obtain a second equation (with the inverse of λ now used), it will be x = (y - a)/b. This is intuitively appealing for a correlation, since it shouldn't matter which variable sits on the x axis. Additionally, with estimates of σ_X and σ_Y, one can compare these to the gage error. If they are off by more than 20%, then there should be a high suspicion that the gage study was not done correctly (e.g. short-term study for the gage study, but long-term data for the correlation).

In applying the results in a practical way the Black Belt should not just assume the resultant equation is correct. In many instances one is correlating two testers that are expected to measure exactly the same. This sets up a basic hypothesis test that 1) the slope = 1.00 and 2) if the slope = 1.00, then the offset, a, equals 0 (that is, the two testers measure nearly identically). Doing this test requires a little bit more algebra. First define k and S_{uu}:

$$k \equiv b/\lambda$$

$$S_{uu} \equiv S_{xx} + 2kS_{xy} + k^2 S_{yy}$$

Then the standard error of the slope, S_b, is:

$$S_b = \frac{|1+kb|\, S_e}{\sqrt{S_{uu}}}$$

And the standard error of the offset is:

$$S_a = S_e \sqrt{\frac{1}{N} + \frac{(\bar{x}(1+kb))^2}{S_{uu}}}$$

Remembering that the standard error takes into account the sample size, our hypothesis test can now be completed. The test is:

$$|1-b| \le t_{\alpha/2, N-2}\, S_b \ ?$$

If this is true, we choose to run under the assumption that the null hypothesis is true, and that the slope = 1.00. There is, however, one additional problem (which occurs for all hypothesis tests when the conclusion is to accept H_o), and that involves the Type II error. If the sample size is small, S_b can be very large and we will never reject the null hypothesis. For this reason, it is prudent to have either a good enough fit (from small measurement errors), a very wide spread of the correlation data, a large enough sample size, or a combination of all three so that $S_b < .03$. If it is larger than .05, then the Black Belt should not feel comfortable in declaring the slope = 1.0.

Given that we have inferred that the slope = 1.0, we can then test the offset. Do not use the standard error of the offset, S_a, for this test! Instead run a simple paired t-test on the data. Typically if the sample size is large enough to limit the slope error appropriately, the sample size is sufficient for limiting the offset error.

As commercial software improves, all of these options should eventually become available. But they are easily programmed into MS Excel. The following diagram provides a layout for doing the calculations; of course the Black Belt will have to use the formulae given previously, and an estimate of the ratio of the two measurement errors for λ will have to be part of the input.

Coefficients			1476.45	=Sxx	0.340	=lambda
Slope	0.73972		710.59	=Syy	208.19	=Syy-λ*Sxx
Intercept	3.44050		744.30	=Sxy	2.174	=k
Calculated Error			5	=N	8070.5	=Suu
X	12.5200		48.59	=x bar	11.794	=Se
Y	7.3033		39.38	=y bar	417.329	=Svv
					11.794	=Se
R-Square	0.5280					
Error(Slope) =	0.34241					
Error(Int.) =	17.45307					

The diligent Black Belt will ask the important question of what sample size should be used for correlation. This can be most accurately answered by doing back calculations, which ultimately depend on the actual slope and the quality of the fit. But in the most likely scenario where the slope is expected to equal 1.0 and the measurement errors of the two testers are equal (both are assumptions!), the sample size can be approximated as a function of R, the square root of the regressions R^2.

$$N \approx 2 + \frac{4(1-R)}{(1+R)S_b^2}$$

R^2 will be a function of both the width of the region investigated and the measurement error. For a desired error of .03 and an R = .9 (that is, R^2 = .81), the required sample size is 236.

For a broader case where the errors are not necessarily equal, one can make estimates of sample size in a different way. Let:

$$\sigma_{Comb} = \sqrt{\sigma_{Gage\,1}^2 + \sigma_{Gage\,2}^2}$$

and let Ratio = the range in sample values divided by σ_{Comb}. Then, depending on how the correlation data is chosen (uniform or normal) the sample size needed to detect a slope change of .05 is outlined in the following table:

Ratio	Uniform	Normal
50/1	10	19
25/1	32	67
10/1	187	402

This alternative approach still demonstrates that the worse the gage error is, the greater the sample size needs to be.

A Few More Thoughts on Correlation

The common practice when doing correlation of testers has been to apply regression. If there is a master gage, then that data became the X variable and the new tester became the Y variable. But is that what really should have happened? Doesn't the engineer want to know what the master tester would read given a measurement on the new tester? This would mean that the regression should have been reversed, with the new tester being on the X axis! Instead, the regression equation would then have been inverted, which has its own errors. And these errors would be compounded if there was a hierarchy of testers, e.g. gold, silver and bronze, which would be correlated in sequence: silver to gold, and then bronze to silver.

The only time such a correlation would give a usable relationship is when the error of the gage on the X axis had a measurement error much smaller than that tester on the Y axis, or when the fit is outstanding, with $R^2 > .98$.

There is one other very important point. Orthogonal regression will provide the best estimate of how the _true_ value of the Y variable relates to the _true_ value of the X variable. This is exactly what the Black Belt wants when doing a correlation, because she is seeking the relationship that could accurately translate the specifications. But OLS regression will provide a better estimate of *predicting* a single _measured_ value of Y given a single _measured_ value of X. Sometimes statistical results seem strange!

Metrics

Perhaps the weakest aspect of judging the goodness of the gage is in the interpretation of the metrics that a gage study produces. Often the advice is that a gage with P/T less than 10% is good and over 30% is bad, with the range in between being "marginal." Essentially, this judges the gage only in terms of the specifications and does not take into account how good the process capability is. P/TV or %R&R only look at the process from a comparison of the gage error to the process spread, and doesn't take into account the specifications. As a result, any interpretation of these two types of gage metrics is misleading and practically worthless.

Furthermore, the gage study software generally assumes that the parts used in the gage study are representative of the process. Obviously, this would be a grave error if the parts were chosen uniformly (as recommended), since it would significantly inflate the denominators of the P/TV and %R&R metrics, making these look substantially better than what they truly are. But even if the parts were chosen randomly, the part-to-part standard deviation would only be estimated with a maximum of 9 degrees of freedom—a very poor estimate with a wide confidence bound. (It's actually even worse than this, since the part-to-part variation is calculated using the even poorer estimate of the inspector-to-inspector variation. More will be said about this in the section on confidence intervals for gage studies.)

What should matter to the process owner is whether the gage is capable of differentiating parts for the process as it exists. That is, the gage should minimize the amount of misclassification of parts. Parts that are truly inside the specs should not be measured outside the specs, and similarly, parts that are truly outside the specs should not be called good. Thus, the appropriate metric is the amount misclassified. This metric is also important from a management standpoint, for "good" parts that are scrapped or reworked represent lost revenue, and "bad" parts that escape may result in customer dissatisfaction. Thus the quantity of material misclassified may be ample financial justification for gage improvement or replacement! The following two graphics illustrate the situation.

Bad Parts Being Misclassified as Good

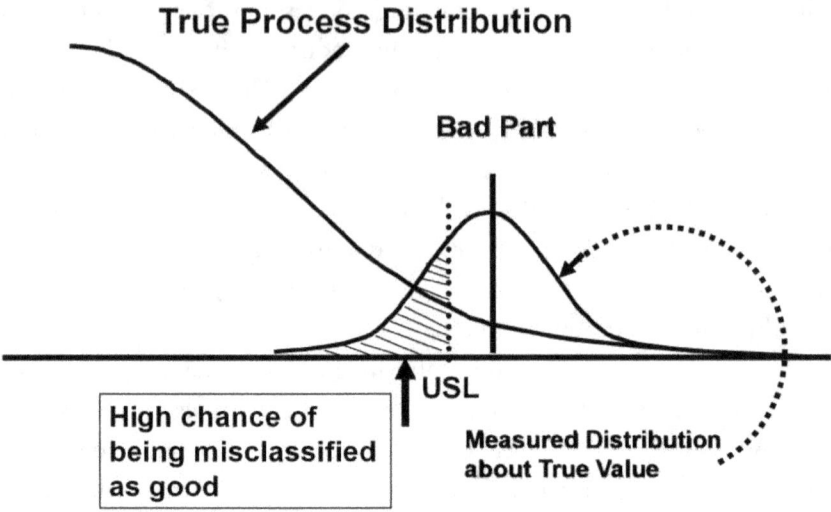

Good Parts Being Misclassified as Bad

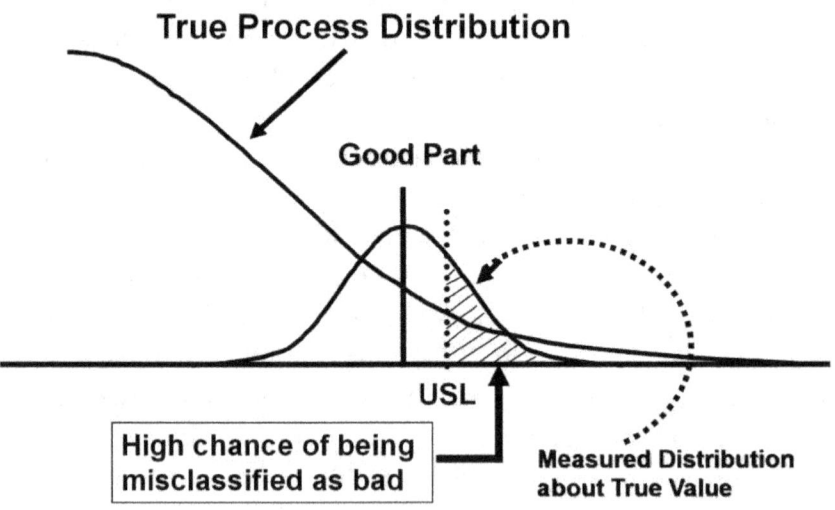

The fraction misclassified is strongly affected by how parts produced near the specifications are judged. Thus, this amount is very dependent on the process capability, since if no parts are manufactured near the specs, then there is almost no chance of misclassifying them. A gage with a large error is adequate for a great process, but even a gage with a small error might not be able to handle a poor process.

The calculation of the amount misclassified requires a double integration which can be done numerically (i.e., not in closed form). Some software programs can provide this estimate, but extreme caution needs to be applied when viewing the resultant numbers. For example, in the standard crossed gage study analysis, as of this writing (2014) Minitab and JMP will provide the fraction misclassified. But unless one specifically requests using the known process standard deviation, it will use the standard deviation of the gage study parts. Furthermore, the program cannot take into account the true mean of the process, so that any offset of the mean will skew the program's results. As said before, the estimate will have a wide confidence-interval band. Furthermore, if uniformly distributed parts are chosen, this part-to-part variation will be greatly inflated, making the process capability look much poorer. There is another glitch that occurs in Minitab, and that is if the standard deviation of the study parts is in excess of the input process standard deviation, it will not continue with the appropriate calculation. Unfortunately, if the parts have been chosen uniformly, this erroneous calculation is extremely likely to occur!

If you don't have access to an appropriate software program, I have used estimates over a wide range of possibilities to create a graph that shows how much material is (totally) misclassified given the one-sided Cpk of the process (as measured) and P/TV. If there is an amount of material out of spec on both sides, than the Cpk needs to be calculated for each side and the two quantities of misclassified material need to be summed.

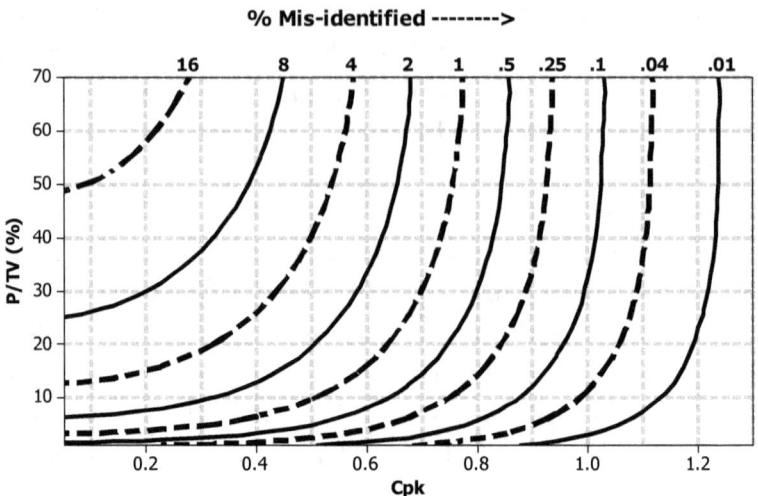

It is very important to note that the process itself needs to be pretty poor (Cpk < .8) before the amount misclassified gets even close to 1%. (Of course, realize that Cpk already has some effects of the poor gage measurement embedded in its calculation.) This graph should be able to provide a reasonable estimate for determining the effect of the gage on misclassification, and hence on the financial impact of a poor gage.

Linearity

It should be obvious that the correlation tool can be used to assess both types of linearity. If the values from the master tester can be relied on to be very close to the true values, then departures from a slope of 1.0 are indicative of a problem with the new gage. Similarly, if the Black Belt does a residual plot versus the predicted values, any non-random pattern will expose the possibility that the measurement error is not constant across its range.

Often, if standards are available across the range of measurements it is better to take multiple <u>replicated</u> measurements of each standard to assess both types of linearity. Software programs have options for doing this and give reasonable results. The problems will always exist that the standards often do not exactly represent the parts that are being measured. This is particularly true in technology industries, where the technology itself frequently is ahead of the ability to measure it accurately; when, in a sense, the product has fallen off the leading edge of technology. This can also lead to a type of error that is relatively rare, but can have a major impact on assessing the process when it exists—a part-dependent, systematic measurement error.

When there appears to be a problem with heteroscedasticity (inequality of the standard deviation across the range), it might be advisable to perform two separate gage studies, each concentrating on the two ends of the specifications. That is, one gage study should involve parts measuring only near the lower specification and the other using parts at the upper specification. Separate misclassification values can be approximated, and a plan of action can be created to address the largest contributors to imprecise gage effects. In one case in which I advised, the gage error on an electrical test was unequal at the two specifications. But the problem wasn't one of linearity; instead the error was so huge that the measurement was essentially meaningless, and the engineer eventually eliminated that particular test.

Part-Dependent, Systematic Measurement Error

While working with a client performing a correlation between two different types of testers, an unusual problem occurred that defied the standard orthogonal regression analysis. A further investigation revealed an insidious type of measurement error that cannot be uncovered by standard analysis. In this specific case, the tester method involved shining narrow laser beams of three different wavelengths upon a limited area of a ceramic surface. The interference patterns provided the data to ascertain the measurement of interest. However, the illuminated polished ceramic surface was composed of a limited number of grains, and it turned out that the orientation of the grains provided a spectrum of different reflectivity characteristics. The interference pattern was affected depending on which grain orientation dominated. Thus, besides a random measurement error dependent on the system, there was also a fixed offset of the measurement depending on the part. Replicates of a part's measurement at the same location might then have a different random component of error, but always had the same fixed bias offset due to its grain orientations. For example, a part whose true value was 12.4 units might read with a bias of +.3 and give an average of 12.7 units for multiple measurements.

What should be evident is that this new error is a component of the overall gage error that cannot be found by any conventional gage study. Whereas the original model for the measurement had been

$$X_{obs} = X_{true} + \varepsilon$$

the actual model is:

$$X_{obs} = X_{true} + \varepsilon + \beta(X)$$

where $\beta(X)$ is a non-random component of the measurement system which is dependent on each individual part. I have given this error the name the "Part-Dependent, Systematic Measurement Error." The term "systematic error" historically refers to an inaccuracy not due to chance, but inherent in the measurement system. For simplicity we can shorten the name to the PDSME.

Another example of the occurrence of such an error would be when trying to measure the width of a photolithographic pattern. The tops of the patterns can be rounded, or the sides slanted as in the following diagram that shows cross sections:

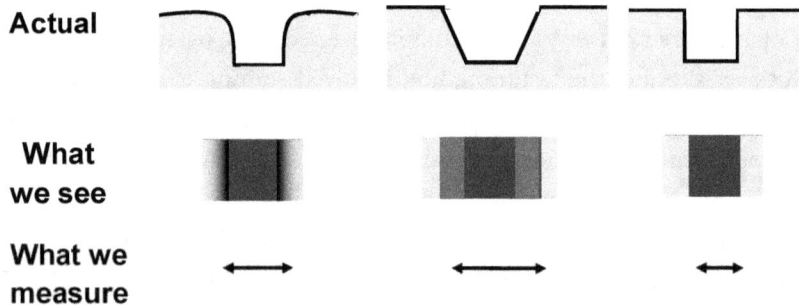

The character of the wall pattern will always produce a fixed effect on the optical measurement system.

In some cases, the physics of the measurement itself might suggest the existence of the PDSME. But it is most likely to show up when doing a correlation and realizing that the measurement error which is output by the orthogonal regression analysis is much bigger than that calculated from a gage study. But there is another trap that the Black Belt might fall into. Often, correlation data is taken over a very short period of time, and so the measurement error of the parts may not include all the components of reproducibility that are present in the system. Furthermore, since some of these components would be "fixed" over a short period (e.g. one inspector, one fixture, one tester calibration), another bias could enter into the data. This is an aspect of MSA that will be expounded on later in this chapter. However, when the calculated error exceeds the "known" gage error by 30%, a careful analysis of both the gage study and the way the correlation data was taken should be done to be sure that the disparity is not due to the PDSME.

When a PDSME is suspected as a significant component of the measurement system, there are two potential ways to quantify it—but it requires a second measurement system that does not possess the equal bias that is present in the first system. (The second system may have the same type of bias, but the specific part bias needs to be random compared with the first.) Estimating a solution also requires that one have an Excel correlation program as indicated in the Correlation section in this chapter. It is important to note that once the data is input (so that N, S_{xx}, S_{yy} and S_{xy} are known), the correlation line depends solely on λ, the ratio of the two measurement error variances. In looking at this in reverse, if the slope is given, then λ can be calculated. This simple dependency will be exploited to perform several important, but novel, statistical calculations that are not generally known, but can be extremely useful.

The first way would involve actually knowing the measurement error of the second system, and that it doesn't contain its own PDSME. (Such a measurement might be far more expensive and not be appropriate for daily production; but it might be available on a short term basis for uncovering the PDSME of the primary tester system.) Then one could input this known error, and by using Excel's "Solver" routine, force the Calculated Error of that second system to equal the input error by allowing the first system's measurement error to vary. This will provide an estimate of the entire gage error of the first system; if the random part of the gage error is known, it can be subtracted off to provide an estimate of the PDSME:

$$\sigma_{PDSME} = \sqrt{\sigma_{Total}^2 - \sigma_{Gage\ Study}^2}$$

The second way requires that something be known about the second measurement system. For example, it may have its own, unknown PDSME, but because the measurement itself uses identical physics, the investigator may believe that the slope of the correlation line should equal 1.0 (or know that it is some other value). Here, the Solver routine can force the slope to be equal to the "known" value by varying either of the two input measurement errors—essentially allowing lambda to vary until the slope equals the known value. Alternatively, the investigator may know that the measurement systems are identical except for the fact that the PDSMEs are arrived at randomly for any given part. Then the ratio of the errors, λ, should equal 1.0, and the resultant calculated errors will contain both the random component and the PDSME component.

In the actual problem that originally uncovered the existence of the PDSME, there was a second measurement system available (which an outside vendor was trying to sell) which used similar physics in its measuring, and so a slope equal to 1.0 was assumed. This provided an estimate of the PDSME which was extremely large relative to the part population's true variability, and proved that the old system was inadequate for dispositioning parts. Furthermore, the improved estimate of the part's true variability now agreed with finite element analysis.

Some of the motivation for addressing this problem came because there was concern regarding the true distribution of the parts being made. Since the measurement was so poor because the technology was being pushed to its limit, mathematical modeling was being relied upon to provide the manufacturing requirements. Yet the knowledge of the true distribution remained elusive. Given that a second measurement system became available for which a correlation line with a slope equal to 1.0 could be assumed, a simpler approach would have sufficed to provide an estimate of the true part's distribution. If the parts were randomly chosen and measured by both systems, a variance component analysis with Parts as a random component would have provided the variance of Parts. However, this is a very specific application, and the use of orthogonal regression allows a more generalized approach, including not using randomly chosen parts.

Destructive Testing

One of the most vexing problems facing a metrology engineer involves the situation in which the measurement itself destroys or significantly alters the part so that it cannot be re-measured with the expectation of obtaining the original measurement (with its gage error). Since all standard gage studies are based on the assumption that subsequent measurements of a part will vary only due to a gage error, destructive testing precludes using the standard approach. Thus, for destructive testing situations, something less than perfect will need to be implemented.

The only way that any kind of gage study can be performed is if measurements can be done on parts (or locations) that are very similar to each other so as to appear replicated:

- Different location on the same part. An example is hardness testing where an indentation is made and the depth measured. Other indentations could be made on the same part but at different locations.
- "Sister" parts—parts from the same lot or produced very closely in time. Often with batch processes, within-batch variation is much smaller than the batch-to-batch variation. Parts from the same batch might then be considered sister parts. Similarly, operations might be such that parts made sequentially are very similar to each other. Such might be the case with wire bonding operations at the same location.
- Surrogate parts—totally different parts which will measure in the same way, but which can be made more uniformly. For example, in tensile strength testing, using segments of the same wire should result in breaking strengths that are quite similar.

In all these cases these similar parts or locations will be substituted for the given part that they are to represent in the gage study. Thus, for a breaking strength study, ten different wires could be cut into 9 separate segments. Three different operators would then measure three each of the segments from a given wire, and the gage study analysis would be performed as if each wire ID would be the Part ID.

The limitation of such studies basically rests on how similar these parts or locations actually are to each other, for any differences between the sister parts will be added to the calculated repeatability term. If the gage study produces evidence of an adequate gage, the engineer can be confident in the gage. However, if the study indicates an inadequate gage because of repeatability, the engineer will not know whether the poor result is due to the sister part-to-part variation or the actual repeatability.

As with the standard gage study, efforts should be made to choose the groups of sister parts such that they span the range of the measurement likely to be seen in production so as to uncover any evidence of linearity problems.

There is one additional approach that is available when multiple sister parts are hard to obtain (e.g. when only 2 to 4 such parts can be made similarly to each other at a time). In these cases, it may be necessary to use a "nested" gage study. Unfortunately, these studies are even more inferior to the method just described because they do not allow for the analysis of any Part × Operator interaction term (the effects again become part of the repeatability term).

Confidence Intervals and Gage Sigmas

As with most statistical analyses, point estimates of parameters are given, but there is always uncertainty in these estimates. Unfortunately, the possible range in which the true value may fall is usually ignored, and the point estimate is announced as if there is no uncertainty in its value. A good statistical practice is to always provide a confidence interval of a point estimate when it is available; this will help either assure the eventual user or warn them. Perhaps nowhere is this practice ignored more than in Measurement Systems Analysis!

There are two reasons for this. The first is that any estimate of the confidence interval is quite difficult to obtain. It is mathematically intractable, and only estimation techniques are available. It is complicated by the fact that the variances are determined from differences between the Mean Squares in the ANOVA table, and that the actual degrees of freedom are not the straightforward values as given in the ANOVA table. Secondly, the standardized gage study is set up to primarily find repeatability, and the reproducibility elements of Inspector and the cross term 'Inspector × Parts' are determined with so few degrees of freedom that the confidence interval would often be shocking. This is particularly true when the reproducibility terms are of the same magnitude—or higher—than the repeatability term.

A colleague and I had put together an Excel spreadsheet that used both the approximations for the corrected degrees of freedom and a Monte Carlo analysis to make estimates of the confidence intervals. However, recent improvements in commercially available software now will provide good estimates of the confidence intervals for all the components of a standardized gage study. The Black Belt now only needs request the confidence interval option.

If the results indicate a high contributor to the gage error due to a reproducibility factor which has a limited count, the investigator should seriously consider re-running the gage study with a substantially greater number of levels of that factor. This will give both a better point estimate and a smaller confidence interval on the gage error. And remember, the CI should also be included in any report.

Isolating Repeatability Error

When the gage is found to be inadequate for its purpose in discriminating parts, the main cause might be due to a high repeatability component. To make any improvement, it becomes necessary to determine the greatest source of the error. Recall that the components of repeatability are 1) loading the part into the fixture, 2) locating the part in the measuring device so that it can be measured, and 3) making the actual measurement. Thus, the model is:

$$\sigma^2_{Repeatability} = \sigma^2_{Loading} + \sigma^2_{Locating} + \sigma^2_{Measure}$$

The first step is to isolate the variation associated with fixturing the parts. This is done with the first of several modified gage studies, where you use one inspector with five or more parts.

1. Load the part in the fixture, locate, and measure.

2. Remove the fixture, and then relocate and re-measure 2 or more times *without* unloading the part from the fixture.
3. Unload the part and repeat steps 1 and 2 with the remaining parts.
4. Repeat steps 1 through 3 twice more.

As long as you set this up with "Load" as a variable in an ANOVA analysis, the residual error (we'll call it "Error 1") will be an estimate of the Locating and Measuring errors combined. That is,

$$\sigma^2_{Error\ 1} = \sigma^2_{Locating} + \sigma^2_{Measure}$$

The second step isolates the Measure component. Here it is advisable to perform a gage study with one inspector and five or more parts:

1. Load a part in the fixture and position (Locate) the part to measure. Then measure it.
2. Without removing the fixture, re-measure the part at least twice more.
3. Unload the part from the fixture, and repeat steps 1 and 2 with the remaining parts. Use the same fixture.
4. Repeat steps 1 – 3 two more times. If additional fixtures are available, it is probably best to use them instead of the first fixture.

By running another ANOVA with Fixture and Part as fixed factors, the residual error (call it "Error 2") will just be an estimate of $\sigma_{Measure}$. Now the analysis finishes up by using the information from the three different gage studies. From the original gage study we have an estimate of $\sigma_{Repeatability}$. So just do the backwards calculations:

$$\sigma_{Measure} \approx \sigma_{Error\ 2}$$

$$\sigma_{Fixturing} \approx \sqrt{\sigma^2_{Repeatability} - \sigma^2_{Error\ 1}}$$

$$\sigma_{Locating} \approx \sqrt{\sigma^2_{Error\ 1} - \sigma^2_{Measure}}$$

As an example, a computer storage device disk was being tested for an acceleration parameter. The original gage study (units have been changed for proprietary reasons) gave a reproducibility error sigma of 5.89, while the repeatability error turned out to be about three times larger at 17.1. To investigate further, the second suggested gage study was performed, providing a $\sigma_{Error\ 1}$ value of 4.57, which is an estimate of measurement error in locating and measurement combined. The third gage study provided a residual error, $\sigma_{Error\ 2}$, value of 5.06. Deconvoluting:

$$\sigma_{Measure} \approx \sigma_{Error\ 2} = 5.06$$

$$\sigma_{Fixturing} \approx \sqrt{\sigma_{Repeatability}^2 - \sigma_{Error\ 1}^2} = \sqrt{17.1^2 - 4.57^2} = 16.5$$

$$\sigma_{Locating} \approx \sqrt{\sigma_{Error\ 1}^2 - \sigma_{Measure}^2} = \sqrt{4.57^2 - 5.06^2} = ?$$

As sometimes happens, calculations when subtracting variances can turn up impossible negative values under the square root. This happened here. The standard way of handling this is to assume that because of random error (in our case of Error 1 and Measure), the two should be about equal, and so the error due to Locating is considered to be "insignificant," that is, presumed to be 0. The end result showed that the primary contributor to repeatability is fixturing the part, and if there is a desire to decrease the overall measurement error, the fixturing error would have to be improved.

Isolating Reproducibility Error

The Comprehensive Gage Study can be extremely useful in demonstrating that there exists reproducibility elements which are strong contributors to the overall gage error. If the overall gage error is unacceptable, then it becomes necessary to identify those factors so that they can be improved. This could become a Six Sigma project in its own right! When Cause & Effect Analysis or a Process Map identifies only a single likely candidate, it is easy enough to run a modified standardized gage study. Instead of using the standard 3 or 4 Inspectors as the reproducibility factor, the Black Belt could substitute a minimum of 8 levels of the suspected culprit factor instead and run only two measurements per combination. Thus the design would be 10 parts × 8 "factor levels" × 2 replicates.

The astute Black Belt will note that such a gage study would then entail 160 measurements, with the purpose of getting an estimate of the reproducibility component error having only 7 degrees of freedom. This would be a foolish and unnecessary design, and it should come to mind that a special technique exists for reducing the number of trial runs when we are looking at a "full factorial" design: Design of Experiments. Traditional DOE with fractional factorial designs has usually focused on multiple factors at two, or maybe three, levels. But there are many other types of designs, called "incomplete block designs" or even modified incomplete block designs, which allow multiple factors to be looked at with fairly high numbers of levels—without breaking the bank in having to do an excessive number of measurements.

Most such designs fall under the purview of DOE, and much more will be said about doing special gage studies in that chapter, but the following illustrates a good example. Assume that we have already performed a "good" gage study so that we have a decent estimate of the repeatability error. And now we suspect that fixture may be a strong contributor as a reproducibility element. Then using just 8 random fixtures and 8 parts (these should be chosen uniformly) and only making 32 measurements we can get an estimate of the gage error due to fixture (with 7 degrees of freedom, so it won't be terrific). The following grid represents the gage study:

	1	2	3	4	5	6	7	8
A		X				X	X	X
B	X			X		X		X
C		X		X	X			X
D	X	X	X				X	
E	X				X	X		X
F			X	X		X	X	
G	X			X		X		X
H		X	X		X	X		

(Make sure to randomize the measurements!) The numbers across the top represent one of 8 parts that are measured, and the letters A – H represent the 8 fixtures that are used. An "X" at an intersection represents that the part is to be measured with that fixture, whereas a blank indicates that combination is not to be measured. Thus, fixture E will be used to only measure parts 1, 4, 5 and 7; and part 6 will be measured only with fixtures A, B, F and H. Here each part gets measured four times and each fixture has four measurements done with it. A Variance Components Analysis using Fixture and Parts will provide 1) an estimate of the variance of the fixture effect on the measurement error and 2) a residual error that will encompass both the repeatability and also the Part × Fixture interaction. An F test should be used to compare this latter value with the repeatability established in a previous gage study. If this turns out to be significant, first check for outliers, and then the value can be estimated using the standard "RMS" method:

$$\sigma_{Interaction} \approx \sqrt{\sigma^2_{ResidualError} - \sigma^2_{Repeatability}}$$

If this interaction term is large, further work should be done to understand why. The magnitude of the variance of the factor levels should be compared to the expected reproducibility (hopefully from the Comprehensive Gage Study). If it doesn't explain the majority of the reproducibility error then further work is required to identify other potential sources. Warning: because of the limited levels of the factors involved, incomplete block design experiments or gage studies usually result in estimates of variances with fairly wide confidence intervals. This should be taken into account before proceeding. It is generally wise to perform follow-up studies to verify the results.

Stability

Perhaps the most widely ignored activity regarding the measurement system falls in the Control Phase: maintaining the stability of the gage. Of course, this can be done by performing frequent gage studies or checking the gage against known standards. This needs to be only an infrequent activity if the gage or the process is quite capable. Major shifts would show up in an obvious way. But if the process is producing an unacceptable amount of material and the gage isn't great, then the use of special control charts may be beneficial. This topic will be covered more appropriately in the SPC chapter.

Short-Term and Long-Term Concerns

The problem often exists that gage studies are performed over short periods of time, yet are supposed to provide values of the gage error that are applicable to the measurements done over a long period of time. On the other hand, a long-term study, such as the Comprehensive Gage Study is done over a long period of time, but the results may then be applied to a situation when the error only has short-term influences. Thus caution always needs to be applied when interpreting the results.

For example, a Black Belt may perform a short-term study on a parameter, giving the parts to an individual inspector who measures them on one tester in an hour's time. Here specific biases might creep in to the measurements which aren't averages of the whole gage error. The inspector might use only three fixtures which by accident all provide a bias to lower the measurement; the inspector may bias the readings, too. And the temperature might be lower than normal which could also lower the parameter's measurements. The result could be a calculated statistically significant difference which, in reality, doesn't exist. Understanding the sources of the gage error should guide the Black Belt into how the measurements should be taken.

Similarly, correlation studies may use data which was measured short term, but the long-term gage error would look large in comparison to what the orthogonal regression provides, leading the investigator to conclude that there might be a PDSME where none exists.

Composite Gage Errors

Sometimes the value that is obtained for the parameter of interest is the result of combining two or more different variables that are derived independently. In this case, an estimate of the final gage error must take into account this defining function. A very simple example would be calculating the error in estimating an area, which is the result of multiplying the length and width.

Both the length and width measurements have their own measurement error, so figuring the final measurement error of the product of the two becomes more complicated. Other cases may involve addition, subtraction, or division. Or, in fact, the functions could be even much more complicated.

To approach this problem we will need to use some basic probability calculations involving the propagation of the standard deviations. The following table shows some important relationships:

Function	**Mean**	**Variance**
x + y	$\mu_x + \mu_y$	$\sigma_x^2 + \sigma_y^2 + 2\rho\sigma_x\sigma_y$
x - y	$\mu_x - \mu_y$	$\sigma_x^2 + \sigma_y^2 - 2\rho\sigma_x\sigma_y$
xy	$\mu_x\mu_y + \rho\sigma_x\sigma_y$	$\mu_y^2\sigma_x^2 + \mu_x^2\sigma_y^2 + 2\rho\mu_x\mu_y\sigma_x\sigma_y$ *
		or for $\rho = 0$
		$\mu_y^2\sigma_x^2 + \mu_x^2\sigma_y^2 + \sigma_x^2\sigma_y^2$ {exact}
x/y	μ_x/μ_y	$[1/\mu_y^2]\sigma_x^2 + [\mu_x/\mu_y^2]^2\sigma_y^2 - 2\rho[\mu_x/\mu_y^3]\sigma_x\sigma_y$ *

Here ρ is the correlation coefficient between x and y, and the starred (*) For products and ratios, the reader can see that the variances also depend on the means.

For addition and subtraction we might also have to take into account constants that we find in the formulae. Thus for:

$z = ax + by$ $\quad \sigma_z^2 = a^2\sigma_x^2 + b^2\sigma_y^2 + 2\rho ab\sigma_x\sigma_y$

$z = ax - by$ $\quad \sigma_z^2 = a^2\sigma_x^2 + b^2\sigma_y^2 - 2\rho ab\sigma_x\sigma_y$

or when $\rho = 0$ (that is, x and y are independent)

$z = ax \pm by$ $\quad \sigma_z^2 = a^2\sigma_x^2 + b^2\sigma_y^2$

There is one other relevant formula when the relationship involves raising a variable to a power. Let $z = \lambda x^\alpha y^\beta$, with λ a constant, x and y independent, and α and β positive. If the σ's are small relative to their means, then:

$$\left(\frac{\sigma_z}{\mu_z}\right)^2 \approx \left(\frac{\alpha\sigma_x}{\mu_x}\right)^2 + \left(\frac{\beta\sigma_y}{\mu_y}\right)^2$$

These formulae can be extended for combining three or more variables by using these basic formulae and combining them appropriately. There are actually other approximations for handling virtually any other functional relationship, but it's likely that the above relationships will suffice for most readers.

The task of computing the composite gage error is compounded by the fact that we necessarily must include the process standard deviation as well into our calculations. But if we "know" both the gage errors for each single variable as well as the observed standard deviations of each variable, we can do some back calculations to estimate the overall gage error. The procedure is as follows:

- Knowing that $\sigma^2_{Total} = \sigma^2_{True} + \sigma^2_{Gage}$, we back calculate to get $\sigma^2_{True} = \sigma^2_{Total} - \sigma^2_{Gage}$ for each variable.
- We now calculate the composite standard deviation for the combination using both a) only the true standard deviation and b) the total standard deviation (which includes the measurement error). This gives us estimates for both σ_{True} and σ_{Total} for the composite situation.
- Finally, we back calculate using $\sigma^2_{Gage} = \sigma^2_{Total} - \sigma^2_{True}$ which provides an estimate of the composite gage error.

It is true that we could compute this in closed form for each simple case, but the approach outlined above greatly simplifies the calculations. Realize also that these are only point estimates for the gage error, and any confidence interval on the composite error would likely be fairly large. This procedure should only be used when the contributing gage errors are very well known.

As an example for these types of calculation, consider the following case. Suppose that we have a variable z that is the simple product of two other variables x and y. What we know about x and y are:

Process	Mean	Process σ	Gage σ
x	100	10	6
y	25	5	3

By back calculating we compute that $\sigma_{x\text{-True}} = 8$ and $\sigma_{y\text{-True}} = 4$. Now we use the formula for multiplication (with x and y uncorrelated so that $\rho=0$).

$$\sigma_z^2 = \mu_x^2 \sigma_y^2 + \mu_y^2 \sigma_x^2 + \sigma_x^2 \sigma_y^2$$

First we calculate it for the as-measured, total process:

$$\sigma^2_{z\text{-Total}} = 100^2 \cdot 5^2 + 25^2 \cdot 10^2 + 10^2 \cdot 5^2 = 315{,}000$$

Then we calculate it for the true process:

$$\sigma^2_{z\text{-True}} = 100^2 \cdot 4^2 + 25^2 \cdot 8^2 + 8^2 \cdot 4^2 = 201{,}024$$

Subtracting the Total variance from the True variance provides the composite gage error:

$$\sigma^2_{z\text{-Gage}} = \sigma^2_{z\text{-Total}} - \sigma^2_{z\text{-True}} = 113{,}976$$

So that $\sigma_{\text{Gage}} \approx 337.6$. Although this appears to be quite large, we must realize that the overall mean is 2500, being the product of x and y.

A General Word of Caution

When variances are being added together or deconvoluted from each other, the formulae being used follows the general pattern of $\sigma^2_{\text{Total}} = \sigma^2_1 + \sigma^2_2$. These statements of equality are valid only when we know for certain what the values of these variances actually are. The reality is that we obtain these values from samples, and thus we only obtain approximations of the true values. But additional errors in our estimates are compounded when some of these variance estimates involve few degrees of freedom. Although this shortcoming was highlighted in the section of MSA confidence intervals, it exists any time we do calculations from samples. When possible, the Black Belt should always strive to obtain estimates by using variance component analyses. Even then she should recognize that the final results are only point estimates with wide confidence intervals unless all the variances were calculated with a large number of degrees of freedom (i.e. a minimum of 30).

---

[1]   Deming, W.E. *Statistical Adjustment of Data.* Dover Publications, 1943.
[2]   Mandel, John, "Fitting Straight Lines When Both Variables are Subject to Error." *Journal of Quality Technology*, 16, #1, 1984.

CHAPTER 6

PROCESS CAPABILITY

*Process capability metrics are all based on specifications.
And specifications imply that anything inside specs always works and
anything outside always fails. This is nonsense! Until we focus on
more meaningful metrics—ones that emphasize being on target with
minimum variation—our Six Sigma efforts will always fall short.*

Perhaps nothing in Six Sigma has been developed more poorly than the study of process capability. The reason is simple. Virtually all analyses depend on the concept of the specification. The basic interpretation of specifications is that parts made inside the specifications always work and those outside specifications will always fail. This interpretation is easily demonstrable by going back to the fundamentals of classical Six Sigma which declare the latter parts are "defects" with the usual requirement that such parts be scrapped or reworked. If the folly of this isn't self-evident, then consider a situation where the specs are at 6 and 8. Do you believe that a part that is truly (not just measured there) at 7.99 always works and a part that is truly at 8.01 always fails?

A better definition of a specification should take into account reality. And that reality almost always entails some optimum value for a given parameter on a part, called the "nominal" (and sometimes the "target"), and an increasing probability of failure as the value gets further from that nominal value. (Exceptions exist, but they are extremely rare.) The specification could

67

then be that value at which the probability of failure is excessive, and the cost involved—either to the manufacturer or the customer—is perceived as "too much." But even that view is warped, first because it doesn't declare what should be done with such parts, and second and more importantly, most parts belong in an assembly, and the functional capability of a part is dependent on the width of the distributions of the other parts with which it must work. The tighter the distributions of the associated parts, the lower the probability of failure for the part in question.

This chapter will suggest two related solutions to this dilemma, as well as highlight some other problems with the way process capability analyses are conducted and interpreted.

Short-Term versus Long-Term Capability

It is very much to their credit that the founders of Six Sigma highlighted the existence of the difference between long-term and short-term performance. The idea that there should be two different sets of metrics, the short-term Cp and Cpk and the long-term Pp and Ppk to differentiate them, was smart. But unfortunately, and to the detriment of the success of Six Sigma endeavors, these same founders introduced a false concept that was supposed to connect these different sets—the 1.5 σ shift. The fallacy is transparent. Long term process behavior is proposed to act as if the short-term distribution is permanently shifted by 1.5σ. Those responsible for the process must be blind, for anyone using SPC would uncover such a shift in one or two cycles.

Again, to give the founders credit, I believe that they were just looking for some construct which would differentiate long- and short-term performance. And once they settled on wanting a process whose mean was 4.5σ away from the spec, adding the additional 1.5σ would result in a much sexier name—Six Sigma. (Would the methodology have taken such a popular turn if it had been named "4.5 Sigma?") But the untold damage this did to the implementation of the methodology cannot be counted, as I witnessed at IBM in the earlier 1990's.

In fact, it would have been far more sensible to suggest the use of an inflation factor applied to the short-term performance variability to estimate what the long-term performance would be. And a reasonable value for that factor would be 1.3. That is, $\sigma_{\text{Long-term}} \approx 1.3\sigma_{\text{Short-term}}$. Of course, this is only to be used when little or no long-term data is available! Otherwise, it should be calculated from that long-term data. The reason this makes sense is that typically a process will see its mean shift about, even out to 1.5σ on rare occasions. And this will add another component of variation onto the overall distribution by adding a σ_{Mean}. Furthermore, the short term standard deviation will also vary which would likely inflate the overall standard deviation. However, for its practical use each facility should look at its own process and process controls to better estimate a historical inflation factor. A well-run factory will usually run at a value less than 1.3.

In exposing the problems with the 1.5σ shift, it should be apparent that I am highly discouraging the use of the "sigma" metric—the measuring of the process mean from the nearest spec in standard deviation units and then adding on an extra 1.5 when the data is taken short term. (To make matters worse, I have even seen the practice of adding together the fraction defective material from both sides of the specifications, calculating a sigma that corresponds to the total, and then adding on the extra 1.5.) These practices only obscure the reality of the actual situation, generating lots of heat but no light. It is far better to truthfully claim what is actually known. If only short-term information is available, provide the process behavior in the appropriate metric (e.g. Cpk, sigma$_{\text{short-term}}$, or hopefully something better) and claim it is short term. If pressed for a projection of long-term performance, claim whatever inflation factor seems best.

Improvement Targets

Traditional Six Sigma suggests an improvement target of 70% in Black Belt projects, that is, a decrease of 70% in the amount of defective material being produced. It is here where the split between continuous improvement and the Six Sigma strategy's "break-through" improvement lies. But it is important to consider this goal with regard to what is called "entitlement," the performance exhibited by a process which would run with a Ppk equal to Cp. If Cp is fairly small in relation to the present Ppk, then the project should be quite simple, and probably is a good candidate for a novice Black Belt. If instead Cp is relatively close in value to an unacceptable Ppk, then the project is likely to be quite difficult, and should employ a more experienced Black Belt, for a reduction in the inherent standard deviation is much more difficult to achieve than to find levels of factors which contribute to mean shifts.

Unfortunately, as Six Sigma becomes ingrained into a company's culture, the opportunity for these 70% improvement projects begins to diminish; the low- and medium-hanging fruit has all gotten picked. At this stage it becomes necessary to begin shifting the focus of projects away from significant financial gains and towards improved customer satisfaction, which may mean giving more emphasis on cost and delivery, and even anticipating better what the customer will want in the future.

The ultimate goal of a process having its long-term performance be at 4.5σ is also unrealistic in today's world. If a company is making essentially the same product over five or more years, then a concerted effort might be able to produce the idealized process. But is it worth the cost and effort to achieve as little as a 15 dppm improvement to get to the elusive 3.4 dppm? And in the technology industry a product's useful life hardly exceeds two years; in reality, the technology changes or the specifications tighten, forcing a reduction in the process capability. It is far better to become practical and weigh the value of gain versus the cost to achieve it.

Non-normal Data

It is fairly common that processes exhibit distributions that are not normal. In some cases there are obvious reasons: the data is a count, rate or fraction defective so that it is governed by either Poisson or Binomial statistics; there exists a lower physical limit (or rarely an upper limit) so that the tail cannot extend in that direction as with Weibull, Gamma or Log-normal distributions; or the data is so composed of individual groups that it is actually a multimodal distribution. Other times it isn't clear at all as to why the distribution doesn't take that ideal Gaussian shape—which might be uncovered in a Six Sigma project.

In some cases, a transformation of the data results in a normal distribution; or if the distribution is known, then some leeway can be given to estimate process capability. But the reality is that the use of the C and P metrics in most of these cases fails to adequately capture what is happening. The conventional approach is to find a dppm and convert it to a Z score which can then be converted to a C or P metric. But this is counter-productive because it forces the receiver of this information to almost assume and interpret the result as if the underlying distribution was normal. I would suggest that it in these case is far better to only report the dppm, and give some underlying explanation of the parent distribution. In fact, for reporting purposes the dppm might be a better metric than the C or P metrics.

Statistical Specifications

One of the great difficulties that exist with the conventional C and P metrics is that they do not emphasize the nominal value enough, thereby permitting the mean to wander without having a consequence when the standard deviation diminishes. This is easily illustrated with a simple diagram that shows two process distributions with equal Ppk:

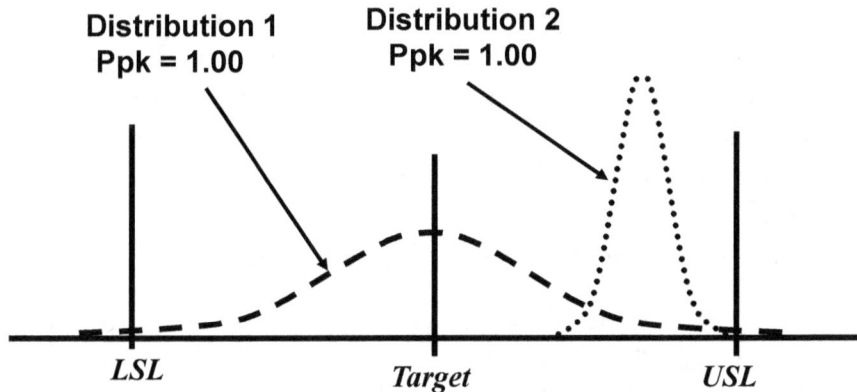

Distribution 1 probably represents what the designers intended in creating the specifications. Parts made with this distribution will have a high probability of working in the assembly. However, because the extreme Distribution 2 has so many parts stacked near the upper spec, it is quite likely that a large number will not work. I have actually seen something like this where the two distributions were the result of parts received from two different vendors. Yes, both distributions met the requirements. Yet Manufacturing found that they had to totally adjust the process to be able to use the parts from the noncentered distribution, and even then there were lots of subsequent problems. As an interesting observation, note that Distribution 1 has twice the dppm as Distribution 2!

To many engineers this kind of situation occurs often, but they feel they can't do much about it because the parts are "meeting specifications." At IBM, I met with two engineers, Jerry Coffey and Pat O'Connor, and together we came up with a solution. What is radical about it is that it puts requirements on the entire distribution and not on individual parts. There is a strong degree of logic in this approach, since it is the entire distribution of parts which must interact with the entire distributions of other parts in the assembly.

The approach follows more closely a technique which Six Sigma has been pretty mute about: acceptance sampling. Acceptance sampling was a way of testing the incoming material of vendors to see if the quality level was acceptable, and it was usually a part of the purchase agreement. Most such plans involved looking at a specific number of parts, and if too many of these sampled parts were out of spec the lot failed. Failed lots were supposed to be returned. Now it is considered an old technique, since it has been generally superseded by the examination of SPC charts by the supplier engineers. But the technique we developed, even when used with SPC charts, was a superior way to guarantee quality. And it was reasonable to apply it to internally made parts as well.

There are two requirements that are placed on the distribution:

1. **Tails Criteria**. There is an upper limit on the allowable percent of the distribution outside the tail limits.
2. **Mean Criteria**. The mean must fall within an allowable range.

The approach then is to take a homogeneous set of parts (such as an incoming shipment), take a random sample of a reasonable size, and test it against the two statistical criteria to see if it passes. Thus, the application of these statistical specifications requires the establishment of statistical tests, including applicable Type I and Type II errors, which the sample from the distribution must pass before it is considered acceptable. Because there are two separate requirements, there are two separate tests, and they follow the basic techniques learned when doing hypothesis testing.

Tails Criteria

The following six independent variables must be set in order to define the criteria for controlling the tails of the distribution: α, β, p_1, p_2, Lower Tail Limit (LTL), and Upper Tail Limit (UTL).

- $(1-\beta)$: Confidence that a lot that passes is not of unacceptable quality (see p_2 definition). β is the consumer's risk, and it is recommended to be set at 0.05.
- $(1-\alpha)$: Confidence that a lot that fails is not of acceptable quality (see p_1 definition). α is the supplier's risk. Because we are controlling the Type I error on each side independently, a recommended $\alpha = 0.03$ would entail a maximum risk of 0.06.
- p_1: Fraction outside one or the other tail limits that you want at least a $(1-\alpha)$ probability of passing in an incoming lot.
- p_2: Fraction outside the tail limits that you want at least a $(1-\beta)$ probability of failing in an incoming lot.
- LTL and UTL: Values of the variable the engineer considers the tails, such that it is acceptable that no more than $p_2 \times 100\%$ is below the LTL and no more than $p_2 \times 100\%$ is above the UTL.

The statistical test that is used is called "Sampling by Variables." A summary of this test can be found in many textbooks, and I've taken this from Acheson Duncan's book *Quality Control and Industrial Statistics*. To run the test requires that a value, called k_0, be calculated from the requirements. Also, because the test is completely specified, a minimum sample size can be calculated. These will be calculated from the normal distribution values corresponding to probability values: Z_1, Z_2, Z_α, and Z_β correspond respectively to $(1-p_1)$, $(1-p_2)$, $(1-\alpha)$, and $(1-\beta)$. Then k_0 and the sample size, n, when the standard deviation is generally not known will be calculated as:

$$k_0 = \frac{Z_\alpha Z_2 + Z_\beta Z_1}{Z_\alpha + Z_\beta}$$

$$n = \left(1 + \frac{k_0^2}{2}\right)\left(\frac{Z_\alpha + Z_\beta}{Z_1 - Z_2}\right)^2$$

From the sample, upper and lower values, k_U and k_L, will be calculated:

$$k_L = \frac{\bar{x} - \text{LTL}}{s}; \quad k_U = \frac{\text{UTL} - \bar{x}}{s}$$

If both $k_U \geq k_0$ and $k_L \geq k_0$ then the lot passes. Otherwise it doesn't meet all the criteria and some kind of dispositioning is required.

Means Criteria

This test is just the classical 2-sided test on a mean. The following six independent variables must be set in order to define the criteria for controlling the tails of the distribution: α, β, δ, Lower Mean Limit (LML), and Upper Mean Limit (UML).

- $(1-\beta)$: Confidence that a lot that passes is not of unacceptable quality (see LML and UML definitions). A recommended default value for β is 0.05.
- $(1-\alpha)$: Confidence that a lot that fails is not of acceptable quality (see LML and UML definitions). Again, because we are controlling the Type I error on each side independently, a recommended $\alpha = 0.03$ would entail a maximum risk of 0.06.
- LML: Lower limit allowed for the population mean. LML is the mean value that you want a $(1-\beta)$ probability of failing in an incoming lot.
- UML: Upper limit allowed for the population mean. UML is the mean value that you also want a $(1-\beta)$ probability of failing in an incoming lot
- δ: Increment inside the mean limits. LML+δ to UML-δ is the range of mean values on either side that you want at least a $(1-\alpha)$ probability of passing in an incoming lot.

From the sample, use the average and standard deviation to find the lower and upper pass/fail criteria values:

$$\bar{x}_L = \text{LML} + \frac{t_\beta s}{\sqrt{n}}; \quad \bar{x}_U = \text{UML} - \frac{t_\beta s}{\sqrt{n}}$$

If both $\bar{x} \geq \bar{x}_L$ and $\bar{x} \leq \bar{x}_U$ then the lot passes. Otherwise it doesn't meet all the criteria and some kind of dispositioning is again required.

Combined Criteria

In a simple way, these two sets of requirements are setting up a region in mean-sigma space in which the user wants the distribution to fall. This is illustrated in the following diagram:

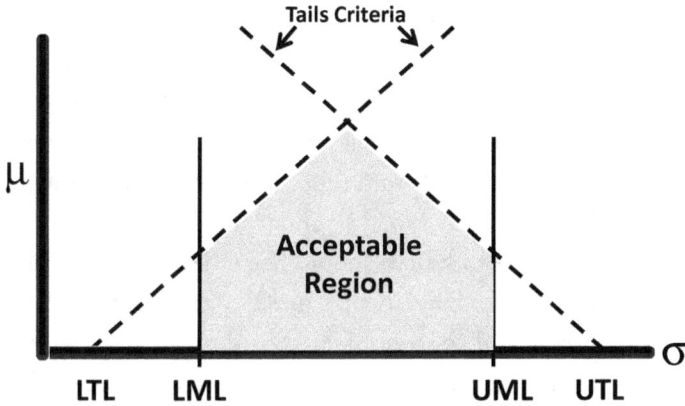

However, in order to pass the two hypothesis tests, the actual region that the *sample* mean and *sample* standard deviation must fall within gets shrunk, and the smaller the sample size, the smaller will be the acceptance region. That region is shown in the following diagram:

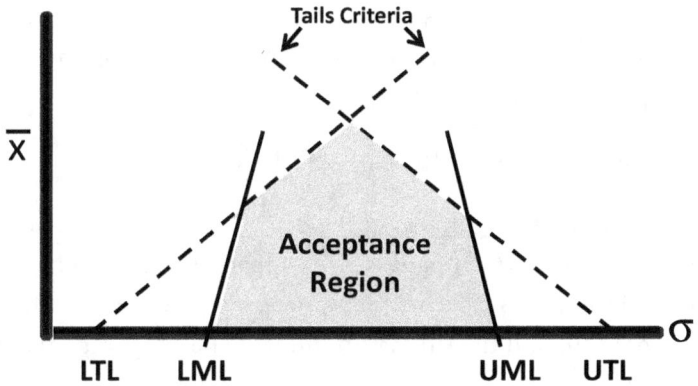

In reality, most of the sample data falls in the upper part of the Acceptance Region, since it is quite rare to have a very low standard deviation exhibited in the sample. Still, the mean limits provide protection, especially against distributions which have been cherry-picked.

The Taguchi Loss Function

Although the previous methodology doesn't provide a process capability metric, it does illustrate—and has the potential to achieve—an important behavior that a manufacturing process should have: producing at the nominal with minimum variation. In one sense, this can be the byproduct of a high Ppk, for a process whose mean is at the nominal and which has a small standard deviation will produce a high Ppk. But a high Ppk does not necessarily guarantee producing at the nominal. And there still remains the strong emphasis on the specification as a good-or-bad boundary.

By this time, most Black Belts should be familiar with the Taguchi Loss Function, originally created by the Japanese engineer/statistician Genichi Taguchi. The fundamental concept of the Loss Function is that a manufacturing process produces parts which entail a cost to society. The lowest cost occurs when the parameters important to the part are all produced at their nominal values, but the cost increases quadratically as the true value of any of the part's parameters get further away from that nominal value. It is described by a simple equation:

$$\text{Part Cost} = k(x - T)^2 + C$$

where x is the parameter value, both k and C are constants describing the cost, and T is the nominal or target value. For an entire population of parts the <u>average</u> part cost turns out to be:

$$\text{Average Part Cost} = k[\sigma^2 + (\mu - T)^2] + C$$

For any group of parts, <u>regardless of the distribution</u>, this equation is valid by substituting $\bar{x}$ and s for μ and σ. It is apparent that the Loss Function shows that minimum cost occurs for a process whose mean is at the nominal and whose standard deviation is minimal. The simplicity and applicability to Six Sigma process requirements makes the Loss Function an ideal candidate to explore to see if this model can be used to create a process capability metric.

On the face of it, there might be some objection to the Taguchi Loss Function accurately describing the value of a process. There might be better models and they may depend intimately on how the process actually works. But surely the Loss Function is vastly superior to the presently accepted model of brick wall specifications where a part just inside the specs is presumed to always work and a part just outside the specs is presumed to always fail. Surely something that is very good and simple is much better than that which is poor or that which cannot be created without intense study of each process individually.

Another objection is that the Loss Function is supposed to represent the loss to *society*. But in today's global market with the extensive communication that surrounds it, virtually all of society's loss now returns to the producing company, so that, in a sense, the Loss Function reflects very well the company's loss. The loss also begins to better reflect the true costs. Traditional specifications merely highlighted the added cost reflected in scrap or rework. But the Loss Function, with increasing costs associated with departing from the nominal, reflect an increasing probability of failure, which triggers not only an increase in the number of failed products out in the field, but also increased customer dissatisfaction and the need for a greater amount of inspection and process oversight. At least the Loss Function indirectly reflects the cost of a lost customer!

The final objection is that the loss is dependent on two parameters, k and C. First C is just a fixed per-part cost and is ultimately irrelevant, for we should be mostly interested in the incremental costs. And we will see in the next section that we can conveniently find a value for k that is quite reasonable.

The Taguchi Loss Function Cost Metric

If we wanted to accurately estimate the quality costs, we would need to know k and C. However, if we are only interested in a *relative* measure of process performance, we can avoid many of our difficulties. In this case, we would probably be most interested in comparing to a process which the designers would want: something operating at the fixed *target* (μ_{Req} = Target ≡ T), and operating with a variation no greater than a *required* standard deviation of σ_{Req}. Then, by ignoring the fixed cost C and comparing present performance to that of a process operating at the design target or goal performance, we get a ratio of these two relative costs in which the k value cancels out:

$$\tau \equiv \frac{k\left[(\mu - T)^2 + \sigma^2\right]}{k\left[(\mu_{Req} - T)^2 + \sigma_{Req}^2\right]} = \frac{(\mu - T)^2 + \sigma^2}{\sigma_{Req}^2}$$

This new metric that I developed I call the Taguchi Loss Function Cost Ratio (TLFCR), or "τ" (Tau) for short, and it simply represents the fractional increase in *total* quality costs above the fixed costs (not just scrap and rework!) over the cost that would accrue if we manufactured at our design targets of T and σ_{Req}. Thus, a process with τ = 1.3 is running 30% higher in incremental quality costs over our intended designed process. With τ = 1.0 we are hitting our goal, and with τ = 0.8 our costs are actually 20% lower than our target.

The assignment of σ_{Req} has some flexibility. If the Design Organization has not specifically provided such a value, specifications can be used to determine it. Depending on how target Ppk's have been created in the past, the width of the specifications can correspond either to a ±3σ process (for Ppk = 1.0) or a ±4σ process (for Ppk = 1.33). For example, if Ppk = 1.0 has been the normal historical criterion for "goodness," then σ_{Req} = (USL − LSL)/6; for a Ppk = 1.33 being "good," then σ_{Req} = (USL − LSL)/8. If we use a specification-based definition, I would recommend that we standardize to the value of Ppk = 1.0 for consistency.

However, another alternative captures one of the principles of Six Sigma process improvement. If we have historical data, it may be possible to establish σ_{Req} based on *entitlement*. That is, from short term studies or from best performance, an optimum capability may be available. Then, σ_{Req} would be the standard deviation of this "best" distribution. This is illustrated below:

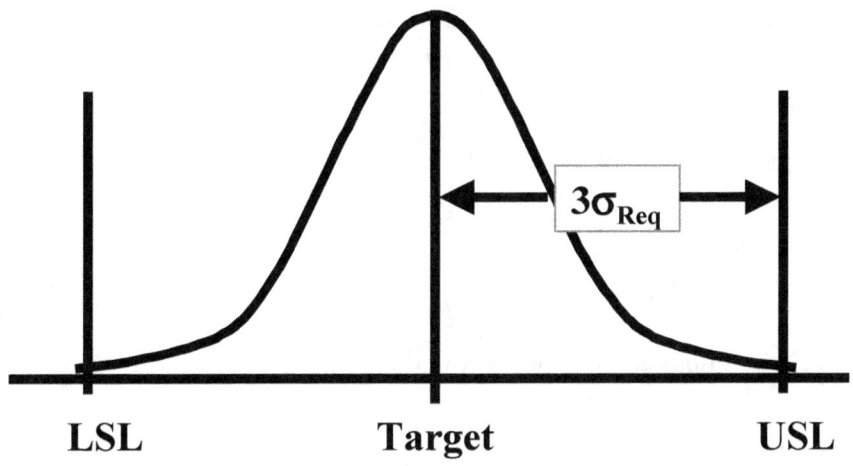

Process which originally required a Cpk = 1.00

Because we may often not have the information about the population to calculate μ and σ, samples of size of at least 200 (and preferably 1000) can be used. In these cases we just use our sample estimates of $\bar{x}$ for μ and s for σ.

And again, to strongly emphasize a previous point, the evaluation and interpretation of τ is completely independent of the distribution. Can we say something similar about either the C or P metrics? In fact, of the common metrics, only DPPM can be considered independent of the distribution, and it is pathetically inadequate in controlling the distributions.

Other Applications

The τ definition given above represents a process situation where there is a known target, and the loss in quality is assumed to be symmetric about the target. However, the concept of the Loss Function and the definition of τ can be expanded to include several other situations:
- Lower is better
- Yield
- Outliers
- Higher is better
- Asymmetric weighting around a target

The modifications, if any, are outlined below.

Lower is better

The previous formula still applies, with our target probably equal to 0. Then:

$$\tau = \frac{\mu^2 + \sigma^2}{\sigma_{Req}^2}$$

This relationship is also independent of the distribution.

Higher is better

In these cases, there is no upper limit on the parameter. The best approach is to transform the data to y = 1/x. Then the standard formula still applies for the transformed variable, and again our target value T is probably 0. Then:

$$\tau = \frac{\mu_y^2 + \sigma_y^2}{\sigma_{yReq}^2}$$

This relationship is also independent of the distribution. In this formula, however, it may be a little more difficult to determine σ_{yReq}, since the process will need to be considered in the transformed units. [Note: Some texts, such as Phillip Ross's *Taguchi Techniques for Quality Engineering*, state that a "mathematically equivalent" identity exists, where the average loss equals $k(1/\bar{x}^2)(1+3\sigma^2/\bar{x}^2)$. But in fact this is only an approximation, and fails drastically when some values are close to 0.]

Asymmetric Weighting

This case is slightly more complex. In standard processes, we might see this when we have an established target value with specifications, but the specifications are not equidistant from the target. Here we have to go back to the original definitions of the Loss Function:

$$\text{Average Part Cost} = \frac{\sum_{i=1}^{N} k(x_i - T)^2}{N}$$

In this case, however, the k values will differ depending on whether x_i is less than the target or greater than the target. Obviously, it will not be possible to use simple summary statistics because of the asymmetric weighting. We can handle this in the following way: for $x_i < T$, then $k_{lower} = 1/\sigma(lower)_{Req}$, and for $x_i \geq T$, then $k_{upper} = 1/\sigma(upper)_{Req}$. The $\sigma(lower)_{Req}$ and $\sigma(upper)_{Req}$ will come from the required distance between the target and the lower and upper specifications. If we keep the standard of requiring a Ppk = 1.0, then $\sigma(lower)_{Req} = [Target - LSL]/3$ and $\sigma(upper)_{Req} = [USL - Target]/3$. Please reference the following figure:

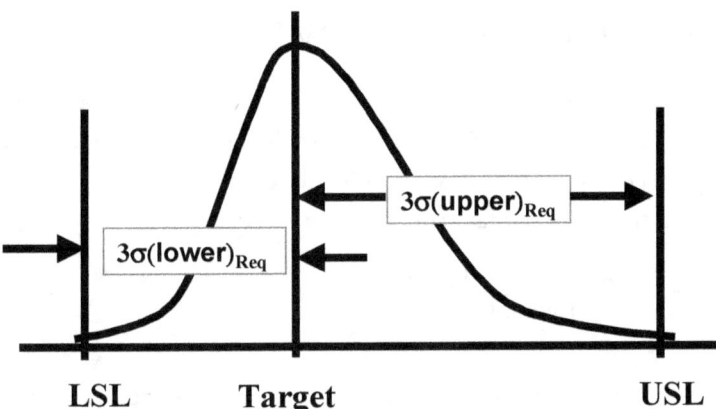

Process with Asymmetric Requirements

To compute the average loss, we have to literally add up all the contributions, and divide by the number of points:

$$\tau = \frac{\dfrac{\sum_{x_i < target}^{n_1}(x_i - T)^2}{\sigma^2(lower)_{Req}} + \dfrac{\sum_{x_i \geq target}^{n_2}(x_i - T)^2}{\sigma^2(upper)_{Req}}}{n_1 + n_2}$$

Here, n_1 refers to the number of parts less than the target, and n_2 is the number greater than or equal to the target. (For those parts exactly at the target, the group that they are in doesn't matter, since their contribution to the loss is 0.) Since this equation is an exact calculation, Tau as defined here will again be totally independent of the distribution.

Yield

Sometimes a process is measured only insofar as the unit passes or fails. In such cases, there really aren't parametric specifications, and the basic Taguchi approach loses some of its validity. The definition that I recommend is based on an empirical model I created of the Loss Function corresponding to a normal distribution with brick-wall specifications. More details can be found in "Special Notes: Correlating Yield to Tau" at the end of this chapter. First:

$$\text{Average Part Cost} \approx k[-0.38 - 9.86/\ln(1 + \varepsilon - \text{Yield})]$$

Epsilon (ε) is a very small number, required only so that the function remains defined for all values of yield. Epsilon should be set at about 1 billionth (0.000000001), and is unnecessary for yields less than 1.00.
Taking the ratio to get the tau value:

$$\tau = \frac{0.38 + 9.86/\ln[1 + \varepsilon - \text{Yield}]}{0.38 + 9.86/\ln[1 + \varepsilon - \text{Yield}_{Req}]}$$

Here, Yield_{Req} is the previously defined value that the yield is expected to achieve so that our quality levels are being met. Yield_{Req} is not expected to be equal to 1.00 unless the base yield is already perfect. Two options are available for Yield_{Req}: Yield_{Req} = 0.99865, corresponding to a Ppk = 1.00 process using variables measurements, or Yield_{Req} could be assigned the value of the *entitlement* yield, in the spirit of Six Sigma capability as discussed previously.

Another approach when the yield is quite good is to measure fallout rather than yield. In this case, we can utilize the lower-is-better metric with a target of 0. Daily fallout will correspond to individual values, and the mean and standard deviation can be computed over time. The value of σ_{Req} will be a bit more difficult, but if we could establish an undesirable fallout value (e.g. when corrective action is considered) we could assign σ_{Req} as 1/3 that value.

Outliers

Frequently, rogue points show up in the data. There are two types. The first type includes those 4σ or 5σ parts that clearly can be part of the distribution. Since these are a normal part of the continuous distribution, and regular inspection could let them be passed on, they need to be included in the standard Tau calculations.

However, there is another group of outliers that are clearly dissimilar to the predominant distribution. These parts are usually easily found through inspection, and are often characterized by their total inability to function in an application. One simple example would be resistance in a device circuit, where opens and shorts are clearly different than the rest of the population, and are usually easily detected.

The inclusion of such points in the calculation of Tau through the square of their deviation from target will vastly overstate their contributions to the quality cost. A better approach is to separate the body of data into two groups. A fraction, P, of the population falls into the normally acceptable distribution—which has its own Tau value, τ_{Good} —whereas 1-P represents the outlier population fraction. Then the effect of each of these two groups can be added (and averaged) separately using the following relationship:

$$\tau = P\tau_{Good} + (1-P)\left[\frac{1}{P}\right]^2$$

Here, $1/P^2$ is a rough approximation of the cost to discover these outliers in downstream processes. (A simple term like $1/P$ instead of $1/P^2$ would only cover the additional starts necessary, and would understate the costs.)

Averaging Multiple Processes

It is sometimes desired to report a single roll-up value that describes the overall quality of multiple processes. Tau is ideally suited to this application. Since each τ equals the increase in quality costs over the required value, then the average of all the τ's produces the *average* increase in quality costs. Neither Ppk nor Z scores can do this.

Of course, averaging the τ's means that the values all have the same weighting. But if any process is deemed more important, that τ value can be weighted more heavily without diminishing the interpretation of the average. That is,

$$\bar{\tau} = \frac{w_1 \tau_1 + w_2 \tau_2 + ... + w_n \tau_n}{w_1 + w_2 + ... w_n}$$

For example, if I have four processes with respective τ values of 1.6, 3.2, 1.2 and 0.8, then the average increase in quality costs is just the average: 1.7. However, if I deem that the last process is twice as important as the others, then:

$$\bar{\tau} = \frac{1.6 + 3.2 + 1.2 + 2(0.8)}{5} = 1.5$$

Application

The actual implementation of the TLFCR into a manufacturing line is a radical step! Companies have relied on brick wall specifications for decades, and even though they *know* that the specification approach is fundamentally wrong, its use is ingrained. Furthermore, the TLFCR operates in a way that is dissimilar to the standard metrics. A lower Tau represents an improved process, whereas lower C and P metrics indicate a process that is worse. This, too, is a prejudice that must be overcome, for the very basis of the meaning of Tau is the ratio of the present quality cost to the required quality cost, and inverting the number for the sake of conformity would be ridiculous.

For a short period of time the TLFCR was adapted where I worked (regrettably, a change in management brought about the return of business as usual). But there were several lessons learned in that time. First, a plan needed to be established for processes which did not meet the minimum requirement for Tau. A simple Excel computer algorithm was written to determine truncation limits from the sample data. Parts measuring outside these limits were to be removed, allowing the shipped distribution to have τ = 1.0 For symmetric requirements these limits are equidistant from the target. However, it was later discovered that these parts that were unacceptable for one group would later be put back into a subsequent group whose Tau was better than needed. I don't agree with that practice, but Manufacturing was being judged also on material passed through the process line. If the TLFCR is adapted, I would suggest that special disposition plans be drawn up to handle these parts, with the foreknowledge that such parts have a higher probability of failure.

Secondly, it becomes incumbent on the Design organization to perform modeling of the multiple parameters to best determine optimum-for-manufacturing distributions, for in most cases trade-offs of performance can be made. For example, Process A may be hard or expensive to control, whereas Process B is easier. If the final product relies on their combined variances, it would be less expensive to allow a wider A distribution and force a narrower B distribution. This also forces a shift from vague specification to a set of specific σ_{Req}'s.

Summary

Specification-based measures of quality often fall short of describing a true process situation, since the requirement of "just meeting specs" does not adequately take into account any of the interactions with other parts in the assembly, inspection costs, engineering attention, dissatisfied customers, and other performance related concerns. In short, they do not really take the distribution of the parts into account. The Tau metric, based on the Taguchi Loss Function goes much further in taking these concerns into account, and actually gives a value that could relate to *overall* quality costs.

Furthermore, whereas the interpretation of the specification-based metrics usually relies on the assumption that the underlying distribution is normal, τ is generally calculated and interpreted independently of the distribution. Finally, the average of the τ values over many processes can be clearly interpreted as the average fraction of quality performance above that level which is required. Averages of other metrics—except DPPM are generally meaningless. These three advantages overcome any slight increase in complexity in evaluating process performance, making τ a clear choice for a quality metric.

Special Note: Correlating Yield to Tau

The following is relevant only to demonstrate that the equation relating yield to Tau is reasonable. This model was based on a simulation. Points were generated from a normal distribution with varying means and standard deviations. These were compared to a target mean value and a one-sided specification to determine the "yield" (the amount outside specifications). Then, based on a requirement that Cpk = 1, a Tau value was also calculated. Specifically, the following values were used:

Target = 0   USL = 3 σ_{Req} = 1.00
Means varied uniformly from 0 to 2
Standard deviations varied uniformly from 0.6 to 2.5

Using regression analytical techniques, several potential empirical functions were created that approximated the scatter of points. One function that seemed to adequately describe the simulated points was Tau = $-0.38 - 9.86/\ln(1 - \text{Yield})$ where "ln" refers to the natural logarithm. A graph of the fit is provided below:

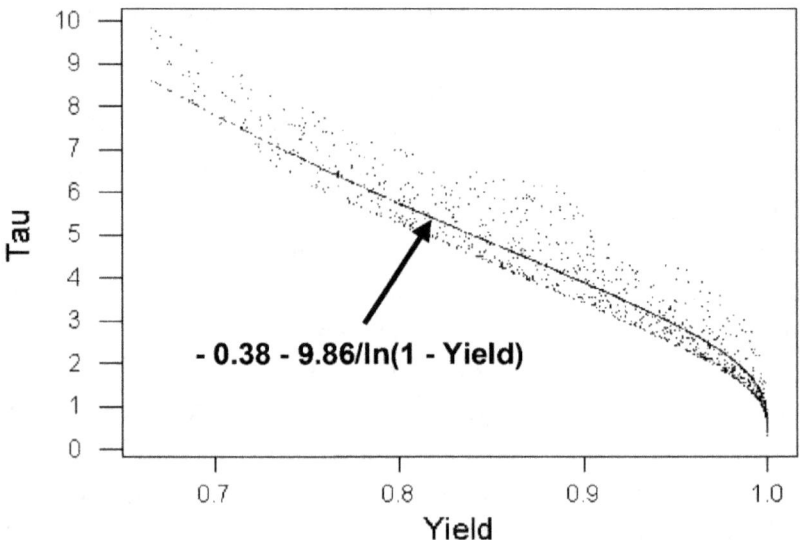

In order to make sure the function remains defined and positive for all values of Yield, a small adjustment needs to be added to the function, so that the suggested function now becomes:

$$\text{Tau} = -0.38 - 9.86/\ln(1 + \varepsilon - \text{Yield})$$

An epsilon (ε) of 1 billionth (0.000000001) is sufficient, and provides a τ with a minimum value of .096.

Generally speaking, this yield definition of Tau should not be based on small sample sizes, since 100% short-term yields are misrepresented with this functional definition.

Cpm

Up to this point there has been no mention of another quality metric which seems to have some of the advantages of rewarding a process for producing at the nominal with minimum variation. This is the metric Cpm:

$$\text{Cpm} = \frac{\text{USL} - \text{LSL}}{6\sqrt{\frac{\sum (x_k - T)^2}{n-1}}}$$

Other than a slight modification using n-1 instead of n, this appears to have much in common with Tau. In fact, if σ_{Req} is defined as (USL-LSL)/6, then Cpm ≈ 1/τ. Cpm does follow the paradigm of "higher is better" common to the C and P metrics. But it lacks all the versatility that the TLFCR has: specification of a different σ_{Req}, a rational explanation of its meaning directly in terms of quality, definitions for non-symmetric specifications (including lower is better), handling straight yield and outliers, and finally the ability to roll up many metrics together. But from the standpoint of the Six Sigma goals, it is better than Cpk and Ppk!

---

[1] Ross, Phillip J. *Taguchi Techniques for Quality Engineering.* McGraw-Hill Inc., 1988, p. 18.

CHAPTER 7

PROBABILITY

*"I was playing draw poker last night and was dealt 4 queens.
What are the odds of that?"*
*"Since the event already happened, the probability appears to be 1.
Had you asked that question before a specific deal—which I doubt
that you did—the probability would have been 1 in 54,145."*

In a sense, the foundation of all statistical analysis is probability theory. Data is taken, and the investigator tries to reach some kind of conclusion regarding various features of the population, such as the mean or standard deviation. But because there is variation in that data, these conclusions cannot be certain; there is some chance, or probability, that the conclusions are wrong. Statistics helps us quantify the likelihood of being wrong, and in that sense, statistics is the science of the study of uncertainty.

Still, the very concept of probability—especially as it applies to their work—is not very straightforward for the physicist or engineer. The mathematics and engineering courses that were taken in college invariably included problems and assignments that came up with exact answers; there was no uncertainty. Furthermore, management often requires specific recommendations for actions as if there are clear black and white answers. Yet when faced with the actual variation they see in the data, such clear-cut conclusions become elusive. It is in this sense that the full appreciation of probabilities becomes important.

Fortunately for most engineers the probability concepts that are essential are not very complicated. These are: 1) a gut-level understanding of what a probability value is; 2) the insight and capability to calculate simple probabilities; 3) knowledge of how tails of distributions provide probability values; 4) the ability to calculate expected values. Certainly a greater depth of knowledge in probability theory can be useful in some circumstances, but these opportunities are rare.

What is a "gut-level understanding" of a probability value? It involves knowledge such as that a probability value of 0.05 corresponds to the chance of something happening in 1 out of 20 opportunities. But it also puts that calculated chance into a practical perspective. If there is a 1 in 20 chance that disaster will strike if one takes a particular action, that is irresponsible. But if only 1 out of 20 engineering decisions that are made are incorrect might that be considered commendable?

This gut-level understanding also takes into account the fact that because millions of events are occurring at any one time, some of these will seem to occur with a very low probability. Sometimes these rare occurrences will involve processes that the engineer is responsible for. When playing poker a person may be pleasantly surprised at being dealt four jacks, but they shouldn't presume the deck is stacked because such an event is rare. Similarly, when something odd happens in an unmonitored process, that occurrence also doesn't mean the process is faulty and needs immediate corrective actions. But it should perhaps lead to future monitoring. (More will be said about this in the chapter on Hypothesis Testing).

Engineers also need to be able make certain simple calculations of probabilities. In my Black/Brown Belt classes I always include the "Let's Make a Deal" problem. Prior to the presentation, I choose one good prize and two "stinker" prizes. Using cards, envelopes or boxes labeled 1, 2 and 3, I place the prizes randomly in the containers (however, I do know where the good prize is located). During class I then call up one student to the front as a contestant to offer them the following deal: "There are three "doors" represented by the three [envelopes, cards, boxes] which are labeled '1,' '2' and '3.' I've randomly placed one good prize behind one of the three doors; behind the other two are not-so-good prizes. Please choose one of the doors."

After the contestant makes their choice, I then proceed to uncover what is behind one of the other two unchosen doors, and reveal that it contains a stinker. I then follow up by offering the contestant the opportunity to switch their choice; they can give up their original pick and switch to the remaining door.

More than half decide to retain their original choice. But is this the best choice?

The contestant should switch, since there is a 2/3 probability that the prize is behind the remaining door. There are three explanations that I usually provide. The first is straightforward. Their original choice had a 1/3 chance of being correct. There is a 2/3 probability that it is behind one of the two remaining doors. The fact that I showed that one of those doors concealed a stinker revealed nothing new that the contestant didn't already know. They knew one of the doors contained a stinker. They also knew (or should have concluded!) that I didn't choose the door that I revealed randomly, and that I wouldn't show them a door if it contained the good prize. Thus, the remaining unchosen door acquired the full 2/3 probability of containing the good prize.

Secondly, I provide a different scenario where there are 100 doors, one with a good prize and 99 with stinkers. After their original choice, I would reveal 98 of the remaining 99 as having stinkers. It should be obvious that a switch should be made.

If some people still aren't convinced, I finally show the entire probability table. There are 9 possibilities covering the 3 possible original choices and the 3 possible actual locations of the good prize. Three of the nine combinations reveal winning by retaining the original choice; whereas the other six would have resulted in a winning choice by switching. Still, even after these explanations, there have been a few "stragglers" who doubt the result, and I offer to play the game at a bar for real money (theirs) after class. I've had no takers.

Although I've been careful in my wording of the offer, some still think there is a psychological aspect to the whole episode. Why wouldn't I try to get them to switch to a loser if their original pick was correct? (Which is more in tune with the real "Let's Make a Deal" show.) I can appreciate that thinking, but I don't believe it should cloud the judgment regarding the calculation of the probabilities if it isn't a trick.

There is one more important aspect to this exercise, and I propose it in what appears at first to be fairly confusing language. I state that there are two types of decisions involved. There is the "correct" decision, and then there is the "right" decision. The difference is that the "correct" decision results in actually winning the prize, but the "right" decision is the one that had the highest probability of winning the prize. Right decisions result in correct decisions more often. And as engineers they should strive to make the right decisions rather than hope in luck that they make the correct decision.

The third aspect of importance in probability is knowing that the area in the tails of a distribution can be used to compute probability. This should be in the foundational knowledge of the Black Belt. The details should be well known for various probability distributions, but there should also be some knowledge of how these areas can be calculated for non-normal data distributions so as to calculate the amount out of specifications when the standard brick-wall specifications are used.

Expected Values

Finally, the fourth item of importance is knowing how to compute expected values. Ultimately, a good engineer needs to be able to make good choices regarding the financial outcomes of any given decision. The concept is simple in principle. One multiplies the probability of an event times its (financial) effect. Then he adds up all these products to determine the net cost. If there are several potential options, the engineer should tend toward the one that provides the greatest likely return.

For example, suppose that there are three potential actions that can be taken. We'll label these A, B and C.

- The probability that A is a success is 10%, and will return $250,000; however, if it's wrong (a 90% chance), it will cost $10,000.
- The probability that B is a success is 50%, and will return $40,000; however, if it's wrong (a 50% chance), it will cost $2,000.
- The probability that C is a success is 5%, and will return $800,000; however, if it's wrong (a 95% chance), it will cost $20,000.

Let's now compute the expected values (EV):

- For A, EV = (.1)*$250,000 − (.9)*$10,000 = $77,460
- For B, EV = (.5)*$40,00 − (.5)*$2000) = $21,000
- For C, EV = (.05)*$800,000 − (.95)*$20,000) = $178,885

From these, the financial decision that is likely to make the most money is option C. That still, of course, does not mean it is the decision that should be made, since the amount of potential loss could have other repercussions, such as creating the inability to continue operations or missing other potentially lucrative opportunities. Decisions must never be made in a vacuum.

I provide an exercise for my Advanced Statistics class that directly relates to expected values. For the first day of class I ask each student to bring both a $5 bill and a $10 bill. And then I present to them this problem:

"I have three 2-sided cards. One of these has a black dot on each side. The second has a red dot on each side. The third has a red dot on one side and a black dot on the other." I then ask a student to come up, take the three cards and shuffle them up, including flipping them around. I take these behind my back and place one of them in an envelope with a hole on one side. I put the other two cards away where they can't be seen. I then show them the envelope, which reveals the color of one side of the chosen card.

I then force them to bet: "You can bet that the color on the opposite side of the card is the same color. If you are right, you win $10; if you are wrong you lose $15. Alternatively, if you think the other side has the opposite color, your bet will win you $15 if you are right, but will cost you $10 if you are wrong." I essentially force them into making one bet or the other, usually using language that implies that they are always betting the company's money without a direct consequence, so that making a bet with their own money in a learning experience should be fully acceptable. A large majority usually chooses to bet that the other side of the card has the opposite color.

So what are the probabilities so we can compute the expected values? Very simply, the original probability of choosing a card with the same color on both sides is 2 out of 3. The fact that the students see a specific red or black dot doesn't affect that original probability, for the same betting proposition would have been offered. Alternatively, if, say, the red dot shows, there are three surfaces that could reveal a red dot. Two out of three of these occurrences would have happened with the card that had red on both sides. Still, many students conclude that a red dot could only show on one of two cards and believe the probability is 50%.

To complete the computation of expected values to highlight the importance of making a "right" choice, I demonstrate:

- EV(same side) = (.667)*$10 − (.333)*$15 = + $1.67
- EV(diff side) = (.333)*$15 − (.667)*$10 = − $1.67

As a side note, when I ask the students who bet "wrongly" why they made that decision, some say that they were more reluctant to lose $15 versus $10, and that thought affected their decision. It would be interesting to see if this misguided parsimony colors their business decisions! Finally, before I reveal the card in the envelope I call the deal off, avoiding the accusation that I am making the students gamble in class. But once again I emphasize the importance in treating the company's money more like their own, and that every time they make a decision they are gambling with that money.

Finally, one other very important application of expected value computation arises in choices regarding the Type I and Type II errors for hypothesis testing. But a discussion on this will be postponed until that chapter.

Bayes Theorem

There is one additional tool of probability that has an occasional use for the Black Belt, and that involves the result of Bayes Theorem. To utilize this correctly requires a little more theory in probability. First there is the definition of "conditional probability," that is the probability of an event A happening given that a second event B has happened. The shorthand designation for this conditional probability is P(A|B), sometimes termed "the probability of A given B is true." For example, we may want to know the probability of a part being out of specification given that a particular mean shift has occurred in a process. We can also define P(A|B) as:

$$P(A \mid B) = \frac{P(A \text{ and } B)}{P(B)}$$

For this relation to work, $P(B) \neq 0$. If $P(A|B) = P(A)$ then events A and B are independent. There is another piece of shorthand notation, and that is if there is a prime (') after the letter, it means "not happening;" thus $P(A')$ is the probability that A doesn't happen. Because all probabilities add up to 1.0, $P(A) + P(A') = 1.0$. Finally, let us suppose that B can have more than two outcomes, such as $B_1, B_2, \ldots B_k$. Then

$$P(A) = P(A|B_1)P(B_1) + P(A|B_2)P(B_2) + \ldots P(A|B_k)P(B_k)$$
and
$$1 = P(B_1|A) + P(B_2|A) + \ldots P(B_k|A)$$

Now Bayes Theorem says:

$$P(A|B) = \frac{P(B|A)P(A)}{P(B)} \quad \text{again } P(B) \neq 0$$

And for k mutually exclusive and exhaustive events regarding A (that is, A can happen as $A_1, A_2, \ldots A_k$)

$$P(A_m|B) = \frac{P(B|A_m)P(A_m)}{\sum_{j=1}^{k} P(B|A_j)}$$

Now how can these relationships be useful? Let's see a couple examples.

Example 1: Consider a semiconductor manufacturing process. Let C indicate that a chip was subjected to "high" levels of contamination and F indicates that the chip failed the test. Assume the following are observed:
- $P(C) = 0.20$ [the probability the chip experienced high levels of contamination equals 0.20]
- $P(F|C) = 0.10$ [the probability a chip failed after experiencing high levels of contamination was 0.10]
- $P(F|C') = 0.005$ [the probability of failure with no contamination]

We are now interested in $P(C|F)$, the probability that a failed chip experienced contamination (which might imply that our failure analysis work should look for contamination as the cause). We need to do some preliminary work to find $P(F)$.

- $P(C') = 1 - P(C) = 1 - 0.20 = 0.80$
- $P(F \text{ and } C') = P(F|C')P(C') = (0.005)((0.80) = 0.004$
- $P(F \text{ and } C) = P(F|C)P(C) = (0.10)(0.20) = 0.02$
- $P(F) = P(F \text{ and } C) + P(F \text{ and } C') = 0.02 + 0.004 = 0.024$

Then using Bayes' equation:

$$P(C|F) = \frac{P(F|C)P(C)}{P(F)} = \frac{(0.10)(0.20)}{0.024} = 0.833$$

The probability that a chip that has failed has experienced high levels of contamination is 0.833, and so that should be the first failure mode that is investigated.

Example 2: A screening test correctly identifies a defect 99% of the time when it exists, and correctly declares no defect 95% of the time when no defect exists (which means there is a 5% false positive rate). The incidence of defects in the general population is 0.01% (0.0001)

If the test should indicate a defect, what is the probability that a defect actually exists? (You can also think of this in terms of medical testing, where false positives can occur; e.g. you've just been tested for Disease XYZ, and the test came back positive. What's the *real* chance that you have the disease?)

First, what do we know? Let's use the nomenclature that T represents that the test shows a failure, and D represents that a defect actual exists. We know

$P(D) = 0.0001$
$P(T|D) = 0.99$
$P(T'|D') = 0.95$

And we want to know P(D|T). To use the Bayes equation we will need to find out:
→ $P(T) = P(T|D)P(D) + P(T|D')P(D')$ [with only 2 possibilities] and
→ $P(T|D') = 1 - P(T'|D')$ [also with only 2 possibilities].

Since $P(D') + P(D) = 1.0$, $P(D') = 1 - 0.0001 = .9999$. Then
$P(T) = P(T|D)P(D) + \{1-P(T'|D')\}P(D')$
$= (0.99)(0.0001) + (1-0.95)(0.9999) = 0.050094$, and

$$P(D|T) = \frac{P(T|D)P(D)}{P(T)} = \frac{(0.99)(0.0001)}{0.05009} = 0.001976$$

This means that there is about 1 chance in 506 that the tested part actually has a defect. This example emphasizes the apparent paradox that even tests with very good discrimination can have results that need follow-up tests when the general population experiences a very low rate of an undesirable characteristic.

CHAPTER 8

HYPOTHESIS TESTING AND SAMPLE SIZE: 1 AND 2 POPULATIONS

Never draw statistical conclusions from data that has been brought to your attention because it is unusual. Instead, let that data suggest a hypothesis that can be tested with future data.

There is probably nothing in inferential statistics that is more important for the engineer to learn than the basic methods of hypothesis testing using the appropriate sample size. These fundamental building blocks allow the engineer to finally make important decisions based on known risks that can actually be controlled by the investigator. Certainly, along with this knowledge comes the appreciation of (and ability to calculate) confidence intervals, which helps quantify the uncertainty in the estimates, and may provide insight into how good those estimates or conclusions actually are.

The methods of hypothesis testing are well covered in Black Belt training for the one- and two-sample cases of means and standard deviations. Of course for the two-sample means test the investigator must first determine whether the two standard deviations are equal. But present software allows quick calculations that produce p-values that can then be compared to the pre-chosen α value.

To briefly summarize the procedure to determine the appropriate testing, all one needs to do is specify each of the following three components:

1. Statistic of interest: means (σ unknown), standard deviations, proportions, or rates (or counts)
2. Levels being compared: one population, two populations, three or more populations; these are usually labeled "samples" rather than "populations," and so I will adhere to convention and use "sample;" e.g. 1-sample, 2-sample or 3-or-more-sample tests.
3. Type of alternative hypothesis: greater than, less than, or not equal.

Indeed, I have never run into a case where the standard deviation is known (although it may be reasonable estimated) but the mean is not. The combination of these three components represent 36 different possibilities (38 if we count the cases of unequal variances for the two and three-or-more samples for means), and the Black Belts must make sure to choose which is correct for their situation. In this chapter, I will only deal with the 1- and 2-sample cases, leaving the methods for the more complex 3-or-more-samples situation for the next chapter.

Type I and Type II Risks

Ideally, any time a hypothesis test is being contemplated, preliminary planning is required. Of course this includes how data should be taken so that the sample data is random and representative. But in order to make full use of the power of statistical testing, the sample <u>size</u> needs to be appropriate. To do this correctly, the investigator first needs to define a difference that he believes is important to find and which is large enough so that there is some reasonable possibility that it exists. This is usually called the "critical difference." For means and proportions this difference can be stated directly. However, for standard deviations and rates (or counts), the difference needs to be specified as a ratio. [Of course one could always state it as a difference, but it will get translated back into a ratio in order to compute the sample size.]

Next null and alternative hypotheses need to be created. Usually the null hypothesis is based on a statement of equality. Traditionally, the alternative hypothesis is based on a statement that implies inequality. Thus, we could have the following for a simple one-sample mean test:

Ho: $\mu = \mu_0$
Ha: $\mu < \mu_0$

with μ_0 being a specific value. Strictly speaking, this would be incorrect, since it doesn't account for the situation where $\mu > \mu_0$, so a better way to write this is:

Ho: $\mu \geq \mu_0$
Ha: $\mu < \mu_0$

Our Type I Error is defined as rejecting the null hypothesis when it is true; the Type II Error is accepting the null hypothesis when it is false, or alternatively, rejecting the alternative hypothesis when it is true. Practically speaking, these designations of the hypotheses are only adequate for the situation where the data has already been taken (but not looked at), and the testing is only performed against a pre-chosen α risk. Before data is taken with the intention of first choosing an appropriate sample size, it is better still to write the hypotheses so that they include the critical difference, Δ:

Ho: $\mu = \mu_0$
Ha: $\mu = \mu_0 + \Delta$

Designating our hypotheses this way is essential in order to compute an appropriate sample size and understand our α and β risks. Now we can make the specific statements that 1) if the null hypothesis is exactly true, there will be only a $(1-\alpha)$ chance that we will reject Ho; 2) if the alternative hypothesis is exactly true, there will only be a $(1-\beta)$ chance that we will reject Ha.

This brings up the very important point of what conclusions we can make after we run the statistical test on the data and obtain our p-value. There are three possible outcomes:

1. If $p < \alpha$, then we reject Ho and declare that we are *at least* $(1-\alpha) \times 100\%$ confident that the true mean $\mu > \mu_0$.
2. If $p > \alpha$, then we reject Ha and declare that we are *at least* $(1-\beta) \times 100\%$ confident that the true mean $\mu < \mu_0 + \Delta$.
3. If $p = \alpha$, then we continue our calculation of p with more precision (decimal positions) until we get an inequality.

Note that at no time can we make a declaration of equality! If we fail to reject Ho, that does not imply that Ho is true and $\mu = \mu_0$. We may choose to operate under that assumption, but it is exactly that—an assumption. And before we even think about making that assumption, we should create a confidence interval on the mean based on the data and verify that it contains μ_0. As I've told my students:

Statistics means never being able to say "equal."

much to the disappointment of engineers who want a "pure" result.

These conclusions can be illustrated with an example that could have several possible outcomes. Suppose my hypotheses are:

Ho: $\mu = 30$ with $\alpha = .05$
Ha: $\mu = 40$ with $\beta = .05$

Now I calculate the appropriate sample size, take the data, and find that based on the sample standard deviation that the 90% two-sided confidence interval is ±5.0 (this would correspond to a 95% one-sided value). Suppose I obtain any of the four following results for x-bar:

a) $\bar{x} = 32$; I conclude that $\mu < 40$, and I may choose to operate under the assumption that $\mu = 30$.

b) $\bar{x} = 38$; I conclude that $\mu > 30$, and I may choose to operate under the assumption that $\mu = 40$.

c) $\bar{x} = 21$; I conclude that $\mu < 40$, and I would be foolish to operate under the assumption that $\mu = 30$.

d) $\bar{x} = 49$; I conclude that $\mu > 30$, but I would be foolish to operate under the assumption that $\mu = 40$.

For these examples I have taken the simplest case of a one-sample mean test. But the set-up and types of conclusions are essentially analogous for any of the one- and two-sample statistics tests.

Getting back to trying to compute an appropriate sample size, once the critical difference or ratio is determined, the engineer is now ready to establish the acceptable probabilities for erring in his decision based on the data. This means assigning a specific value to α, the probability of rejecting Ho when it is true, and a specific value to β, the probability of rejecting Ha (missing a difference as big as the critical difference) when it is true. Although default values of α = .05 and β = .1 are often used, these are the historical remnants from statisticians without process knowledge who have had to arbitrarily assign these probabilities for engineers who don't want to take the responsibility for assessing the risks themselves.

The superior way to assign these probability values is to try to calculate expected values with regard to the decisions. If there is a difference as big as Δ, what is the cost in lost opportunity if we miss it in our testing? If there is no difference, what does it cost to proceed with a change (or to more thoroughly check out the possibility of a change) when no difference exists? Here the engineer also will need to make an educated guess as to what the chances are that there is a difference as big as Δ. The engineer will also need to realistically factor in the cost of taking the sample.

In this age of limited resources, the sample size itself may be limited. Here, using available software, the Black Belt can calculate various scenarios using multiple combinations of α, β and Δ to determine if any of them are practical based on assumed possibilities of sample size. In some instances where the sample size is significantly restricted, α or β may become so large, or Δ so small, that it might not even make sense to try to obtain data. However, in my experience I have noted that when an engineer is told that some number is the *minimum* sample size to use, it is generally interpreted that this is the *maximum* sample size that he will plan to use. I believe this parsimonious attitude is wrong, since too often something goes wrong in the generation of the data so that the advised sample size is not achieved, or certain assumptions are violated (such as non-normality, unequal variances, or a higher-than-expected standard deviation such that the critical Δ is practically too large).

Variables Cases: Means and Standard Deviations

The methods for hypothesis testing are relatively simple. For standard deviations, if the distributions are not normal, then non-parametric tests are required (e.g. Levene's for two-sample). For means, the results of the Central Limit Theorem will support most parametric tests for one- and two-sample tests.

In calculating sample sizes for means for one- and two-sample tests, the straightforward methods work as long as one puts the critical difference in terms of number of standard deviation units (assuming the sigmas are unknown). Currently, I am unaware of software macros that work for two-sample tests when the standard deviations are expected to be unequal. But if a reasonable estimate can be made of the ratio between the two, a spreadsheet program can be made that takes that ratio into account. In work that I've done, the ratio of the correct sample sizes is approximately equal to the ratio of the standard deviations. So a close approximation with present software would be to use the average of the ratio and 1.0 for the expected standard deviation, double that sample size, and reapportion the total so that the ratio of the sample sizes equals the ratio of the standard deviations.

Example 1: Suppose that from a physical interpretation of the relevant data the ratio of sigmas can be estimated to be about 1.6. The properly calculated sample sizes (for α = .05, β = .1, Δ = 1.0 × lower sigma) were 24 and 38. Using common software and inserting 1.3 for the standard deviation estimate, the equal-sigma calculation total is 30+30=60. Reapportioning these would provide 23 and 37. The population with the larger standard deviation should always have a larger sample size taken.

For standard deviations, as long as the distributions can be assumed normal, the Chi-square over degrees of freedom (χ^2/df) distribution and the F distribution work well for the one- and two-sample tests respectively. If the distributions are not normal (but not really radically non-normal), an increase of 10% in the sample size using χ^2/df or F (the software macro assumptions) will usually suffice.

A note of importance when choosing the sample size is to be aware that the ratio of the standard deviations needs to be tested when considering the two-sided test. That is, if you are looking for a 50% increase as the upper Ha value, you cannot look for a 50% decrease on the lower value, or else the sample size is asymmetric depending on which side you are testing. Thus if Ha is σ_2/σ_1 = 1.5 at the upper side, the lower side test should be σ_2/σ_1 = 1/1.5 = 0.667. Similarly, if you test σ_2/σ_1 = 0.5 then you should also be looking for σ_2/σ_1 = 2 at the high end.

Special Cases: Tolerance Intervals and Cpk

As Black Belts develop their skills, other questions and concerns often crop up. One of these important concerns relates to knowledge about the standard Cpk or Ppk statistic. That is, given specifications and a process mean and standard deviation, the capability metrics are usually calculated. But how well does the Black Belt know what the value of those metrics actually are? How can a confidence interval be put on those values, or how can one run a hypothesis test on those values to determine if they are meeting pre-defined criteria? The difficulty arises because of the metric's definition, which involves a ratio where the mean is in the numerator and the standard deviation is in the denominator—and finding joint confidence intervals of both these statistics is quite complicated.

There are two separate approaches to better defining these capability metrics. Both require that the underlying distribution is normal. The first involves what are called "tolerance intervals. The previously referenced ratio is distributed according to what is called a "non-central t distribution," and it is extremely difficult to calculate, such that only recently has standard statistics software been able to produce accurate values (previously these were calculated using approximation formulae). The end result is usually a probability value and a proportion. Thus, if the investigator inputs a process mean and standard deviation, along with the sample size and a criterion value (call it W), then these programs can produce paired values of probabilities and proportions. These outputs would read something like:

"You are 80% confidence that less than 1% of
the distribution falls outside W."

or

"You are 90% confident that less than 2.6% falls outside W."

Generally, the investigator provides either the probability or the proportion, with the other quantity being given by the program.

These can obviously lead to a confidence statement about Cpk or Ppk. For example, if the data were long term and we obtained the results of the second example where W is one of the specifications, we next need to calculate the Z value corresponding to 2.6% out of specification. This value is 1.943.

Dividing this by 3 to get Ppk, we would be able to say we are at least 90% confident that the one-sided Ppk is no worse than 0.648 (not a very proud statement!). Realize that this is only a one-sided statement, so the Black Belt should only run the calculation on the worse side.

A second approach uses an approximation attributable to Bissel[1]. With a sample size, n, of at least 50, the capability metric (call it Cpk just for simplicity) is calculated from the data. A one-sided confidence value, $1-\alpha$, is determined and $Z_{1-\alpha}$ is calculated. Then a value "A" is calculated, with:

$$A = \sqrt{\frac{1}{9n} + \frac{Cpk^2}{2n-2}}$$

And the capability metrics are

$$Cpl \approx Cpk - Z_{1-\alpha} A$$
$$Cpu \approx Cpk + Z_{1-\alpha} A$$

If the Black Belt desires a two-sided confidence interval, then just substitute $\alpha/2$ for α. Once one has confidence intervals, one can also run hypothesis tests, although p-values will not be generated.

Attribute Cases: Proportions and Counts (or Rates)

When dealing with attribute cases, it is important to be able to differentiate the type of data that is being analyzed. Typically, the Black Belt is concerned either with defects or defectives. In the former case, the defects are countable, and it may be possible that a unit possesses more than one defect; the analytical distribution to be used is then the Poisson distribution. If a unit has one or more defect it is considered defective, and the judgment made is binary—the unit is either good or bad; the analytical distribution to be used is then the Binomial distribution.

The methods for hypothesis testing are significantly more complicated when dealing with either proportions or rates for two important reasons. First, the distributions that they are based on are discrete, so that the probability values that are generated fall into non-continuous groups. Second, the distributions themselves are relatively complicated, and only recently has computing power developed sufficiently to handle some of the calculations that can involve numbers like 96! (96 factorial). It is true that software hypothesis tests can adequately provide accurate p-values for 1-sample tests because the true distributions can be used. But things remain much more complex for the 2-sample tests, mostly because there are no statistical distributions describing the difference of two proportions or the ratio of two rates, but also in part because the hypotheses themselves are not always clear.

To illustrate how complex this problem has been for statisticians, consider a paper by Robert Newcombe (1998)[2]. In this paper he compares <u>eleven</u> different methods that have been proposed for dealing with the difference between two proportions. His final recommendation is first a computer solution (because of the computational complexity) and then a fairly complex approximation that can be done algebraically. As I've looked into commercial software solutions, I don't believe these have been incorporated.

In the case for proportions, let's provide an illustrative example. Suppose we are looking for a $\Delta=0.1$ higher difference of π_2 over π_1. Then (using π as a population proportion) we might denote Ho and Ha as:

Ho: $\pi_2 = \pi_1$ or $\pi_2 - \pi_1 = 0$
Ha: $\pi_2 = \pi_1 + 0.1$ or $\pi_2 - \pi_1 = 0.1$

However, we also need to provide a baseline value for the null hypothesis. Let's arbitrarily choose 0.75. The software for a sample size calculation uses an approximation which looks and compares the two situations of equality at p = 0.75 and inequality if p_2 is 0.85. The hypothesis testing software also compares the differences. But there is a second option for analysis called "Fisher's Exact Test" (FET), which calculates the probability of seeing the actual split in counts assuming that the two proportions are equal. Thus, in our example suppose the sample size of 100 was used for both samples, with the first sample showing 70 counts of interest and the second sample 80 counts. Fisher's Exact Test would then assume the real proportion was 0.75 = (70 + 80)/200, and calculate the probabilities of the 75:75, 74:76, 73:77, 72:78, and 71:79 splits, add them together, and subtract from 1.0 to get the p-value. It seems to me that this is a very reasonable way to compute a probability value. At one time, because the calculations were onerous, in order to use FET limits had to be put on the total counts, so that this test was used only in cases with very low counts. But now since computing power has reached an extremely high level of efficiency and accuracy, FET can probably be used in all cases. Note, then, that the assumed hypotheses are somewhat different, since the Ha proportions are spread equally about the null hypothesis value of equality, and π_1 does not maintain its original value.

Assuming that FET is going to be used for analysis, current software (such as Minitab 16) underestimates the appropriate sample size by about 10%. (Realize that you should always avoid the "normal approximation to the binomial" approach.) Although no exact formula is possible for the two-sample proportion case, Casagrande, Pike and Smith (1978)[3] have arrived at a very good approximation. Their formula for the one-sided case, with p_1 and p_2 designated as the two sample proportions, testing $p_1 > p_2$, gives the sample size n as

$$n = \frac{A\left[1 + \sqrt{1 + 4(p_1 - p_2)/A}\right]^2}{4(p_1 - p_2)^2}$$

where A is defined as:

$$A = \left[Z_{1-\alpha}\sqrt{(p_1 + p_2)(1 - p_1 - p_2 + p_1 p_2)/2} + Z_\beta\sqrt{p_1(1 - p_1) + p_2(1 - p_2)}\right]^2$$

For the two-sided case, just substitute $\alpha/2$ for α. However, be careful in the 2-sided case if the average proportion is different. For example, if p_2 is the baseline and you are looking for a $\pm\Delta$ from p_2, the value closer to 0.5 will give a larger sample size, and this larger value should be used. If instead a base value of $(p_1+p_2)/2$ is used while looking for a $|p_1-p_2|=\Delta$ difference, the $\alpha/2$ substitution works correctly.

This aspect of checking both an upper and lower 1-sided sample size using $\alpha/2$ for the null hypothesis should always be done for attribute cases, since the available software might not take the asymmetric nature of these distributions into effect. And this could result in a sample size that is too small.

There is a special case of two-proportions testing that is worth mentioning. Sometimes the investigator doesn't really care which of the two proportions is superior; he only wants a good chance of picking the better of the two. In that sense, there really isn't a null hypothesis that is important, but only the desire to have a large enough sample size so that the error of picking the worse proportion is avoided. Such testing would require a significantly lower sample size than what the standard two-proportion testing method would require. Wendell Carr in a 1985 paper[4] outlines how this can be done and provides a table and a graph with sample sizes appropriate to achieve a 90% confidence that the better proportion is chosen in a "pick the winner" strategy. For example, in choosing a sample size for the case where possibly $p_2 = p_1 = 0.02$, and $\Delta = -0.01$ the conventional sample size would be about 2730, whereas the "pick the winner" size is 480.

For the one-sample rate or count tests, a fortuitous statistical "accident" occurs, in that a well-known continuous distribution, $\chi^2_{df,\alpha}$, equates to the Poisson distribution for certain values. Let $P(\lambda, x \leq c) = \alpha$ equal the Poisson probability of obtaining a value of c or less given that the mean is λ. (For example, with $\lambda = 4.7439$ and c=1, P(4.7439, c $\leq$ 1) yields a probability of exactly 0.05.) Then $(\chi^2_{df=2c,\ 1-\alpha})/2 = \lambda$. This can be used in the following way. Suppose in a process I find exactly 3 defects in 100 ft² of material and I want to know what the 90% level upper limit there is on the true mean of defect occurrence. The value equals $(\chi^2_{df=6,\ 0.9})/2 = 10.6446/2 = 5.3223$; I am at least 90% confident that the true average occurrence of defects is less than or equal to 5.32 per 100 square feet.

This relationship allowed me to create a sample size method for 1-sample Poisson problems well before these became integrated into present commercial software. Such a problem and its solution would be posed:

I wish to prove with $(1-\alpha)\times 100\%$ confidence that the true defect rate is less than 1/N. Also, if the true defect rate =1/kN, I would like to pass the test with $(1-\beta)\times 100\%$ confidence.

To solve, one needs to find the lowest even value of degrees of freedom (df) such that:

$$\frac{\chi^2_{df,1-\alpha}}{\chi^2_{df,\beta}} \leq k$$

Then the sample size equals $\frac{1}{2}N\chi^2_{df,1-\alpha}$

And if $c = df/2 - 1$ or fewer defects are found you conclude that the true rate of defects is less than $1/N$ with $(1-\alpha) \times 100\%$ confidence.

Example 2: I might wish to be 95% confident that my true defect rate is less than 1 in 100 units (0.01). But if the true defect rate is actually 1 in 300 units (0.0033), I wish to "pass" the test 80% of the time. Then $\alpha = 0.05$, $\beta = 0.20$, $N = 100$, and $k = 3$. Looking down the columns of the χ^2 table for 0.20 and 0.95 probabilities, the ratio $\chi^2_{.95}/\chi^2_{.20}$ is less than 3.0 for df = 10. Since an even degrees of freedom are needed, I can use df=10. Since $\chi^2_{df=10, .95} = 18.3$, sample size = ½(100)(18.3) = 915, and I will declare a lower rate than 1/100 if I encounter (10/2) − 1 = 4 or fewer defects in my sample.

The two-sample Poisson comparison also has many difficulties, and Lloyd Nelson (1987)[5] provides two approaches that are legitimate. In general, as with the two-sample binomial test, one should avoid using the "normal approximation to the Poisson" approach for analysis (although this may be one way to calculate a sample size). However, this method is sometimes used as the first method in software programs. In the same way that Fisher's Exact Test is used for proportions, a similar approach can be applied to the outcomes of rate tests if the null hypothesis involves equality, but the alternative hypothesis involves a split around that equal value. In general, when "exact" options are available in software, these should be chosen, if only to avoid the normal approximation being used.

Finally, as a last step in the hypothesis testing procedure, it is always advisable to create a confidence interval about the statistic of interest. Sometimes, especially when the null hypothesis has not been rejected, these CIs are so large that making any assumptions of equality are absurd. This happens usually in instances when a sample size less than an appropriate value has been taken.

Sampling, a Special Case

As has been written in a previous chapter, all samples need to be representative and random. By representative is meant that the sample is taken in such a way that the population being tested is well represented by the sample—that is, that the characteristics that are present in the population are also very likely to appear in the sample.

Almost as important is that the sample is randomly taken, such that each part has an equal chance of being chosen (with the exception being when stratification is advised). Usually, the random parts are chosen over a period of time to be able to capture the time element involved in the population. But a problem might arise when the total time of sampling is not known, and parts cannot be stored until such time that the random sample is drawn from the entire group.

I devised a method for being able to take a random sample when the total number of final parts is unknown. (I've since become aware of others who created a similar method.[6]) It allows every part to have an equal chance of being chosen and yet allows parts to pass on before all parts have been made. The procedure uses the following definitions:

- M = desired sample size
- n = the sequential number of each unit
- $U(n)$ = a random number assigned to the nth part, uniformly distributed on [0,1]
- ROUNDUP(y) = next higher integer $\geq y$

Then the following algorithm will choose a random sample:

1. Designate the storage compartments for the M units of the sample size as $S(1)$, $S(2)$, $S(3)$, ... $S(M)$. Fill these compartments with the first M units.
2. For the nth sample (n > M), generate Q = ROUNDUP(n·U(n)).
3. Based on the value of Q:
   ◦ If $Q < M + 1$, place the unit corresponding to $X(n)$ in the compartment $S(Q)$, replacing the previous contents. (The replaced part can move on for further processing.)
   ◦ If $Q > M$, pass that unit on.

When all units have been made, the M storage compartments will contain M units, and each produced unit had an equal probability of being chosen regardless of the population size. Unfortunately, in practice it may be difficult to spend time generating random numbers and placing and replacing parts in registers. However, a table could be created from a computer that would identify specifically which parts should be removed for possible use in the sample and which register they would go in. If some minimum population size could be postulated, such as 300, then the first M samples could be specified by order, and random numbers generated "on the fly" could be avoided for the first 300.

---

[1]   Bissel, A. F. (1990), "How Reliable is your Capability Index?" *Applied Statistics,* vol. 39 Issue 3, pp. 331-340.

[2]   Newcombe, R. E. (1998). "Interval Estimation for the Difference between Independent Proportions: Comparison of Eleven Methods." *Statistics in Medicine* 17, pp. 873-890.

[3]   Casagrande, J. T.; Pike, M. C.; and Smith, P. G. (1978). "An Improved Approximate Formula for Calculating Sample Sizes for Comparing Two Binomial Distributions." *Biometrics* 34, pp. 483-486.

[4]   Carr, W. E. (1985). "An Exciting Alternative to Fisher's Exact Test for Two Proportions." *Journal of Quality Technology,* 17, pp. 128-133.

[5]   Nelson, L. S. (1987). "Comparison of Poisson Means: the General Case." *Journal of Quality Technology,* 19, pp. 173-179.

[6]   McLeod, A. I.; and Bellhouse, D. R. (1983). "A Convenient Algorithm for Drawing a Simple Random Sample." *Applied Statistics,* 32, no. 2, pp. 182-184.

CHAPTER 9

HYPOTHESIS TESTING AND SAMPLE SIZE: THREE OR MORE POPULATIONS

"What difference, at this point, does it make?"

—*Hillary Rodham Clinton*

The tests used to determine if there is a difference between three or more populations using sample data are significantly different than what has been used for the 1- and 2-sample tests. However, the Black Belt will occasionally encounter such problems, particularly with regard to means. But Black Belts should also have available in their arsenal of tools the ability to handle multiple populations when it comes to standard deviations, proportions and rates.

Variables Case: Means

The method of Analysis of Variance (ANOVA) is the well-known statistical technique used to test the means of multiple levels, or populations. When there are two or more groups of levels, the overriding variable is called a "factor." (Thus Factor A may have 3 levels and Factor B may have 4 levels.) For want of any further guidance, the significance value α of 0.05 is almost always used. Still, an α value might be more correctly assigned based on the cost of concluding the means are different and taking action when no action is called for.

ANOVA's two main assumptions are that the standard deviations across the multiple levels are both equal and normally distributed. The latter assumption is generally unimportant when there are sufficient observations per level, since the Central Limit Theorem assures normality of the means. The former assumption is usually specifically ignored, since it is hard to test because there are not enough observations per level. And so the basic verification principle involves looking at the residuals of the fit and testing these for normality and unusual patterns. If these are only mildly violated (and looked at in more detail for special causes), the investigator can still legitimately use the results of the p-value if it is low enough, such as 0.02. The odds are still quite in favor that a significant difference is present.

However, there is an important consideration in reaching any conclusion when the p-value is low. And that is that the null hypothesis actually being tested with ANOVA is not $\mu_1=\mu_2=\mu_3=\ldots=\mu_n$. Instead, it is $\sigma_\mu = 0$, and that is why it is called the Analysis of <u>Variance</u>. The significance test or tests are run by checking the probability of the F statistic of the ratio of the variance of the means over the variance of the "noise," or the within-groups variation. Thus, when the p-value is low, we can only claim that $\sigma_\mu > 0$. This may be caused by a single odd mean, a bimodal distribution of the means, or even just a relatively broad spread in the means.

However, given $p < 0.05$, the Black Belt will still be interested in whether any of the means are different than the others. Once again, multiple statisticians have investigated methods for determining this situation, and each method has both advantages or disadvantages over the others. Today, commercial software generally offers several choices, and I don't have any to recommend in particular. But there are some details worth mentioning, since the methods generally fall under two different categories that control a given pre-determined error: "individual error rates" and "family error rates." The individual error rate methods usually make pairwise comparisons at some predetermined value, so that there are many comparisons (for example, if there are 5 different levels with their means, there are 10 different two-way comparisons). Let's call this possible individual error γ (gamma). Given that each comparison involves this error, the overall random chance of incorrectly calling a difference significant is approximately $1-(1-\gamma)^n$, where n is the number of comparisons. This latter probability is the family error rate. Regardless of which method is used, the family error rate should be constrained to a low value—at least less than 0.10 and better still to 0.05.

Another feature about ANOVA that affects the conclusions is whether a factor is "fixed" or "random." Fixed factors are pre-chosen levels whose specific means are tested against each other, and the conclusions regarding these levels involve only the levels tested. Random factors involve levels which have been randomly chosen from a larger set of potential levels, and the conclusions of the ANOVA apply to the standard deviation of the means of the *entire* group of levels. To illustrate, I may have 4 machines that make parts and I test these to see if their means are different. This is a *fixed-effects* model. Any conclusions I make about differences will be applied specifically to those 4 machines, such that I may be able to say something like "there is a high probability that Machine #2 is operating at a lower mean than the others." Alternatively, I may have 25 fixtures that I use for making the parts, but I randomly choose 6 of them to test their mean levels. This is a *random-effects* model. If the p-value is low, I will conclude that the entire population of fixtures is operating with mean biases that can create offsets—and this could lead to the possible identification that fixture is a critical KPIV, just as Machine #2 could be identified as such in the fixed-effect investigation.

When there are two or more factors, one can also check for two-factor interactions between different combinations of the levels. When factors are fixed, these interactions and their main-effect factors are compared to the residual error to determine significance. However, if any of the factors are random, any two-factor interaction is also considered random. These two-factor interactions are compared to the residual error for significance. However, the main effect factors are compared to the variance of the interaction and not the residual error. Furthermore, if there are multiple two-factor interactions involving a given factor, the general method tests against a specially balanced combination of the two-factor interactions. In such cases you may get a note implying it's not a real F test.

With fixed factors, the means of the levels are considered important. With random factors, if terms are considered statistically significant, the standard deviation (or variance) of the factor is what is considered important.

As described in the chapter on MSA, gage studies generally fall under the category where all the factors are considered random. Even if the parts have been specifically chosen uniformly, it is still advisable to designate the factor as random. However, when uniform parts have been chosen for the study, the standard deviation calculated from the tested parts should never be used in gage metrics calculations!

Perhaps the most important circumstance which arises for the Black Belt is when the data is unbalanced. Standard ANOVA methods assume that there are equal numbers of observations for each possible combination of the levels of the multiple factors. This would be called a "balanced" design, and any deviation would be considered "unbalanced." The worst cases of being unbalanced occur when several 2-factor combinations have no observations; the most trivial unbalanced case is when all combinations have several observations, some being different by only one count. In the former case, extreme caution needs to be taken in making any conclusions, since those specific missing interaction terms could have made a big impact on the level means had they been included. In the latter case, there is almost no chance of making an error in the conclusions of significance.

Two different methods have been devised to handle the unbalanced ANOVA situation. The first method is called "General Linear Models" (GLM for short), and has a long history of development, with different approaches being applied for different situations involving the nature of the design being unbalanced. The more the design is unbalanced, the more the Black Belt should be skeptical of the results, and should probably consult a statistician regarding what can truly be concluded.

When specific combinations of factor levels are missing in the data, GLM will not output a p-value for the interaction corresponding to that combination. Ideally, the Black Belt would return to the equipment and try to recover data for these combinations. But this is often not feasible.

However, there is a "trick" that can be used when only a couple combinations are missing but there is still a desire to see if some interactions may be present. As an option in the ANOVA analysis, the investigator can choose macros that estimate the means of the different levels of the factors. With an unbalanced design, simply calculating the means by level or combination is incorrect. However, there is an option called "Least Squares Means" or "LS

Means" which accounts for the missing values (while assuming there are no interactions) and balances the calculation. By outputting these LS Means and noting their individual effects, one can compute an expected value for missing combinations. A single artificial observation can be inserted into the data set for each missing combination and now a term generating a p-value corresponding to the interaction can be generated. Realize that a low observed artificial p-value is almost certainly higher than any p-value that would have been generated had we been able to obtain the additional data that would have produced an actual balanced design. Thus, such a low value should trigger further investigation into various combinations as KPIVs.

The second method for handling unbalanced data uses the technique of "Maximum Likelihood Estimation" (MLE). Because of the complexity of the calculations which involve iterative techniques, this method is only recently being used in some current commercial software. In general, MLE usually provides better estimates for probabilities, although the mechanism is much more opaque to the user. Furthermore, although GLM can estimate confidence intervals regarding the different levels, I have not seen similar output for the MLE approach. Again, as computing power increases, this shortcoming is likely to be overcome.

One further capability that these advanced ANOVA methods provide is that of handling "mixed models." These are models that contain factors with multiple levels (which may shift the mean) and variables that are continuous and require a regression-like approach. Usually, if there is no investigation for interactions between factors, standard regression techniques using indicator variables is recommended, since the diagnostics provided by the software programs are better. In the GLM option, the continuous variables may be designated as "covariates." Because the models correct for overall mean levels, to get the most power in analysis, the investigator should always "normalize" the continuous variables before the analysis. There are several options for normalizing, but the most common is to find the mean and standard deviation of the input variable (call it "x"), compute its Z value, where $Z \equiv (x - \bar{x})/s$, and use Z as the input variable. Normalization is a necessity when checking higher order terms of x, i.e., use Z and Z^2 rather than x and x^2.

Sample size calculations for ANOVA situations where there are more than one factor are complex because the results will be greatly influenced by the number of replicates at each combination and the number of levels of each factor. In a sense, the methods calculate the ratio of two standard deviations, yet the output of interest is in checking if any single level has a different mean than the other levels. I don't know of any alternative techniques, so I believe using commercial software should provide reasonable sample size estimates.

There is one other technique for checking a single factor or two factors and their interaction to see if the means of its levels are different. This technique is taught in some Six Sigma Black Belt classes and not others, so I will include it for completeness; plus it has other uses. This technique is called "Analysis of Means" or ANOM.

ANOM uses a technique quite similar to control charting for SPC in that an $\bar{x}$ chart is created for each level (or interaction), the overall mean becomes the center line, and limits are put on the chart. But there are major differences. SPC limits are placed at ± 3 sigma; ANOM limits are placed at values corresponding to ± $\alpha/2$, where α is pre-chosen, often at a 5% level. SPC generally uses its limits based on an historical in-control process to test future subgroups; ANOM tests all the subgroups that make up the chart together, and therefore takes into account the bias that occurs because some aberrant means will contribute to offsetting the overall mean.

ANOM's null hypothesis is that all the levels have the same mean, with the alternative hypothesis being that at least one level has a mean different from the collective mean. Although this sounds like the traditional hypotheses put forth for ANOVA, we've seen that ANOVA really tests variances. In an analogy, ANOVA tests to see if there is criminality in the group; ANOM tries to identify the specific criminal. In this sense, ANOM could be used to test the means against each other when ANOVA results are statistically significant. The α chosen for ANOM will correspond to the family error rate, which also has its advantages. Still, just because ANOVA shows significance doesn't mean that ANOM will actually detect specific levels that don't belong, since ANOVA is testing the overall standard deviation of the levels.

The assumptions that are made for ANOM are the same as those for ANOVA: each treatment level is normally distributed and all levels have the same standard deviation. For groups of data with relatively high numbers of observations, the assumption of normality is less important because of the Central Limit Theorem.

Variables Case: Standard Deviations

The techniques used to test standard deviations are straightforward. If the data is normally distributed, Bartlett's Test is to be used. If the data is not normally distributed, then Levene's Test is advised. The basic difference comes in the power of the test: if Bartlett's Test can be used, it is more likely than Levene's Test to find a difference if one exists for the same sample size.

I know of no methods for choosing an appropriate sample size. That size should depend somewhat on how many levels are being tested against each other, such that the greater the number of levels the lower should be the sample size necessary for each level. An upper limit on the size needed per level would result by using the technique for a 2-sample standard deviation test.

Special Consideration: the Chi-Square Goodness of Fit Test

Strictly speaking, the Chi-square Goodness of Fit Test is a non-parametric test that has nothing specifically to do with testing means, standard deviations, proportions or rates. Yet it is a tool that can be used in a variety of ways to overcome some of the difficulties that are faced when no reasonable parametric test can be brought to bear on a problem. The principle under which it operates is simple. For a proposed distribution, that distribution can be divided into "n" specific regions. For a given number of total counts in the data, an *expected* number of counts can be calculated for each region. The more the actual counts observed in that region differ from the expected number of counts, the more likely it is that the proposed distribution is incorrect in describing the data. The test is run in the following way:

Let us propose a distribution and divide it into n regions. Also, let the sample size of our data equal "m." Based on the proposed distribution and sample size we would expect to see the kth region have E_k counts (E_k can be a fraction). However, the data shows an observed count of O_k. The sum of all E_k's and O_k's must equal m. We now compute the Chi-square value:

$$\chi^2 = \sum_{k=1}^{n} \frac{(O_k - E_k)^2}{E_k}$$

This computed χ^2 value is compared to the Chi-square distribution with n-1 degrees of freedom to determine the probability of it occurring by chance. Typically, a p-value greater than 0.05 is considered statistically insignificant, and the null hypothesis that the true distribution is the proposed distribution cannot be rejected. The general requirement for the test to be valid is that all E_k's are at least 5. However, it has been shown that if 80% or more of the E_k's are at least 5 and none are less than 3, the test still works pretty well. Often, if that size requirement cannot be fulfilled, regions are combined so as to increase an E value, although this then reduces the degrees of freedom for the χ^2 statistic.

An early common use for the Chi-square Goodness of Fit Test was to actually validate a proposed continuous distribution for observed data. However, since then better tests have been devised for this purpose (such as the Anderson-Darling test). The Chi-square Goodness of fit Test is usually considered to have a low power. That is, it has a relatively high probability of falsely accepting the null hypothesis when it is not true. As such, it is usually used as a last resort in statistical testing.

Attribute Case: Proportions

There are two approaches possible when testing multiple proportions against each other. The first uses the Chi-square Goodness of Fit Test. This test is actually a catchall technique that works in a variety of attribute cases. Its advantage is that it accurately produces a p-value that can be compared to the desired Type I error. Unfortunately, little can be deduced about its Type II error. When the Goodness of Fit Test is used to analyze proportions, it is actually applied to a two-way table, involving 2 factors, which is sometimes called a Contingency Table. For proportions, one of the factors only has two levels (e.g. pass/fail, good/bad, yes/no), and these levels apply to the count of pass or fail, good or bad, etc. The other factor designates the different levels of the proportions being compared. Again, the observation count requirements that need to be fulfilled for using this test: at least 3 observations in every grouping, and most observation counts should be 5 or more; no more than 20% of observations should have counts less than 5. Commercial software usually has a two-way table Chi-square test available.

A second, and more powerful technique can be applied when there are at least 5 observations in each of the two categories (e.g. a minimum of 5 passes and 5 fails) for all levels, and the sample size is equal for all levels. For then the normal approximation to the binomial can be used, and ANOM can be applied. This method also facilitates identifying which proportion(s) may be outside the average of the group. ANOM will still work reasonably well for slight departures from equal sample sizes (perhaps 3% differences). Commercial software is likely to have an option for ANOM using proportions. The Chi-square Goodness of Fit Test does not require equal sample sizes, and therefore has broader applicability.

Attribute Case: Counts or Rates

Just as in the proportions case, there are two approaches to testing multiple rates against each other: ANOM and Chi-square. With ANOM it is very important that sample sizes (sometimes called "units," thereby obtaining rates of defects per unit) are equal or very close to each other (the assumption the commercial software makes is that they are equal), and that there be at least a count of 3 at each level. Commercial software is likely to have an option for ANOM using rates or counts.

The method involving the Chi-square Goodness of Fit Test has the advantage that the opportunities do not have to equal each other, but it is much more complicated to apply. A procedure outlined by Nelson (1987)[1], whose paper was already referenced in the previous chapter, is presented below (since I am unaware of present commercial software that performs this test). However, I am simplifying his presentation to apply only to the case where we are looking for equality of rates for all levels.

Suppose there are n levels of interest (that is, n different rates to compare simultaneously). Let $C_1, C_2, \ldots C_n$ equal the observed counts of interest, and $O_1, O_2, \ldots O_n$ be the number of units corresponding to those levels. Define $B_k = O_k/O_1$. Now calculate their respective fractions, P_k for each of the n levels:

$$P_k = \frac{B_k}{\sum_{j=1}^{n} B_j}$$

Check to make sure the sum of all the P_k's equals 1.0. Let "m" equal the sum of all the C_k's. Now calculate all the expected values $E_k = m \cdot P_k$. (The sum of all the E_k's equals m also.) Now calculate the Chi-square statistic value:

$$\chi^2 = \sum_{k=1}^{n} \frac{(C_k - E_k)^2}{E_k}$$

Finally find the probability of this value occurring with n-1 degrees of freedom. Note that this method can readily be put into a spreadsheet for ease of use.

Example: A clean room is being checked to see if the contamination level, as measured by particle count, is consistent across five different tool types used. Tools are swiped with a swab across equal exposed areas, and the swabs are sent to a scanning electron microscope with EDX to determine counts. Since all tools were swiped with an individual swab and there are more of some tools than others, the sample size is unequal. The results of total counts and total tools is as follows:

Tool	#Tools	Total Particle Count	Rate
#1	5	42	8.4
#2	5	21	4.2
#3	2	11	5.2
#4	6	44	7.33
#5	5	24	4.8

Average rate = 142/23 = 6.17
We now need to calculate the B_k and P_k values:

$$B_1 = O_1/O_1 = 5/5 = 1$$
$$B_2 = O_2/O_1 = 5/5 = 1$$
$$B_3 = O_3/O_1 = 2/5 = 0.4$$
$$B_4 = O_4/O_1 = 6/5 = 1.2$$
$$B_5 = O_5/O_1 = 5/5 = 1$$

The denominator, $D \equiv \Sigma B_k = 4.6$ and
$$P_1 = B_1/D = 1/4.6 = 0.2174$$
$$P_2 = B_2/D = 1/4.6 = 0.2174$$
$$P_3 = B_3/D = 0.4/4.6 = 0.0870$$
$$P_4 = B_4/D = 1.2/4.6 = 0.2609$$
$$P_5 = B_5/D = 1/4.6 = 0.2174$$

With total counts = 142, we now compute E_k:
$$E_1 = 142 \cdot P_1 = 30.87$$
$$E_2 = 142 \cdot P_2 = 30.87$$
$$E_3 = 142 \cdot P_3 = 12.35$$
$$E_4 = 142 \cdot P_4 = 37.04$$
$$E_5 = 142 \cdot P_5 = 30.87$$

Finally we can compute the chi-square contributions:
$$\chi^2_1 = (C_1-E_1)^2/E_1 = (42-30.87)^2/30.87 = 4.013$$
$$\chi^2_2 = (C_2-E_2)^2/E_2 = (21-30.87)^2/30.87 = 3.155$$
$$\chi^2_3 = (C_3-E_3)^2/E_3 = (11-12.35)^2/12.35 = 0.147$$
$$\chi^2_4 = (C_4-E_4)^2/E_4 = (44-37.04)^2/37.04 = 1.306$$
$$\chi^2_5 = (C_5-E_5)^2/E_5 = (24-30.87)^2/30.87 = 1.529$$

The sum of all these is 10.151. Checking the probability of this occurring by chance with 4 degrees of freedom, the p-value equals 0.038. Based on a "standard" alpha value of 0.05, we conclude that the occurrence of contamination is not uniform across tools, and because tools #1 and #2 were the highest contributors of the five χ^2 values, we should investigate why. Here, #1 has the much higher rate, while #2 has the lowest rate. Are there special causes?

Sample Sizes for Multiple Proportions, Rates and Goodness of Fit Tests

Unfortunately, there are no standard methods for computing sample sizes for these multiple attribute tests. Certainly using the sample sizes resulting from a 2-sample test—per level—will be sufficient. But by using these 2-sample sizes for multiple levels the Type II error will likely be significantly reduced. One method I have used to try to improve on the sample size is to use Monte Carlo simulation to see what a reduced sample size might produce given both no difference and at least one difference of a significant size. This can be time consuming, but if resources are restricted, it may lead to a less costly sample size.

---

[1]   Nelson, L S (1987). "Comparison of Poisson Means: the General Case." *Journal of Quality Technology*, 19, pp. 173-179.

CHAPTER 10

BATCH PROCESS STATISTICS

In a sense, most manufacturing operations can be considered to occur as batch processes. It is imperative that the Black Belt always considers this possibility.

A computer disk drive is a very complex device. In very simplified terms, a "head" is suspended extremely close over a spinning disk. Electrical current pulses are put into this head which creates a magnetic field, which in turn magnetizes a tiny area (called a "bit") on the spinning disk. This is the "write" operation. Also, the new magnetic field of the bit can create a magnetic field in the head, which produces an electrical current which senses the up or down state of the bit, yielding a binary value of information. The information of multiple bits is combined to produce meaningful output that can be interpreted in a realistic way. These heads are actually very tiny, now being the size of about a millimeter at their longest dimension.

At the Seagate facility in which I worked, the main product was called a "wafer." Each wafer was patterned using thin film techniques so that thousands of heads could be cut from that wafer. Presently, these wafers undergo more than 1000 separate operations, and a finished wafer can provide over 16,000 heads. Obviously, the end-product wafer is quite expensive and takes a long time to process. Still, engineers needed to know if their wafers were meeting the requirements of certain variables; or when a change was being contemplated, how many wafers needed to be checked. Even to check for a simple 1-sigma difference on a 1-sample test requires a sample of 13, and this number of wafers was considered totally impractical.

It became clear that the overall standard deviation of heads was influenced by both a wafer-to-wafer variability and a within-wafer variability. In a broader sense, the wafer could be considered a batch, and the problem being faced was how to handle hypothesis testing when dealing with batch processes. This becomes practically important when producing a batch is either very expensive or time consuming, but the parts within a batch are relatively cheap or easily available once the batch had been made.

Because of the importance of this problem I came up with an approximation that seems to handle this issue. I state that this is an approximation because the only way to fully encompass the standard deviation of the process for a hypothesis test is to test the full number of batches corresponding to the correct sample size. By taking less than that number, there is a greater risk that the overall standard deviation is not being estimated appropriately. Still, the practical demands of the problem, plus the likelihood that good decisions can still be made, override statistical rigor.

Both confidence intervals and hypothesis testing are based on the standard error: $s/\sqrt{n}$, where n is the overall sample size. Yet in our special case, this s is based on both the within- and between-batch variation:

$$s^2_{Total} = s^2_{Batch-to-Batch} + s^2_{Within-Batch}$$
$$= s^2_B + s^2_W$$

where "B" is used to indicate "batch-to-batch" and "W" to represent "within-batch." Now let "M" equal the number of batches and "N" equal the parts measured per batch. Then:

$$\frac{s}{\sqrt{n}} = \frac{\sqrt{s^2_B + s^2_W}}{\sqrt{n}} = \sqrt{\frac{s^2_B}{M} + \frac{s^2_W}{M \cdot N}}$$

Let's simplify this by defining "ϕ" such that:

$$s^2_W = \phi s^2_B$$

Then:

$$\frac{s_B\sqrt{1+\phi}}{\sqrt{n}} = \frac{s_B}{\sqrt{M}}\sqrt{1+\frac{\phi}{N}}$$

or:

$$\frac{1+\phi}{n} = \frac{1}{M} + \frac{\phi}{M \cdot N}$$

thus:

$$n = M \cdot N \left[\frac{1+\phi}{N+\phi}\right]$$

Now we have defined the required sample size in terms of both the number of batches and the parts per batch. However, to take full advantage of this, we will still need a good estimate of ϕ. Presumably, if the process has been running successfully, we can use past data to reasonably estimate ϕ. We can verify this also after the data has been taken.

Since we typically want to keep the number of batches low for cost purposes, how can we estimate the minimum number of batches, M_{Min}, needed? If we take that last equation and let $N \to \infty$, we get

$$n = M_{Min}(1+\phi)$$

or equivalently

$$M_{Min} = n/(1+\phi)$$

We also have:

$$N = \frac{n\phi}{M(1+\phi) - n}$$

Now since the true M_{Min}, $M_{True\text{-}Min}$, must be an integer, $M_{True\text{-}Min} = M_{Min} + \varepsilon$. With the lowest number of batches, this leads to the greatest number of parts we will ever need per batch, N_{Max}:

$$N_{Max} = \frac{n\phi}{\epsilon(1+\phi)}$$

Example 1: You are analyzing a batch process and you want to run a 2-sample, 2-sided means test with α = .05 and β = .10. Also, previous data indicates that $S_W \approx S_B$, and you want to detect a critical difference equal to 1 sigma ($\sqrt{s_B^2 + s_W^2}$) of the process. Given that the normal sample size would equal 23 (from software), and $\phi = 1$, then $M_{Min} = 11.5$ and $M_{true-Min} = 12$. Also, $\epsilon = .5$, so

$$N_{Max} = \frac{n\phi}{\epsilon(1+\phi)} = \frac{23 \cdot 1}{.5(1+1)} = 23$$

You would need a minimum of 12 batches, and no more than 23 per batch. Of course this is 12 times bigger than the original required sample size, but only about half the batches are necessary. This is the type of tradeoff that will occur with batch processes.

There is a strange aberration in the above calculation that actually works in our favor. When one works through the algebra for a regular sample size, the actual computed value doesn't necessarily become an integer. Usually it is an integer and a fraction. But because the actual sample size needs to be an integer, the value is rounded up. In our example, the necessary sample size is 22.05. When we insert this into the equation defining M_{Min} we obtain $M_{Min} = 22.05/(1+1) = 11.025$. This is still fractionally above 11 so we still must assign $M_{Min} = 12$ (had the numbers been just a little different, we might have gotten away with $M_{Min} = 11!$). But we still haven't lost out yet. With n = 22.05, ϵ now equals 0.95,

So N_{Max} is now reduced:

$$N_{Max} = \frac{n\phi}{\epsilon(1+\phi)} = \frac{22.05 \cdot 1}{0.95(1+1)} = 11.61$$

That is, we should only need to measure 12 parts per batch (since we need to round up).

Unfortunately, most Black Belts do not have the sample size formulae to do this improved calculation, so I will offer it here for the two cases:

One sample: $n = \dfrac{(t_{1-\alpha,n-1} + t_{1-\beta,n-1})^2 s^2}{\Delta^2}$

Two samples: $n = \dfrac{2(t_{1-\alpha,2n-2} + t_{1-\beta,2n-2})^2 s^2}{\Delta^2}$

These calculations are iterative, since the degrees of freedom in the t statistics depend on the sample size, but the calculations quickly converge.

Realize that these calculations provide for the lowest number of batches. If we took more batches, the number of parts per batch will diminish. In our example if we took one additional batch (13 total), then substituting this in to our equation for N we would get either 7 (for n=23) or 6 (for n=22.05). Adding just one more batch usually reduces the number of required parts per batch dramatically.

[In truth this method only approximates the true α and β risks (but which we really can never know). There is a more conservative approach to using this methodology which probably slightly improves the actual α and β risks closer to what they are estimated to be. This would involve using M-1 as the degrees of freedom in our t-statistics calculation for sample size instead of n-1. To now calculate n will require more complex iterations, since for every n we get during an iteration we would have to recalculate an M. In our example, our first iteration would use 2M-2 = 24-2 = 22 degrees of freedom for our t-statistics. This yields a self-consistent $M_{True-Min}$=12 (no more iterations needed), which is what we started with, but the fractional n we obtain is 23.05 instead of 22.05. This calculates to an N_{Max} equal to 12.13, which we round up to 13. The reader can appreciate that this "better" method only marginally increases the sample sizes. But it would have a significantly bigger impact in cases where the sample sizes are calculated to be much smaller, and the t-statistics much more sensitive to the degrees of freedom. From now on I will use only the simpler method for further calculations.]

One extremely important use for this sample size calculation capability is to invert the equation to solve either for the β risk or the critical difference, Δ. That is, it allows the engineer to use pre-selected batch sample sizes to estimate either the β risk of missing an important difference, or to calculate the sensitivity of the test with regard to any difference given the pre-selected β risk. However, for clarity it should be pointed out that there is a difference in how we look at "n." When we were trying to figure appropriate sample sizes of M and N, we started with a required sample size, which we called "n," that could be calculated ahead of time. When we now "reverse engineer" to calculate an expected Δ or β, we will need to first calculate the "equivalent sample size," or "n_{equiv}" from our M, N and ϕ values, essentially using the old formula modified for this purpose:

$$n_{equiv} = M \cdot N \left[\frac{1+\phi}{N+\phi} \right]$$

So given the inputs of number of batches (M), parts per batch (N), and expected ratio of the variances (ϕ) for the batch-to-batch and within-batch variability, n_{equiv} can be calculated. Now with n_{equiv}, α and either the critical difference (in terms of the ratio of Δ/s_B) or the β risk, one can calculate the missing parameter using one of the following equations:

<u>One Sample</u>

$$\frac{\Delta}{s_B} = \frac{t_{1-\alpha,n-1} + t_{1-\beta,n-1}}{\sqrt{n_{equiv}}}$$

$$1-\beta = \text{Inv}(t_{1-\beta,n-1}) = \frac{\Delta\sqrt{n_{equiv}}}{s_B} - t_{1-\alpha,n-1}$$

<u>Two Samples</u>

$$\frac{\Delta}{s_B} = \frac{2(t_{1-\alpha,2n-2} + t_{1-\beta,2n-2})}{\sqrt{n_{equiv}}}$$

$$1-\beta = \text{Inv}(t_{1-\beta,2n-2}) = \frac{\Delta\sqrt{n_{equiv}}}{s_B\sqrt{2}} - t_{1-\alpha,2n-2}$$

Where the "n" in these t-statistics refers to n_{equiv}. For 2-sided tests, just substitute α/2 for α.

Example 2: A Black Belt has suggested changes to a process which could have the side effect of lowering the mean of a second variable, amplitude. This would be detrimental to performance. This is a batch process where the within-batch standard deviation of amplitude has typically been about 20% higher than the batch-to-batch standard deviation. Given that the Black Belt is only allowed 4 batches to determine if there is a reduction in the mean of amplitude, what is the sensitivity of this test to a shift with a Type II error of 20%? (Assume an α error of 0.05.)

First, we note that $S_W = 1.2S_B$, so that $\phi = 1.44$. Also, to start we do not have to concern ourselves with how many parts per batch we may need; that can be calculated later. So for now we will see what the lowest Δ is, given that we can take as many parts per batch as we need. Using the formula defining n_{equiv} as $N \to \infty$, $n_{equiv} = M(1+\phi) = 4(1+1.44) = 9.76$. (Realize now that this $n_{equiv} = 9.76$ is the maximum effective sample size that we can achieve for this problem—regardless of the number of parts per batch—given that we only have 4 batches to deal with.) For our t-statistic we will have to use df = 9-1=8 since we can't use fractional values. Using our formula:

$$\Delta = s_B \frac{t_{1-\alpha, n-1} + t_{1-\beta, n-1}}{\sqrt{n_{equiv}}} = s_B \frac{t_{.95,8} + t_{.8,8}}{\sqrt{9.76}}$$

$$= s_B \frac{1.860 + 0.889}{\sqrt{9.76}} = 0.88 s_B$$

From the information we have, $s_{Total} \approx \sqrt{1 + 1.44} s_B = 1.56 s_B$, and thus the Δ sensitivity can be less than s_B, and can be as low as $(0.88/1.56)s_{Total} = 0.564 s_{Total}$, depending on how many parts per batch are measured.

In choosing the number of parts per batch, there are several approaches. If we would compromise so that we get a smaller number of parts per batch but still achieve high sensitivity, we can set our n_{equiv} to 9.0 (so as to still maintain 8 degrees of freedom for our t statistics). This gives the parts per batch as:

$$N = \frac{n\phi}{M(1+\phi) - n} = \frac{9 \cdot 1.44}{4 \cdot (1+1.44) - 9} = 17.05$$

Increasing this to the next higher integer, 18 parts per batch, now provides an n_{equiv}:

$$n_{equiv} = M \cdot N\left[\frac{1+\phi}{N+\phi}\right] = \frac{4 \cdot 18 \cdot 2.44}{18+1.44} = 9.037$$

And the new sensitivity becomes:

$$\Delta = s_B \frac{t_{1-\alpha,n-1} + t_{1-\beta,n-1}}{\sqrt{n_{equiv}}} = s_B \frac{t_{.95,8} + t_{.8,8}}{\sqrt{9.037}}$$

$$= s_B \frac{1.860 + 0.889}{\sqrt{9.037}} = 0.91 s_B$$

This sensitivity (Δ) is only marginally worse than the "infinite" number of parts per batch we had used in our earlier calculation.

If we wanted to decrease the number of parts per batch further—at the cost of increasing Δ, we would use an n_{equiv} equal to 8, which would result in the number of parts per batch of 7 and a sensitivity equal to $0.981 s_B$ (the calculation is left to the reader).

One concern the Black Belt should have in this case is how well the present baseline is known. Usually, the value varies a bit depending on incoming material, and a more appropriate test would require a 2-sample test.

Example 3: The Black Belt in Example 2 realizes that she should run this as a two-sample test, but she can only obtain 4 batches run in each configuration. Now what is the sensitivity of this test to a shift with a Type II error of 20%? (Assume an α error of 0.05.)

As in Example 2, $n_{equiv} = 9.76$, but we have to use the 2-sample formula:

$$\Delta = 2s_B \frac{t_{1-\alpha,2n-2} + t_{1-\beta,2n-2}}{\sqrt{n_{equiv}}} = 2s_B \frac{t_{.95,17} + t_{.8,17}}{\sqrt{9.76}}$$

$$= 2s_B \frac{1.740 + 0.863}{\sqrt{9.76}} = 1.67 s_B$$

The best the Black Belt will be able to detect 80% of the time is a mean shift of $1.07 s_{Total}$, depending on how many parts are measured per batch. Again, minimizing the number of parts per batch but maintaining an n_{equiv} at least of 9.0 yields the same requirement of 18 parts per batch and an n_{equiv} equal to 9.037. This increases the sensitivity to $\Delta = 1.74 s_B$. The Black Belt will have to assess if this sensitivity is sufficient to implement the improved process if the null hypothesis is not rejected.

Hypothesis Testing with Batch Processes

Based on what we have covered so far, the extension to the actual hypothesis testing of means is straightforward. First, we need to obtain estimates for the between- and within-batch standard deviations. This can be achieved by using the method of variance component analysis on our data (which was covered in the chapter on MSA) to obtain actual values of the standard deviations. However, we will also need to check to see if ϕ is consistent with our historical estimates, and in the case of a 2-sample test, whether the ϕ's can be considered equal. If not, we will have to continue under the assumption of unequal sample sizes.

Second, rather than using the actual sample size we will have to convert to an equivalent n using our basic formula

$$n_{equiv} = M \cdot N \left[\frac{1+\phi}{N+\phi} \right]$$

Third, we calculate the mean or means from our data. If the data is completely balanced, then the mean will simply be the overall mean. If the data is only slightly unbalanced (e.g. all the within-batch sample sizes varying by only ±15%), the mean should be calculated weighting their effect by the within-batch sample sizes. For more unbalanced designs, all within-batch sample sizes should be at least 20.

Finally, to perform the hypothesis test and obtain a p-value we just run standard software, using n_{equiv} for our sample sizes and s_{Total} for the standard deviation. We are still somewhat at risk of misrepresenting s_{Total} because the degrees of freedom truly defining s_B are quite limited. To have more confidence in the results of the test—especially when the p-value is close to (but less than) our α value, it is advisable to use the degrees of freedom related to the number of batches rather than n_{equiv}.

Other Batch Process Scenarios

Attribute hypothesis testing often does involve batch processes, but it is rarely recognized as such. For example, when we sample a process to determine the proportion corresponding to yield, we usually make the basic assumption that any sample we take has a constant probability of having defectives. Yet when we look at the process in depth we may notice that the process itself is somewhat batch oriented (e.g. we can only run 500 parts at a time), incoming material may arrive in batches, the process is time based so that any KPIV influenced by time may create a batch effect, or we may use different machines, fixtures, operators or measuring devices. Of course the Black Belt is on the lookout for any critical KPIV, but some KPIVs with a lesser effect may have undue influence. It is probably wise to check for the possible existence of a batch effect by performing ANOM or any of the other techniques provided in the previous chapter.

Unfortunately, if there are batch effects occurring in an attribute situation, I am unaware of any straightforward way of dealing with it in the planning stages. Probably the best approach for sample size is to treat it as a multiple attribute testing scenario, although this is extremely conservative (meaning that it requires a sample size in excess of what should really be needed if we actually knew how to solve this problem). When the null hypotheses of equal rates or proportions cannot be rejected, then the component values can be merged (again weighting by sample size). If the null hypothesis is rejected, then it becomes necessary to determine if there are special causes. This might also be done via control charts (see the chapter on SPC).

Even if the batch means vary, there still might be an overall rate or proportion that governs that distribution. The determination of a "true" overall proportion or rate will require a very large number of batches, and a high number of parts per batch. For example, if we chose only 50 parts per batch in a proportions case and the overall proportion was 84%, the 90% CI on any batch mean would be about a raw ±10%, which isn't very good discrimination; and then we would also have to worry about the underlying standard deviation of those batch means. It would be very difficult to anticipate how to do this properly. However, as an option we can approach the problem as a means test, where each batch's mean is used as an individual point. To plan for such a test would require the Black Belt to anticipate that the overall standard deviation of the means will take into account both the within-batch standard deviation (which can be estimated) and the batch-to-batch standard deviation (which is unlikely to be known or even estimated reasonably). Because of the required resources to do all this, I would doubt that many would undertake such a study.

CHAPTER 11

REGRESSION

Regression is one of the most powerful statistical tools that an analyst possesses. Unfortunately, it is easily misused—which is most of the time.

Perhaps the statistical tool most abused by non-statisticians—and even some statisticians—is regression. Software has made it easy to apply ordinary least squares regression (OLS) to virtually any situation where there is matched data of some kind, whether it be matched pairs, or an output variable of interest coupled with the measurements of all the other variables for that part. Thus, cause-and-effect relationships that don't exist are routinely found, someone creates a predictive relationship that has so much uncertainty that it is essentially useless, and real predictors are regularly ignored because they "don't fit the model."

This chapter will show why all these errors occur and how to avoid them. In some cases, an improved approach is required, while in others, being aware of the right rules of regression will lead to better models. Because Black Belt training does not necessarily cover all of these aspects, this chapter may have sections of redundancy for some readers, such as when it talks about C_p, VIFs or Cook's Distance. But these topics can shed a great deal of important light on a regression problem, and it would be remiss to neglect them.

Linear One-Variable Regression

It would seem that this topic must certainly be well covered in Black Belt training, since it provides the backbone of multiple-variable regression. Unfortunately, there are still some holes that need to be exposed and plugged. To begin, there are the basic assumptions that go into a one-variable regression model:

1. A model of the form y = a + bx actually exists. It seems like common sense, but if the true relationship is more complicated, the value we obtain for b in the regression is almost certain to be incorrect.
2. Each observation pair, especially the variable being predicted (we'll call it y for convenience), that is (y_k, x_k) for the kth observation, is independent of all the others. There are many situations where parts or measurements made sequentially are biased in the sense that the previous value can affect the next value. These can be the result of circumstances like batch processes or single fixtures being used for the measurement of all the regression parts. The wary investigator should always check the circumstances of data gathering to uncover possible sources of bias.
3. The error variability seen in y, $\sigma_{\varepsilon y}$, is constant for all y values, and is normally distributed. Although the normality assumption isn't critical, the homogeneity of variance is. Also, these errors must also be independent of each other.
4. There is no error in the predictor variable, x. That is, these x values are perfectly known.

Hopefully, there is something in the physical science supporting the real model of Assumption #1. Assumptions #2 and #3 can most easily be checked by performing a residual analysis. This analysis can also uncover points having high residuals or being leverage points. Leverage points can have a strong influence on the regression equation, and must <u>always</u> be investigated both for their validity and for their effect. If the regression equation changes substantially when these observations are excluded from the analysis, the Black Belt needs to do more verification work on the best model.

There is an insidious error that can occur when we choose to regress using observational data. We usually don't know the background of this data very well, and it might be that other variables acted upon the data we obtained in a way that will change the relationship that we obtain with our regression. Furthermore, it may be that the data itself "suggested" that a relationship existed; that is, when we plot the data we notice what looks like a relationship and so we pursue it with regression. Regression relationships that result from observational data should always be followed up with verification studies!

Unfortunately, Assumption #4 is almost always violated! Just as the y values are measured with some measurement error, so too are the x values. If that x error is small relative to the overall spread of the x values, then the effect is minor, as it is when the R^2 value is very high (i.e. greater than 0.95). [I'm assuming the reader knows about R^2 and R^2-adj, as well as the RMSE, which is the standard deviation of the fit.] Here there arises some subtle but important points. When there is no error in the predictor variable x, the linear relationship resulting from the standard regression method, OLS, provides the best relationship. When there is error in the predictor, more care is needed. OLS provides the best capability of predicting a *measured* output variable given a *measured* input variable. However, this capability is rarely required by the Black Belt. Instead, he or she usually wants to know the true relationship between the two variables: what the real value of y is given a real value of x. Why is this so?

Generally, a Black Belt studying a process understands the measurement errors. As such, he would rather apply the effect of the gage error to the process after estimating the true process parameters. He can estimate what the input distribution is supposed to look like, and then translate that using the correct relationship to the output distribution. From there he can then estimate the observed output distribution by applying the gage error. An estimate of the true relationship is also something that can be compared to physical models for verification. Unfortunately, OLS almost always provides a slope that is too low.

Since OLS usually does not provide the true relationship, another statistical tool is required: orthogonal regression. We have seen and used this tool in performing correlation analysis as part of our Measurement Systems

Analysis. [The reader is encouraged to review that section before proceeding.] Given that we have the matched data, the only other input needed is the ratio of the error standard deviations: $\sigma_{\varepsilon y}/\sigma_{\varepsilon x}$ (although we square it to get λ). When we used it for correlation, we either implied that we might know both $\sigma_{\varepsilon x}$ and $\sigma_{\varepsilon y}$, or that we might be able to assume what the ratio might be—such as $\lambda=1.0$ for identical measuring systems. With a regression system we may no longer have that luxury. If only the measurement errors produce the variability seen in the data, then the proper application of orthogonal regression with the correct λ is appropriate. Unfortunately, the variability that is seen in our output variable is usually not just due to the measurement error, but also to *lack of fit*. That is, there are probably other variables acting on the output besides the x variable we have chosen for our regression. The variation due to these other variables provides a contribution to variation that exists in y that exceeds the measurement error and that cannot easily be quantified. Thus, we usually cannot know what $\sigma_{\varepsilon y}$ really is, and so we cannot directly apply the method of orthogonal regression.

But there is a trick that we can use to get around this apparent roadblock. If we study the formulae used in orthogonal regression, we can see that two of the outputs that we can obtain are estimates of $\sigma_{\varepsilon x}$ and $\sigma_{\varepsilon y}$. Given that we have a good estimate for $\sigma_{\varepsilon x}$, we can back-calculate to get our orthogonal regression relationship, as well as an estimate of $\sigma_{\varepsilon y}$. If we try to do this algebraically, the math gets fairly messy. And in practice it is unnecessary. If we have already set up our equations in spreadsheet form, we can use a tool like Microsoft's Excel Solver to do the back-calculation for us! This is done by merely allowing λ to vary until Excel's estimate of $\sigma_{\varepsilon x}$ equals our estimate. The solution, if it exists, is unique. (It is possible that no solution exists if our estimate of $\sigma_{\varepsilon x}$ is wrong by being too high. In the graph of y versus x data there is a fixed amount of error represented by the variation around the line. It may be that our estimated x error exceeds that which is available in the data.)

Example: Suppose we have the following 10 points of data (of course this is inadequate for doing any kind of regression, but it may allow the user to see how the tool is used):

X	Y
6.81	22.37
10.02	24.34
6.42	20.72
6.77	15.2
2.16	10.37
1.16	5.09
5.04	14.07
4.45	12.27
8.09	25.56
5.82	20.94

A graph of the data looks like the following:

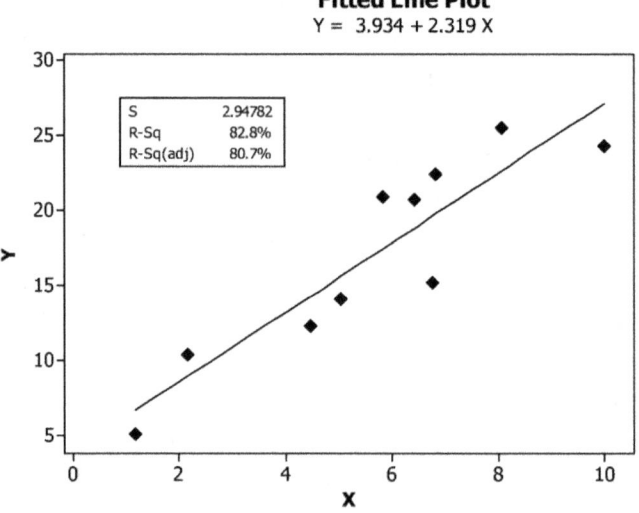

Now suppose that we "know" that the X variable has error, and that a good estimate of it is 0.90. By using the Solver routine in Excel, and setting the estimated sigma value to 0.90, we obtain a different linear relationship of Y = 2.41 + 2.59X. In this artificial case, the true slope was 2.5, but our technique has reduced the actual error in our slope's estimate from 7.2% to 3.6%.

This method will almost always provide a better estimate of the slope of the linear relationship between y and x, since the OLS slope can easily be in error by $1-\sqrt{R^2}$. But caution is needed. We need to input an estimate of the measurement error $\sigma_{\varepsilon x}$ that applies to the data when we obtained it for the regression. If the data was long term, then the best estimate for error would come from a Comprehensive Gage Study; if the data was short term, then we need an estimate that reflects measurement error over that short term.

Provided that we have properly used the right x gage error for our orthogonal regression, one output will be an estimate of $\sigma_{\varepsilon y}$. If we compare this value to any (appropriate) gage error estimate, $\sigma_{y\text{-gage}}$, we can estimate how much error is unaccounted for through lack of fit (σ_{LOF}). The greater σ_{LOF}, the more likely the need is to use more predictor variables in our regression.

Binned Regression

There is one technique that I saw being used when data had an approximately normal distribution spread, but either the predictor or response variable had high error. This was called "Binned Regression." I mention this only to warn others of this wrong technique. In these analyses, the measured X values were put into equally spaced increments called "bins" centered at their middle value. The means of the output variable were also calculated for each bin; call these $\overline{Y}_{bin}$. Then $\overline{Y}_{bin}$ was regressed against the centered binned X values. A simple example of this would be if we rounded all the X values to the nearest integer to create their bins and found all the Y averages for each corresponding bin. This technique was performed because the R^2 values for the original data were so low, yet were quite high when Binned Regression was used.

This technique doesn't work for basically the same reason that OLS doesn't work when there is error in the predictor. There is more "spill over" of values from the central region into the tail regions than vice versa, since there are more values in the central region. For example, for the right side of a positively sloped line, more lower-valued y values will wrongly be assigned into bins further to the right, lowering the apparent slope; on the left side higher-valued y values will wrongly be assigned into bins further to the left, also lowering the apparent slope.

One other problem is that the bins in the tails have far fewer points making up the Y averages, yet these points are over-weighted in the regression (due to the least squares effect). Natural variation can make these points appear as outliers.

In summary, Binned Regression should never be used. If the error is primarily in the response variable, OLS provides correct results, even if the R^2 values are poor. If there is strong error in the predictor, then the methods corresponding to orthogonal regression will provide results far closer to the real relationship.

Linear Multiple-Variable Regression

Before one begins to delve into the problems of multiple-variable regression, it is usually a good idea to understand what purposes this tool might have:

- *Prediction*: Predict the measured output (y) based on two or more measured inputs (x); e.g. y = F(x_1=2, x_2=7).
- *Variable Screening*: Prior to any designed experiments multiple-variable regression can help indicate which of the variables might be strong KPIVs for the KPOV (y). We might also then eliminate other variables from consideration.
- *System Explanation*: Describe how much of the variability in the output is explained by the input(s). We may have y = F(x_1, x_2) = 1 + x_1 + 2x_2+ε, but how big is the leftover error ε, and how big is R^2 which describes the fraction of the variance in the original output y that the predictors explain? We can also compare the regression results to theory to verify.
- *Predictor Prioritization*: When our predictors have been normalized to have the same range (e.g. ±1), then the magnitude of the coefficient helps describe the strength of the effect of the input predictors on the output. This can help identify the critical KPIVs.
- *Develop a Transfer Function*. The transfer function is the name of the function that allows us to predict a true value of the output variable given the true values of the input variables. In a sense, it a combination of the previous four purposes. Its most important use is in the Design Organization for assessing trade-offs and determining specifications.

We are using the term "linear multiple-variable regression" to indicate that we are investigating multiple variables, but that each term in the regression is linear in its coefficients. That is, we may be looking for something like $y = a + b_1x_1 + b_2x_2 + b_3x_1/x_2 + b_4e^{x_3}$, where a and the b_k's are coefficients we are trying to determine, but not something like $y = a + b_1x_1 + b_2x_2 + b_3e^{b_4x_3}$, which is non-linear in its coefficient of the last term. With linear regression, the method of ordinary least squares methods is applied.

To really unveil the depth of multiple-variable regression techniques, pitfalls, diagnostics and procedures requires a semester devoted to regression. In this chapter I will try to cover many of the relevant topics, but I can't go into the theoretical depth. And worse, I can't demonstrate with detailed examples, since such would require copious quantities of data that would have to be transcribed by the reader. I urge the reader to use this book as an initial reference to these topics (to recognize when they might arise), and then to follow up in one of many more detailed texts on that subject.

Pool of Potential Predictors

The first challenge facing the investigator is to determine which variables to explore as potential predictors of the KPOV. Often, the primary source of this list will be data that is already being taken. This list must be supplemented with other variables that have been uncovered in the initial stages of the project using the tools of Cause & Effect, Process Mapping, FMEA, etc., as well as what physical models may suggest. Thus, it may be necessary to track additional variables for which data is usually not taken.

The next step is to apply common sense! Often we may have a variable, Z, for which data has been taken. That does not mean that we should run our initial regression looking for the coefficient of Z as a linear term. As an exercise in my classes we use automobile gas mileage as the KPOV, and are given eleven pieces of possibly relevant data for multiple cars. Amongst these are car weight, height and width. The first instinct of the students is to throw all eleven variables—as is—into a model to see what drops out. With weight they perceive a negative effect as well as some kind of curvature and want to then add a weight² term. But this is entirely the wrong approach. First, it would imply that as weight increases, eventually mileage would become negative. A quadratic term would also predict absurd results. Instead, with just a little thought, the variable that makes the most sense is the inverse of weight, 1/weight. This also has the desired property of not going negative.

Furthermore, whereas neither width nor height might be significant, physics tells us that a larger cross-sectional area of a vehicle might increase drag and affect mileage. Therefore, a proper variable to try is height × width.

Metrics

Before we get into model selection, we should first discuss some of the different metrics helping us define "goodness" that are used. There are three that should be familiar to the Black Belt, and a fourth that has use under limited circumstances.

- RMSE: The Root Mean Square Error, or the square root of the error variance, σ_{error}. It represents the standard deviation of the residuals "around" the fitting regression surface, or the standard deviation of the fit. Lower is usually better.
- R^2: This is the fraction of the variance in the output variable explained by the predictors. Another view is:

$$R^2 \approx 1 - \frac{\sigma^2_{error}}{\sigma^2_y}$$

  The smaller the total error, the closer R^2 gets to 1.0. Higher is usually considered better. R^2 may help us in screening variables to find which may be important, but we need caution in declaring that a high R^2 shows a model that is useful for prediction. When we interpret R^2 correctly we can note that an $R^2 = 0.70$ means that we've accounted for only 50% of the standard deviation in our output variable. This is pretty useless for prediction; yet many practitioners are delighted with such a high value. Here is my interpretation of R^2 values:

    - $R^2 > 0.4$: An association definitely exists
    - $R^2 > 0.7$: The relationship can be used with caution
    - $R^2 > 0.9$: A useful relationship for prediction exists
    - $R^2 > 0.95$: The relationship is good for prediction

- R^2-adj: A superior value to R^2 since it penalizes the metric for adding terms that do not sufficiently lower RMSE. Higher is usually considered better.

- There is a fourth metric called "Mallow's C_p," (after its creator) or usually shortened to C_p or C-p. This metric is calculated thusly:
  - Designate the total number of terms under consideration to be "m," and the total number of data points as "n." When regression is run on this model it is called a "full model."
  - Define σ_{full} as the RMSE of the full model.
  - For a regression model using only a specific "p" predictors, we would also obtain an RMSE, which we will designate as "$RMSE_p$."
  - We can now define C_p as:

$$C_p = \frac{RMSE_p^2}{\sigma_{full}^2} - n + 2p$$

Models with $C_p \leq p$ are to be preferred, and lower C_p's are considered better. When m = p, C_p = m. Typically, R^2-adj and C_p usually contain about the same information, and there appears to be no major profit in using C_p. However, there is a particular case where C_p sheds special light, and that is when we have a good estimate of what the actual lowest σ_{error} is supposed to be. This occurs when we have replicated y values for the same set of input variables. The pooled standard deviation coming from these replicates represents the pure error, whereas σ_{full} is only our best estimate of that error, even though it may contain lack-of-fit contributors as well as measurement error. In fact, we should probably only use C_p as a deciding metric when we can get a good estimate of σ_{error}, and then our proper goal is C_p = p.

There is one final metric of interest, although it cannot be quantified. It is called "parsimony." Its basic thrust is thriftiness: simpler models (fewer predictors) providing nearly the same degree of fit are to be preferred over more complex models. Similarly, models that make physical sense are to be preferred over models that don't make physical sense. Thus, even though R^2-adj may be increased by adding more terms, that alone doesn't justify the inclusion of those terms into the final model. Those terms need to contribute in a <u>practically</u> significant way. The Black Belt needs to realize that the recommended model is likely to be handed off to a process owner; the simpler it is, the more likely it is to be accepted and used.

I've created a general rule of thumb to help guide the Black Belt when considering the prospect of parsimony:

Each additional term should reduce the R^2-adj by at least 20% of what is left from the remaining R^2-adj of the model with one term less.

For example, suppose I have a 3-parameter model with an R^2-adj of 0.70. There is 0.30 left to be explained. Twenty percent of this is 0.06, so I would be hesitant to add a fourth term unless it improved R^2-adj to at least 0.76. This rule needs to be modified as R^2-adj goes beyond 0.90, first because the number of data points may be forcing R^2-adj to not be easily changed, but more importantly, some additional terms may reduce the RMSE to such a point that the model becomes quite good for prediction purposes.

Choosing the Best Models to Explore

There are several tools for discovering which predictor variables might influence the KPOV. The first tool should just be a two-way graph of the KPOV versus each of the variables. This method can uncover important variables, and as in the case for weight affecting mileage, can hint at curvature or suggest other relationships (e.g. 1/x). Once a proper potential variable list has been created, the best method for checking out possible models is called "Best Subsets." [Another set of methods called Backwards Elimination, Forward Selection and Stepwise Selection are inferior. Historically, the Best Subsets method had limitations because it requires a lot of computing power, but these limitations have essentially been eliminated for nearly all practical cases.] Best Subsets will provide the best 1-parameter models, 2-parameter models, etc., up to the n-parameter model specified by the investigator. Best Subsets generally bases its "best" models on the highest R^2 value, but can also provide R^2-adj and C_p.

Based on the R^2-adj values and the application of parsimony, the investigator can usually be led to just a handful of models that provide some prediction power without being ponderous with marginal predictors. If there really is a good estimate for σ_{error}, judging models on the basis of the true C_p

(not usually the one calculated from the full model, but calculated using the formula with σ_{error}) is definitely to be preferred. But there are dangers still to be avoided. And the chief one, multicollinearity, should usually be anticipated before one runs Best Subsets.

Collinearity and Multicollinearity

Perhaps the most insidious error that can occur in multiple-variable regression results when predictor variables can be correlated to each other. In the case of two predictors x_1 and x_2, if $x_2 = a + mx_1 + \varepsilon$, where ε is a relatively small error and m is a constant, we have the case of "collinearity;" essentially x_1 and x_2 are linearly related. In the case of three predictors x_1, x_2 and x_3, if $x_3 = a + m_1x_1 + m_2x_2 + \varepsilon$, we have the situation of "multicollinearity." In our gas mileage example we should be able to anticipate that car weight and engine size (in number of cylinders) are collinear. If we add length as another predictor, then those three exhibit multicollinearity.

The problem that then arises if we have predictor variables that are partial linear combinations of each other is that each one of these "tries" to explain a portion of the same variability in the KPOV, and so they share their explanatory power amongst themselves. In some cases, multicollinear variables will register as not being significant when taken together, whereas any single one would be significant. This "sharing" also shows up in the estimates for the standard error of each coefficient. Recall that the standard error of a coefficient relates to the standard deviation of the estimate, and that a 95% confidence interval on the estimate would be approximately ±2 standard errors. The standard errors may be large and so their p-values high. Yet together their net effect might be highly significant. In these cases, we might call the regression model "unstable," since the coefficients of these predictors can vary substantially without actually affecting the predictive capability of the model very much. This all means we really don't know which variable or combination of variables is important!

Before we actually seek out regression models, we can try to discover which variables are collinear by checking the correlation coefficients between any two of them. We should be wary of any for which R > 0.8. Unfortunately, this method will not uncover multicollinearity. For this we will need to use a special regression metric called the "Variance Inflation Factor," or VIF. These are usually an output option in our regression software. Any VIFs exceeding 5.0 are big warning signs that collinearity or multicollinearity exist. In fact, the Black Belt should never be satisfied with a regression model in which any VIF exceeds 5, and should be cautious even for values exceeding 3.0. Often, when we run a full model we will detect large VIFs. If we can determine which predictors relate to specific other predictors, we will try to avoid having them all be in models that we will explore later as good model candidates.

If we use higher order terms of any of the predictors together with their linear term (e.g. weight and weight^2), we will often fail the VIF test. This is because such variables are usually highly correlated to each other. To better determine the need for these higher order terms in our model, we should always first normalize these variables. [Some investigators recommend normalizing all variables. This has the advantage of allowing us to check the size of the coefficient to determine the actual effect that predictor variable has. And it used to be necessary when computing power was weaker because of round-off error. However, it is no longer necessary, except for higher order terms.] There are several ways to normalize the variables. Perhaps the best way is to find the mean and standard deviation of the predictor values, and then create its normalized version:

$$\hat{x} = \frac{x - \overline{x}}{s_x}$$

By using $\hat{x}$ and $\hat{x}^2$ we have separated them completely and can determine their separate effects on the KPOV without worrying about the collinearity effects between them (but not necessarily between them and other variables). However, to get the proper coefficients later on, we will have to still use the "pure" terms, and ignore the VIFs that involve those term combinations.

Sometimes it will be difficult to tell which of the multicollinear variables to keep in the model. Usually it is almost always better to choose the more practical or physically descriptive, even if there is a small lowering impact to the R^2 value.

Model Checking: Residual Analysis

At some point the investigator will finally winnow down the list of predictors such that there are only a handful of models that seem to be likely good choices. The next step is to check to see if these models are consistent with the assumptions. The majority of this activity involves looking at the residuals.

The Black Belt should be adequately familiar with basic residual analysis and that these should be checked graphically, looking at a histogram of them and checking for normality, and plotting them versus time (run order) and predicted values. Strong indications of heteroscedasticity may be enough to disqualify a model (more later). In multiple-variable regression it is even more important to graph the residuals versus the predictors (to see if higher order terms should be added) and the other predictors that didn't make the cut (again, they may be involved in higher order terms or perhaps in some unusual combination with one of the other potential predictors).

However, there are other type of residuals that have value in model checking, and these should not be ignored. Most of them are available in commercial software but usually require that the investigator request them. They are:

- *Standardized Residuals:* If the residual of the kth point is defined as:

    $e_k \equiv y_k(\text{actual}) - y_k(\text{predicted})$

    then the standardized residual is defined as:

    $d_k \equiv e_k / s(y_k)$

    where $s(y_k)$ is essentially the standard deviation of the fit at y_k.
    - Standardized residuals greater than 2.0 may be outlier points, and probably are when $d > 3.5$
    - Software, such as Minitab, marks with an "R" any standardized residual greater than 2.0.
- *Studentized Residuals*: The studentized residual of the kth point is the standardized residual computed using a model which omits the kth point. As such, a large deviation of the studentized residual from a relatively large standardized residual probably indicates an outlier.
- *Cook's Distance:* Designated as D_k, Cook's Distance is a standardized measure of the squared distance between the parametric space (b_0, b_1, b_2, ...) of a model using all the points and the model *excluding* the kth point.

- High values of D_k indicate the likelihood that the kth point falls outside the general boundaries of the other points, and therefore is likely to be a leverage point in the data. The model coefficients could change significantly if the kth point were omitted.
  - D_k values of 1 or more are highly suspect. Models with and without these points should be evaluated to determine the effect of the kth point.
- *Hat Matrix Diagonals*: Regression analysis involves matrix inversion, and so matrix algebra becomes important. From the matrix, the Hat Matrix Diagonal of the kth point, sometimes designated as h_k, is a measure of how unusual the kth set of observations in the X space ($x_{1k}, x_{2k}, x_{3k}, \ldots, x_{p-1k}$) is from the rest of the input data. (If we could create a p-dimensional cloud of the input data, h_k would reflect the distance of the kth point from the center of that cloud.)
  - When h_k values exceed $2p/n$ (p is the number of predictors including the constant term and n is the number of data points), there is a chance that the observation is a leverage point. When $h_k > 3p/n$, it probably is a leverage point.
  - In Minitab when $h_k > \text{Minimum}(.99, 3p/n)$, the software marks this observation with an "X."
  - Just as with the result of Cook's Distance, these points should be carefully checked to determine their influence. We will see later that some of that influence can be detected using the "Press" statistic.

Generally, good practice would dictate that the investigator take a cautious look at all these residuals. Models that have the best behaved residuals should be preferred as final model candidates.

Model Verification

Before any model is released for general use to either Manufacturing or Development, the model must be verified as being correct. The optimum way to achieve this is to run another entire set of data through the model, obtaining predicted output values, y_{pred}. These are compared to the actual y values by creating $\delta = y - y_{pred}$, and then finding the mean and standard deviation of δ. Ideally, one would have had at least 60 data points for the original model selection and 60 data points for the verification. [Sometimes if there are sufficient data points the investigator can randomly split the data into two groups, one for model creation and one for model verification.] Then one can reasonably accept the model as adequate if the null hypotheses of $\overline{\delta} = 0$ and σ_δ = RMSE cannot be rejected. When the number of available points is less than 60, the Black Belt should check the Type II risk of making a wrong decision, and use judgment as to whether the risk is acceptable for the case at hand.

Quite often, no secondary set of data exists against which the model can be verified, but there is a strong need for an immediate model. The Black Belt still has one more weapon in her arsenal: the PRESS Statistic. If there are n data points, suppose that n different regressions are created (each with different values for the coefficients) in which the kth observation is omitted. For the regression in which the kth observation was missing, the y value predicted for the missing observation, y_{pred-k}, is generated by using that regression's coefficients. The actual y_k observation is compared to y_{pred-k} for these n regressions (with p predictors), such that the sums of squares of differences are calculated:

$$PRESS_p = \sum_{k=1}^{n} [y_k - y_{pred-k}]^2$$

The closer $PRESS_p$ is to the expected sum of squares (which equals n·RMSE^2), the more robust the model is to the individual data points—and hence, the more stable the coefficients are. Similarly, the closer $R^2(pred)$ is to the actual R^2 of the fit, the better the model. A difference of 10% or more should be considered a warning sign. Check especially for leverage points or high residuals, which can have major impacts on the PRESS value.

Thus the PRESS statistic is very useful for determining 1) the "sensitivity" of the model to the data it's based on, and 2) comparing competing models with the same number of parameters, p. In this latter sense, the PRESS statistic could be a tie breaker.

One final step that should be completed by the investigator is whether the model is practically useful. If the model is used for prediction, how well can the model predict? As stated earlier, if $R^2 < 0.9$, the model has limited prediction capability. Check how well the model can predict using prediction intervals of actual or proposed points (especially near specification limits if they exist). Is that capability sufficient for what the model will be used for? [Note that for variable screening the prediction capability is not nearly as important. Supposedly the real effect can be better discerned by performing designed experiments later.]

Common Mistakes Regarding Regression

Although these are routinely covered in Black Belt classes, it is worthwhile to repeat these mistakes that can be made either in using the resultant model or creating them:

1. *Excessive focus on R^2.* The R^2 value reflects the amount of variance in the output variable, y, that the model explains. However, if the y value incorporates a large measurement error, the maximum possible R^2 will be limited. If the y error can be estimated, the investigator should change his expectations of what a "good" model R^2 will be. For example, suppose the investigator obtains her best model, but R^2 equals only 0.70, with an RMSE equal to 10.0 mm. (This means that the original data had a starting variance of $10^2/(1.0-0.7) = 333.3$ mm^2, and the regression accounts for 233.3 mm^2.) However, the gage error for the predicted variable is 9.0 mm. Thus, the left over variance from the regression is 100 mm^2, but the gage error makes up 81% of that. What then would remain unexplained is $100 - 81 = 19$ mm^2. This would be out of an originally unexplained variance of $233.3 + 19 = 252.3$ mm^2. In a sense, this is actually like an R^2 value of $1 - 19/252.3 = 0.925$.

2. *Attributing cause and effect.* When data is observational, there should always be a healthy doubt about whether there actually is a cause-and-effect relationship. If process knowledge cannot verify such a relationship, follow-up experiments should be run.

3. *Extrapolating the relationship beyond the data range.* Predicting KPOV values that involve using x values that fall outside the range that was used in regression is always risky. Sometimes higher order terms are not included in the abbreviated model, yet actu-

ally should belong in the model. Furthermore, variables that have been eliminated may have a significant effect on the KPOV in a different range of the data.

There is one type of extrapolation error that occurs all too often in regression. In many physical situations it is known that at some settings of the predictors the output value <u>must</u> equal 0. Thus the investigator will force the regression to go through zero at those predictor values (often by eliminating the constant term). If this is truly an extrapolation, there is great danger that the predictive capability of the model in the region of the data will be significantly reduced. The problem is that we really don't know what the proper model should be between our "cloud" of predictors and the zero value. There may be some kind of curvature that occurs in that region that is undetectable in our present body of data. Or we may not have included a particular variable in our model because of its low predictive power in our data region, but which has an important effect as the output value should approach zero. Since we don't really know what happens in that region, it is usually wrong to presume our present model must somehow compensate.

One of the most egregious examples of this which I encountered involved something like the following graph:

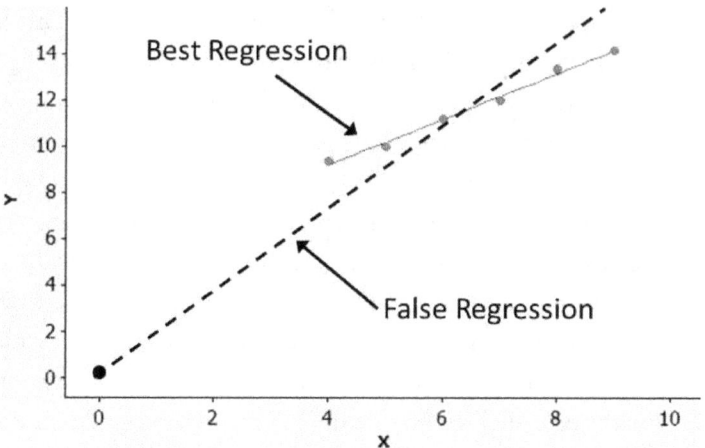

Here the users insisted that the graph had to go through 0 when X equaled zero, and so they ignored the obvious, insisting that the line marked "False Regression" was valid.

4. *Masking real correlations or creating false correlations.* Often the data that is available for performing the regression is not representative of all the data that will be or can be generated by the process. As such, there may be certain factors which contribute, but for which the present data is too limited to detect their effect. For example, only two fixtures might have been used for the data available in the regression, while 10 fixtures are actually used in practice; each fixture could provide a mean shift.

5. *Data collected over too narrow a range.* The wider the range of the input data, the more likely it will be to detect the effect of those input variables. Unfortunately, the common practice is to use data that is available. For some variables this data has already been truncated to meet specifications, and so the net effect of the variable cannot be detected. If possible, always try to generate data outside the normal bounds of production so as to uncover real contributor variables. Sadly, a request for such data is usually rejected because the people responsible "can't intentionally make bad parts."

6. *Accepting models with inadequate residuals.* Certainly, all unusual residuals should be checked. But often the residuals show patterns for which the Black Belt doesn't know how to deal. This happens especially with incidences of heteroscedasticity (inequality of variance across the spectrum of results). There are often no easy solutions to some of these. For example, a "bow-tie" pattern *might* be indicative of an interaction, but this could be hard to find.

However, when the pattern is more of an increasing or decreasing trend in the standard deviation of the residuals, often a transformation of the data can be used. For increasing patterns, a square-root or log transformation might provide much better results; for decreasing patterns, an inverse transformation might be called for. In one difficult regression problem that I was involved with, there were very few potential (available) predictor variables. Not until I took a log transform of both the output variable and one of the input variables did I get a relationship that really worked: $y = Ax^B$.

Error in the Predictor Variables

As mentioned in the section involving single-variable regression, the fundamental assumption of all OLS regression is that there is no error in the predictor variable(s). This assumption is almost universally violated—usually in complete ignorance of the consequences. As a result, the coefficients of the model's variables are almost always under-estimated. When regression is used for variable screening, this is no problem. But it can be disastrous for prediction when at least one of the predictors has non-negligible error. Again, to emphasize, the investigator is usually looking for the model that will predict a true output given true inputs. But even when there are multiple inputs, there is no guarantee that OLS will provide the best estimates of a measured output given measured inputs, since the error on one of the predictors can easily skew the influence of other predictors.

The best solution to this dilemma is to recognize that the predictors have errors, and instead of trying to establish the relationship through regression, use designed experiments with carefully chosen and measured levels. If need be, the input values can be measured multiple times to guarantee known input levels.

There is another path if the previous method appears to be too difficult, or answers need to be generated right away. It involves the application of orthogonal regression, but in an iterative way. Theoretically, it can be done for multiple predictors, but practically, trying to go beyond two predictors is risky. The following is the methodology, which is best done using a spreadsheet. First assume that we have one output, Y, and two predictors, X1 and X2, for which we want to find the best linear relationship $Y = a + b_1X1 + b_2X2$. Assume that we can expect X1 and X2 to be independent of each other (essentially having a very low correlation coefficient), and also that we have reasonable estimates for the measurement errors of X1 and X2. Then:

1. Perform an orthogonal regression of Y versus X1 using the known X1 measurement error (as was done for the linear, one variable

method discussed earlier in this chapter). This provides a linear relationship $Y = A1 + B1_1 X1$. The error we obtain for Y will contain the measurement error of Y, the effect of X2 (which has not yet been accounted for), and any lack-of-fit effects which we won't be able to find anyway.

2. Calculate $Y1 = Y - (A1 + B1_1 X1)$ for all points. This is just the residual of the first orthogonal regression.
3. Now perform a second orthogonal regression, this time of Y1 versus X2 using the known measurement error of X2, which yields another relationship: $Y1 = A2 + B2_1 X2$.
4. If X1 and X2 were totally independent of each other, the best relationship we could get would be $Y = (A1+A2) + B1_1 X1 + B2_1 X2$. However, because of random error, there is some overlap in the determinations, so we need to repeat our orthogonal regressions. Now create $Y2 = Y - (A2 + B2_1 X2)$.
5. Perform a third orthogonal regression, with Y2 versus X1 using the known X1 error. This provides still another linear relationship $Y2 = A3 + B1_2 X1$. $B1_1$ and $B1_2$ should be similar in value, but somewhat different because the output variable has been adjusted for the X2 variable.
6. Calculate $Y3 = Y - (A3 + B1_2 X1)$ for all points.
7. Now perform a fourth orthogonal regression, this time of Y3 versus X2 using the known measurement error of X2, which yields another relationship: $Y4 = A4 + B2_2 X2$.
8. This process can be repeated until both $B1_k$ and $B2_k$ converge: $B1_k \rightarrow b_1$ and $B2_k \rightarrow b_2$. These convergent values then are our best estimates of the coefficients for predicting the true value of Y given true values of X1 and X2.

This method was used quite successfully in a case where standard OLS predicted that the specifications on a particular dimension could be widened—in contrast to what had previously been the Standard Operating Procedure. However, the predicted value of the affected KPOV also involved a second variable, the tip height of a probe, which itself had measurement error. When the two predictor variables were regressed using this type of dual orthogonal regression, the old specifications were proven to be correct.

This method has also been tried in prediction equations where there were three predictor variables—without substantial success. There are several possible reasons why the method didn't work well for these: 1) the estimates of the errors were incorrect, so that the corrected values were not properly adjusted; 2) the variables were not sufficiently independent of each other; 3) there wasn't enough data, or the spread in the predictors wasn't large enough to compensate for the measurement error; 4) the random error in the data itself was not representative enough so that it did not balance out sufficiently.

Does this mean that this iterative orthogonal regression method is ineffective for the three-variable case? Not at all. First it is important to realize that standard OLS regression produces incorrect coefficients when trying to get the true relationship when there is error in the predictor variable data. It almost always underestimates them. OLS is wrong. It is defensible only because there hasn't been anything else to take its place. But that is hardly a good recommendation for the tool. As a result, I can recommend the orthogonal regression method for more than two predictor variables precisely because it does try to take into account the measurement error and therefore will usually give results that are closer to the true relationship. But note that even with two predictors, the measurement error pertaining to when the data was taken must be reasonably known and the predictors must be independent.

Non-linear Regression

There exists one additional type of regression problem that the Black Belt might encounter. These involve theoretical models that imply that certain terms like x^{b_1}, $\sin(b_1 x)$, $b_1 e^{b_2 x}$, etc. might occur. Thus, in the regression equation, the b_k parameter of interest is not simply a coefficient, but is actually imbedded somehow, and so the model is not linear in its coefficients. If there are no additional predictors, a transformation might allow us to uncover a good model. Thus, as cited previously, I was able to develop a model $y = Ax^B$ because I first took the log of the y and x variables: $\log(y) = \log(A) + B \cdot \log(x)$; $\log(y)$ became the output for $\log(x)$ in a linear fashion.

Unfortunately, most practical models can't be simplified, since more than one predictor variable is usually required. Thus we may be seeking a model that might look like $y = a + b_1 x_1 + b_2 x_2 + b_3 e^{b_4 x_4}$. This is intractable using transformations and OLS, and so requires an entirely different approach called "non-linear regression." The general topic is well beyond the scope of this book, and the Black Belt should consult with a statistician (although commercial software programs are getting better able to address non-linear regression).

There is a "back-door" approach that might provide some reasonable estimates when there is only a single non-linear term, but it usually requires that we have some bounds on the unknown parameter showing up in the non-linear term. As an example, suppose we wish to find the best model using our starting model of:

$$y = a + b_0 e^{b1x1} + \sum_{k=2}^{p} b_k x_k$$

Suppose that our "reasonable bounds" on b1 are [β–δ, β+δ], where β is the center of that interval. We now run three different sets of linear regression explorations fixing our b1 value: one using b1=β–δ, one with b1=β, and the third with b1=β+δ. If our original range for b1 is fairly limited, we can probably find a set of b_k's that are fairly close together for all three models. We now also have three separate R^2 values for these three regressions. Assuming that there is some degree of curvature in these R^2 values, we can interpolate a new β' that would predict the maximum R^2. We should then run a second set of b1 values centered at β' with a much smaller δ. If we cannot interpolate a new β', we could try to extrapolate. Since this value will fall outside of the original proposed range, it may be that something is wrong with our assumptions. If we continue to iterate the interpolation procedure, eventually, we should arrive at a reasonable estimate for b1.

Conclusion

I hope after reading this chapter the Black Belt understands why regression is so easily misused. The software is simple to apply, answers are spewed out without comment, and the user can take the resultant equation as if it were the truth and apply it to whatever situation arises. The careful investigator needs to take a much deeper look, and apply the knowledge from this chapter, becoming wary of:

- Predictors not even considered
- Multicollinearity
- Higher order terms
- Parsimony
- Metrics that imply a poor fit
- Assumptions that are not supported by the residuals
- Leverage points that can skew the regression
- Measurement error in the predictor variables

It usually takes a great amount of effort to obtain the appropriate data to be able to support a good regression analysis. The investigator should recognize that the analysis process should not be rushed, and that time invested in creating a reliable regression model is only a small part of the total resources used overall.

CHAPTER 12

NON-PARAMETRIC STATISTICS

Except for the Chi-Square Goodness of Fit Tests, the common Non-parametric methods offer little of value to the Black Belt.

Non-parametric statistical methods are those we can use when our usual assumptions about normality of the data or homogeneity of variances either are not true or there is not enough data to show that they are. These methods extend to situations where the normal distribution cannot be used legitimately, and we can't find continuous distributions to accurately describe the data.

Falling under the first set of potential applications are those situations where we would like to be able to perform 1-sample t tests, 2-sample t-tests, or ANOVA, but we cannot be sure about our assumptions. Generally, if there are at least 10 or more observations in each group, the Central Limit Theorem will permit us to ignore the normality assumption, but we still have to worry about homoscedasticity. Still, it is virtually impossible to prove variances are not equal when one has at most only 10 observations per group! Thus, we rarely reject this assumption; the residual plots from ANOVA would really have to be bizarre.

With these tests we are forced to perform tests on the medians. One main question then becomes, "how important is it to be able to say the medians are different?" In my experience I have found extremely few instances where making any kind of statement about the median—especially without being able to say something practically useful about the confidence interval about that median—has been an important concern for the investigator. Another main question is more practical: "why is it so hard to reject the null hypothesis of equal medians?"

This latter question is important because these non-parametric methods have considerably less power (greater Type II error) than parametric methods, and usually the sample size is quite small. Thus in order to reject the null hypothesis the splits about the proposed median have to be very large; in practical testing the actual p-value is almost always high. With a single sample of 10, the split has to be 9 versus 1 to pass the Sign Test, and close to 8 versus 2 for the Wilcoxon Signed Rank Test. How often will these happen unless the differences are already so big that the investigator would almost trip over them anyway? So the major flaws in these non-parametric methods are that they aren't sensitive, and the test results involve a metric that often isn't of much use. Personally, I think the teaching of them in Black Belt training is generally a waste of time.

However, there is the second type of non-parametric methods that have considerably more merit. Admittedly they suffer from the same lack of power versus parametric methods. But usually the sample size is substantially larger, and so they have a much better chance of uncovering differences when they exist. The primary non-parametric method that I'm referring to is the Chi-square goodness-of-fit test. This test was thoroughly covered in Chapter 9 (hypothesis testing for three or more groups). There it was used primarily for situations that could be described by having the count data be placed in a two-way table.

The Chi-square goodness-of-fit test has even more versatility, being able to handle one-way tables for equality of counts versus an overall mean (for example if we wanted to compare aggregate counts from multiple particle count stations across a week's time). And it can also be used in three-way tables, especially to see if there is independence between the three different factors. Its limitation is that there should be expected values of at least 5 in the majority of the cells (individual 3-way combinations).

In summary, learning the large variety of non-parametric tests probably isn't worth the Black Belt's time, except for the Chi-square goodness of fit test—which should probably get more class time.

CHAPTER 13

EXPERIMENTATION

The purpose of an experiment is to better understand the real world, not to understand the experimental data.

—*William Diamond*

Perhaps nothing in statistics is as fun for the statistician and eye-opening for the practitioner as Design of Experiments (DOE). The statistician sees multiple elements of statistics (hypothesis testing, sample size calculation, data collection, gage error, ANOVA, etc.) joined with aspects of group theory and vector analysis, and finished off with multiple options for applications where creativity rather than rote methods can be utilized. It's exciting! For the Black Belt / investigator, DOE is an awesome tool of efficiency, allowing her to check out a dozen variables simultaneously with the bonus of uncovering interactions all at a mere fraction of the cost of doing a couple one-factor-at-a-time (OFAT) experiments which unveil little.

So because of this power, Black Belt training spends a considerable amount of time in the Improve Phase uncovering the "secrets" of DOE: highlighting the differences between OFAT experiments and the 2×2; expanding to the 2^3 and then the 2^n and full factorials; then revealing the magic of the fractional factorial; and for some Black Belts wrapping up with Response Surface Methodology (RSM) which allows the experimenter to not only peruse the curvature of the response but even reach the Nirvana of finding the settings of the KPIVs which produce the "optimum" value for the KPOV. Along this journey, if the training has been good, the Black Belt will have been exposed to proper analysis techniques (e.g. understanding both statistical and practical significance, reducing the model, checking the residuals), sample size calculations, DOE planning tools and resource considerations, and the dangers of confounding.

In this chapter I will not attempt to repeat the majority of what the Black Belt has already studied. Instead I hope to expand some of the DOE horizons, explore other important DOE points that might not have been covered in training, reveal the "dark" side of DOE, and comment on the actual execution of the experiment.

The Design of the Experiment

When anyone says, "I'm going to run a DOE," I always want to correct them. The meaning of what they said is that they are going to design an experiment, but what they probably meant to say is that they are going to execute a designed experiment. I would like to assume that they know what they're doing, but in many of the cases I've witnessed, the investigator acts as if he is on a fishing expedition hoping to catch the "big one" with this experiment, but planning to move to a different location if this spot doesn't work out. Fortunately, Six Sigma training has brought the DMAIC strategy to bear on the problem so that through the Measure and Analyze Phases the BB has diligently narrowed down potential critical KPIVs and now is either seeking to optimize the process or at least screen out those variables which don't have a significant impact on the KPOV.

It certainly has been emphasized in the training that the experimenter must understand the purpose of the experiment, identify the resources (which include both time and funding), anticipate barriers to success, and outline a general strategy. But there are aspects of the circumstances which can crop up which will affect the results.

First and foremost in importance in running designed experiments is assessing the capability of actually executing the experiment correctly. Theoretically, an experimenter can investigate a huge number of factors in a single experiment. But these experiments become so complicated, that the chance of an incorrect setting for a single trial—which could destroy the validity of all the results—is fairly high. I often counsel my students to avoid anything more than a 5-factor experiment, emphasizing that a 2^{5-1} is an excellent Resolution V design.

Next, having an appropriate sample size is extremely important, since hypothesis tests will be run on the mean differences (or even the standard deviations), and the experimenter should do whatever is necessary to control the Type I and Type II errors. But the right choice of α and β should also be a major consideration. The best experimental practices involve using a structured approach: first screen out the unimportant variables, identify with some degree of certainty which of the remaining variables are actually critical KPIVs, and then find levels of these KPIVs which optimize the process.

In the earliest stages involving the task of screening, the usual practice we use in hypothesis testing of a low α and a medium β needs to be reversed. Typically the Type II error level should be set at 0.05 and the Type I error at 0.2. The reason for this is that during the screening process if a significant factor is eliminated, the experimenter is unlikely to test that factor again. The low β gives us only a 1 in 20 chance of missing a significant variable, while the higher α makes it more difficult to eliminate those same variables. Once the list of potential factors gets reduced, further experiments will better uncover the critical KPIVs.

Usually, sample size is calculated using the *process* standard deviation as a guide, with the critical difference either being put in absolute terms or in some multiple of the process standard deviation. This practice is unnecessarily conservative. The process standard deviation contains all the variation due to common causes, but a good experiment is set up to reduce the effect of many of those noise variables. Typically the experiment is run with a single operator on a single machine using limited numbers of fixtures (if required at all). The runs are generally performed in a short period of time, where environmental effects are minimized. And most importantly, several of the variables which would otherwise contribute to the overall variability are factors in the experiment. Thus, we can expect the standard deviation affecting the experiment to be reduced substantially, usually a minimum of 20%, with possibilities that it is reduced by 40%. This consideration of a smaller sigma can result in a smaller required sample size.

Furthermore, it is important to recognize that in the analysis many of the terms will drop out. Thus, in a full factorial 2^5 perhaps only a maximum of 7 terms (considering only main effects and two-factor interactions) might show up as significant. Since the experiment will then have 24 degrees of freedom remaining for error, the sensitivity will be substantially increased. Similarly, if instead the experiment is run as a 2^{5-1}, with 7 significant terms there would still be 8 degrees of freedom for error left over. In either of these two designs the likely anticipated reduction of the model could possibly reduce the estimated number of required replicates in the sample size calculation—but only if the experimenter presumes this dropping out of terms during the planning stages.

One other consideration can occur when the required sample size is less than that needed for the given design and only specific interactions are likely to be significant. For example, investigating five main effects and one interaction, one might consider a fractional factorial 2^{5-1} design involving 16 trials, but because one is looking for extremely large effects, an eight-trial experiment may suffice. Looking at the confounding columns for a 2^{5-2}, the five main effects would be confounded with 2- and 3-factor interactions, but the two remaining columns have 2-factor interactions confounded only with other 2- and 3-factor interactions. By appropriately designating the variables within the design, the important 2-factor interaction would not be confounded with the main effects.

Example 1: The experimenter wants to investigate in a 2^{5-2} experiment the five factors X1, X2, X3, X4 and X5, and believes that only the X2•X4 interaction is likely to be important. If we create the design (here in Minitab, using default variables A, B, C, D and E) we get the alias table (using "=" to designate aliases):

    A = BD = CE = ABCDE
    B = AD = CDE = ABCE
    C = AE = BDE = ABCD
    D = AB = BCE = ACDE
    E = AC = BCD = ABDE
    BC = DE = ABE = ACD
    BE = CD = ABC = ADE

If we were to simply make our variable assignments as if they were defaults, with X1→A, X2→B, up to X5→E, we would see that the X2•X4 interaction becomes BD, which is confounded with our "A" factor, X1. Instead, if we assign X2→B and X4→C we see that this interaction will only be confounded with one other 2-factor interaction (and two 3-factor interactions). Thus X2•X4 would be "clear" of the main effects, and we could determine the significance of all the terms we considered likely to be important separately.

Next to an appropriate sample size, perhaps the biggest barrier to running a valid experiment involves the cases where the data is produced in batches. From a statistical standpoint the most important consideration occurs when the batch-to-batch variation is a significant contributor to the overall variation seen in the process. If, as is likely to occur in practice, the sample for each trial setting is generated by only a single batch run, whatever mean bias that that particular batch has will raise or lower all observations equally, and we no longer can consider that we have randomized the runs. The experimenter has not generated replicates; he has generated repeats—which are only good for taking the average and considering that average as a single response. Such type of trials may be seen as a time saver when set-ups are complicated, but the results of the experiment will be invalid. As should be emphasized in class, each trial should be generated by its own run. In situations where batch processes operate, the violation of this principle is even more deadly to the experiment.

But the impact of the batch-process phenomenon is even more insidious when attribute data is taken. First, the tendency is to generate all the data for a single trial setting all at the same time. Thus, suppose we have a 2^3 proportions or rates experiment with three variables, and we choose a sample size of 50 for each trial. When we look at the contrasts, we see that we will have 200 values at each of the low and high levels of the experiment. But because each trial's data was taken all at once, we have the bias of the batch process entering in. And then we end up combining the results of one set of four trials for each of the low and high settings. But averaging proportions or rates is not statistically legitimate. Instead, we really need to use each trial's average as a single data point and do a means test. But this may then imply that we need to take much more data to have a valid sample size. [In doing this, one needs to consider the dual standard deviations inherent in the data: the natural variations occurring with the batches and the within-group variation because of the within-group sample size. For example, if one had proportions around 20%, then using a within-group sample size of 50 we could expect an inherent (that is, within-trial) standard deviation of about 0.057, which would be very large!

Highly Fractionated Designs

When the experimenter's goal is screening, she often relies on experiment designs that are highly fractionated. They could simply be a Plackett-Burman design or a 2^{7-4} eight-trial design. To a statistician these designs are things of beauty. But to the practitioner, they can be deadly traps. The primary problem arises in that the experimenter must control each factor's level precisely while making sure that no other outside force acts during the experiment. Simultaneously controlling seven, ten, or more variables requires a constant vigilance that is often difficult to achieve for an engineer who may have to carefully watch over every step. Even then, it is quite likely that some of the variables will be affected by any time-based changes, since a few of the variables must necessarily be set up to be less random in time than others.

Because the result of each trial contributes significantly to the determination of the factor effects upon which a judgment will be made as to whether to screen out the variable, a single erroneous trial will completely destroy the validity of the experiment except in the rare cases where one or two factors have an enormous impact on the response—a situation that should already be anticipated anyway.

The second major problem occurs in processes which have previously been well studied. Here, process improvement efforts have already identified and optimized single factors. (These circumstances often arise in the technology industries.) But what remains to be uncovered are significant interactions. Yet highly fractionated designs are impotent in revealing these. What's worse is that 2^{p-k} screening designs are Resolution III: the interactions may just be mistaken as main effects, and it may be impossible to deconvolute them. Thus, a Plackett-Burman design, which spreads the confounding of interactions across several of the main effects, should be preferred when screening. On the other hand, when significant improvement efforts have already been made, screening designs should probably be avoided in favor of designs that will reveal interactions.

There is at least one feature of interactions that can help them be uncovered in a screening design. Usually, if there is a strong two-factor interaction, at least one of the two contributing factors is likely to show up as statistically significant. However, the experimenter needs to enter into the experiment itself with the expectation of only uncovering important main effects.

Alternative Designs

For brevity sake in this book, a discussion of the details of the possible experiment designs which the Black Belt is likely to be familiar with will be ignored. These include the standard 2-level experiments involving full, fractionated 2^{k-p}, and Plackett-Burman designs, plus the generalized full factorial (e.g. $m^k \times n^j \times p^l$). But there are many other approaches, some simple, and others so complicated, that a statistician should probably be consulted. Perhaps the simplest of these alternative designs falls under the umbrella of "Latin Square" designs.

As implied by their title, these designs resemble squares. As such, the number of levels of each factor must be equal. One of the simplest of these is the 4×4 Latin Square:

	1	2	3	4
I	A	B	D	C
II	D	C	A	B
III	B	D	C	A
IV	C	A	B	D

The leftmost column represents the first factor and its four levels (I-IV), the top row the second factor (1-4), and the third factor is embedded inside the square (A-D). Thus, in 16 trials there are three factors each at four levels. The non-randomized design looks like:

Trial	Factor 1	Factor 2	Factor 3
1	I	1	A
2	I	2	B
3	I	3	D
4	I	4	C
5	II	1	D
6	II	2	C
7	II	3	A
8	II	4	B
9	III	1	B
10	III	2	D
11	III	3	C
12	III	4	A
13	IV	1	C
14	IV	2	A
15	IV	3	B
16	IV	4	D

Latin Squares involving three factors can be made up with 3 through 9 levels. The restriction is that each factor must have exactly the same number of levels as the other factors.

If instead you have four factors—all with the same number of levels—there's a solution for that, too, called "Graeco-Latin Squares." Below is an example of a four-factor Graeco-Latin Square design:

	1	2	3	4
I	Aα	Bβ	Cγ	Dδ
II	Bδ	Aγ	Dβ	Cα
III	Cβ	Dα	Aδ	Bγ
IV	Dγ	Cδ	Bα	Aβ

As with the Latin Square, the Roman numerals, capital letters and regular numbers all refer to levels for the first three factors. The Greek letters (in the present example, α, β, γ and δ) represent the four levels of the fourth factor. Written out, the sixteen-trial experiment represented by the above example would be:

Trial	Factor 1	Factor 2	Factor 3	Factor 4
1	I	1	A	α
2	I	2	B	β
3	I	3	C	γ
4	I	4	D	δ
5	II	1	B	δ
6	II	2	A	γ
7	II	3	D	β
8	II	4	C	α
9	III	1	C	β
10	III	2	D	α
11	III	3	A	δ
12	III	4	B	γ
13	IV	1	D	γ
14	IV	2	C	δ
15	IV	3	B	α
16	IV	4	A	β

There are even more designs which allow for *five* factors—all with the same number of levels—called the Hyper-Graeco-Latin Square design. And finally there is even one 6-factor, five-level design called the Hyper-Hyper-Graeco-Latin Square (or Hyper^2-Graeco-Latin Square). In summary, the number of levels and factors available in designs like these are:

Designs	# Factors	# Levels
Latin	3	3, 4, 5, 6, 7, 8, 9
Graeco-Latin	4	3, 4, 5, 7, 8, 9
Hyper Graeco-Latin	5	4, 5
Hyper^2 Graeco-Latin	6	5

A good text to see all these designs is by Box, Hunter and Hunter[1]. Realize that these designs, especially the more elaborate, are highly fractionated. As a result, any single trial that is mis-run can have a disastrous effect on the analysis. Also, no 2-factor interactions will be available, but will be "buried" within the results. Since there is only a single trial that contains any specific 2-factor combination, if the effect is quite large it might be possible to detect that value as a general outlier in the results.

With regard to these Latin Square designs, in most practical investigations, the experimenter will not have factors all of which have the same number of attribute levels. But there is one particular discipline for which it can readily occur, and that is in performing a more detailed analysis of the measurement system. Unfortunately, the most common gage studies allow few degrees of freedom for the reproducibility factors, yet provide excessive df's for repeatability. But by using a Latin-type Square design, multiple reproducibility factors can be investigated simultaneously. For example with a 7-level Latin Square, we could conceivably look at 7 parts, measured on 7 different fixtures by 7 different measurers using only 49 total measurements. And if we had a fourth factor (loading method?), we could add that factor through a Graeco-Latin Square design for free (well, almost for free, since we'd lose some degrees of freedom for calculating repeatability, which could also slightly increase p-values). With an MSA, we actually don't care about the individual factor levels. Instead, such designs should be analyzed using variance component analysis so that the variance contributions to the gage for the factors can be uncovered. If any factor's variance is high, by outputting the Least Squares Means for that factor, one can determine if any given level is the main cause for the inflated variance and investigated further.

Recognize that all these designs that have been discussed are "balanced" designs. That is, they are all set up in a way that the effects of all the other factors cancel out. But there is one type of unorthodox design that I have used successfully several times. It is an artificially fractionated design that contains at least one factor with a high number of levels. These aren't textbook designs, and I have had to create those that I used. Usually, they are highly unbalanced, but they are set up in a way so that the individual levels can be reasonably estimated. These designs were all used to estimate variance components in gage studies.

One design I used was to investigate a gage which measured multiple parts all at one time (a "Run"), and there were multiple positions (Slots") on the measuring fixture. Nine Runs were used, measuring 16 pre-chosen parts strategically located in the 16 different positions. The following is the design:

	Slot															
	1	2	3	4	5	6	7	8	9	10	11	12	13	14	15	16
Run 1	12	11	13	14	4	6	7	2	1	3	15	8	10	9	5	16
Run 2	4	1	11	3	5	15	14	8	12	10	6	9	7	13	2	16
Run 3	6	5	12	4	11	10	2	8	9	1	14	3	13	7	16	15
Run 4	1	14	3	4	15	2	9	11	5	8	7	6	13	16	10	12
Run 5	8	13	3	12	2	5	6	10	7	9	11	1	16	14	15	4
Run 6	1	2	5	9	12	14	7	3	10	16	13	11	4	8	15	6
Run 7	2	10	15	7	5	6	8	13	16	4	3	12	14	11	9	1
Run 8	14	4	6	2	8	12	16	5	9	10	11	15	3	1	13	7
Run 9	13	2	10	11	16	8	3	6	15	7	4	12	5	14	1	9

The Part number is tabulated within the matrix, with the Run number running down the left column and the Slot number across the top. Note that for each slot, one part was re-measured (the Part number was the same as the Slot number) with a different run so as to (mildly) directly estimate repeatability. This was compared both to the remaining RMSE as well as previous gage study repeatability values to help validate this experiment. If the design had been completely balanced, 16 runs would have had to be used. But the careful assignment of part to position allowed a 44% reduction of runs.

Another design I used was more complex, since it involved delicate parts and the goal was to not have any part measured more than 6 times. The primary reason for the experiment/MSA was to assess the fixtures. Thus in all, 22 different parts were measured using 12 fixtures by 3 operators with 2 trials each. That is, each operator only made a total of 44 measurements (each part twice). The design used is illustrated in the following matrix:

Fixtures		Parts																					
		1	2	3	4	5	6	7	8	9	10	11	12	13	14	15	16	17	18	19	20	21	22
	A		X2		Y1	Z1	Z2			Y2					X1		Z2	Y1		X1	Z1		X2
	B			X1	X2		Y1		X1	Z2							Z2	Z1	Y1		X2	Y2	Z1
	C		Y2	Z1			Y2			Y1	X2	Z2	Z1		X1			X1		X2	Y1		
	D					X2				Y1	Z1	Z2	Y2	Z1		Y1	Y2		X2			X1	Z2
	E			Y1		Z2		Y2	Z1	Z2			X2	Y2						Z1	X1	X2	X1
	F	X2					Y1	Z1	Y2		Y2			Z2	Z1		X1	X2	X1				Y1
	G	Z1	Z2	X1	Z1	X2		Y1	X2			Y1			Y2							Z2	Y2
	H					Z2	Y2			X1	Z1	Y1		X1	X2	Y1	Z1			Y2	Z2		
	I		Z2	Y1			X2	X1		X2			Y2				X1	Z1	Z2	Y2	Y1		
	J	X1			Z2	Y2			Z1			X1	Z2	Y1	X2		X2	Y1		Y2			
	K	Y2	Z1	Y2			X1	Z2			X1	X2	Y1			X2					Z2	Z1	
	L	Y1			X1				X1	X2		Z1		Z2	Y2				Z1	Z2	Y2	Y1	

X1 = Operator 1, Trial 1	Y1 = Operator 2, Trial 1	Z1 = Operator 3, Trial 1
X2 = Operator 1, Trial 2	Y2 = Operator 2, Trial 2	Z2 = Operator 3, Trial 2

The result of the experiment showed (using variance component analysis) that fixtures were significantly contributing to an unacceptable gage error. Analysis using LS Means highlighted likely extreme fixtures which were then carefully measured and found to be out of specification. Notice that only half the 12 × 22 matrix was used for a total of 132 measurements. The full factorial would have required six times that many as well as measuring each part 36 times each, which would have been quite risky because the parts being measured were relatively delicate.

In all these designs I've discussed there has been the implicit assumption that within any experiment, randomness of run or position can be assured. However, from a practical standpoint this is not always possible to achieve. Some factors are very hard, time consuming or expensive to change. It would be far easier to not randomize those variables. For these cases, the "split-plot" design can be applied. In these designs, the troublesome variable is actually treated like a block, and the analysis will have to be adjusted in a special way to account for it. If the Black Belt faces such restrictions, he should consult a good text, such as Montogmery[1], or a statistician before proceeding.

Example 2: A Black Belt wishes to run a 2-factor plating experiment. The first factor involves four different additives in the plating bath. The second factor involves subjecting the plated film to three different levels of heat treatments. After patterning the treated films, they are tested for magnetic properties. To obtain replicates, twelve plating runs will be made, creating a bath with each additive three times.

In a completely randomized design, every part would have to come from a separate plating run. But this is not possible practically. In our example, all parts coming from a single plating run are nested together, and so the statistical model, and hence the analysis must be different. That analysis is beyond the scope of this book, but the awareness of the difference inherent in certain restricted experiments is important for the Black Belt to have.

When the goal of the experiment is to optimize a particular result, the standard approach of finding linear terms in the factors which are significant will only lead to a region that is close to the optimum. (This procedure is called following the "path of steepest descent/ascent," depending on whether the optimum level is a minimum or a maximum.) When center points in an experiment indicate that there is curvature in the response occurring within the design space, new experiments exploring the possible curvature of behavior of factors is usually then required. This is especially true when the transfer function is required. It is here where *Response Surface* designs are required.

Many Black Belt classes include the study of Response Surface methods. But the practical reality is that only a very small fraction of Black Belts ever need this instruction. First, the final area of exploration is usually fairly narrow, and because small differences are sought, much larger sample sizes are required—with the high probability of introducing unwanted bias or execution error. Second, the Black Belt's goal is usually not to discover the absolute best point of performance, but only to achieve something close to that. This is usually achievable through the standard two-level experiments. Perhaps the best target audience for learning Response Surface Methodology would be experimenters in the Design organization, who would benefit from a knowledge and application of these designs. These, as well as Master Black Belts, should be taught their use.

Finally, I've really only discussed standard (and some semi-standard) design approaches. These designs essentially give an equal treatment to each factor of interest. However, there is a whole host of other potential designs that allow for fine tuning the exploration, putting more emphasis on some factors than others, trying to reduce variance estimates, or even trying to optimize a linear combination of factors. These designs often fall under the name of "x-Optimal," where x is any of the following letters: A, C, D, E, G, I, T, or V. Each type of design tries to optimize a certain pre-determined criterion, and can often lead to smaller overall sample sizes. The actual designs are complicated and must be generated by software. Their discussion falls outside the scope of this book, and the interested experimenter is encouraged to do some individual research and consult a statistician.

Design for Robustness

One of the goals of any process improvement effort should be the widening of the process manufacturing window while achieving the quality target. This will produce either capability metrics with better values or permit trade-offs so that less capable inter-related processes can have their specifications widened while more capable processes can be tightened, producing a net gain in overall capability at lower cost. One method for doing this is to investigate the inter-relationships to see if an offset in mean of one process can be made such that another inter-related process mean can be shifted to a region where the manufacturing capability is greatly improved.

For example, suppose that the output of a process is called Y and we have established the relationship of Y to X given other factors. Our situation may be as follows:

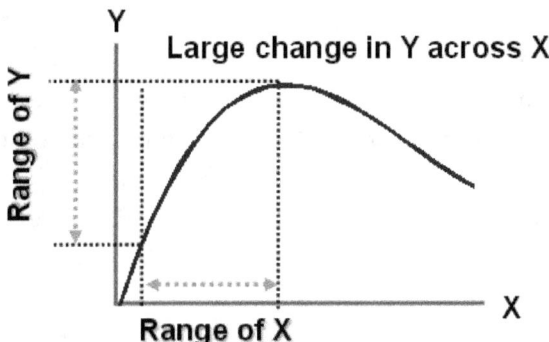

The range that we are operating in for X produces a wide range occurring for Y; that is, the manufacturing output of Y will have a high variance.

However, if by shifting the center area of X by shifting some other parameter, we may obtain:

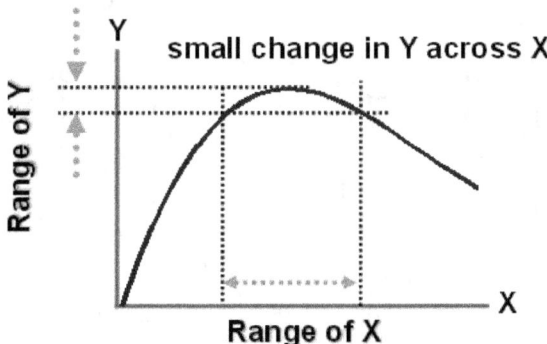

Now, even though we are still restricting X to the same range, the output range of Y is substantially smaller, significantly reducing the final product's variance. Such improvements are often available in systems where multiple factors are added together and the sensitivities of the output variable vary depending on the centering of any given specific factor.

Analysis of Goodness

I first became aware of this simple verification technique when the creator, Bill Diamond, gave a presentation at an internal IBM DOE conference. Analysis of Goodness (ANOG) has since been written up in one of his books[2]. The premise is that in a well-run, complex 2-level experiment, those levels of an experiment that are significant will "rise to the top." That is, if we order the trial combinations from best to worst using the output variable, a pattern will generally emerge, with the level of the most influential variable being mostly in the top half, the second most influential being in the top quarter and then alternating, and so on.

On the follwing diagram is a simple, completed 2^3 full factorial experiment, ordered by results from higher (better) to lower (where, per convention, a "-1" represents the low level of the variable and "1" represents the high level):

A	B	C	Z
1	-1	1	61.12
1	-1	-1	55.57
1	1	-1	48.89
1	1	1	47.44
-1	-1	1	42.02
-1	-1	-1	40.13
-1	1	1	34.08
-1	1	-1	29.16

A straightforward ANOVA analysis would show high A is best followed by low B. One can see that the ordered pattern shows all high A first, followed by an alternating pattern of low B, then high, low, and high. This is the expected pattern when two factors dominate, with one being stronger (A) than the other (B).

If, in fact, it was the AB interaction that was important, the pattern might look more like the following:

A	B	C	AB	Z
1	-1	1	-1	61.12
1	-1	-1	-1	55.57
1	1	-1	1	48.89
1	1	1	1	47.44
-1	1	1	-1	42.02
-1	1	-1	-1	40.13
-1	-1	1	1	34.08
-1	-1	-1	1	29.16

The levels of B now show an altered pattern, but the AB interaction term follows the alternating pattern resulting from secondary significance.

The next diagram is an example of a 2^4 full factorial, with the results ordered by fraction defective. Note that the pattern is not quite as straightforward, yet pretty strong.

A	B	C	D	Defective
-1	1	-1	1	9.36
-1	1	1	1	10.23
-1	-1	1	1	10.44
-1	-1	-1	1	11.49
-1	1	-1	-1	19.66
-1	1	1	-1	19.75
1	1	1	1	19.81
1	1	1	-1	20.64
1	1	-1	1	21.02
1	1	-1	-1	21.6
-1	-1	-1	-1	22.49
1	-1	1	-1	25.62
1	-1	1	1	26.56
1	-1	-1	-1	26.64
-1	-1	1	-1	27.00
1	-1	-1	1	29.41

The evidence here is that the low level of A is best, followed by a high level of D. (If there were an AD interaction, the pattern in D would follow high-low-low-high; alternatively, we could create the AD column and see if it followed the second grouping pattern.) The eighth-level pattern in B suggests that high B may also be preferred. These "pick-the-winner" conclusions would all be borne out by standard analysis.

From the standpoint of determining significant factors, ANOG doesn't offer much. But its true strength is in uncovering those situations where the pattern *does not* occur. That is, if we expect to see a pattern (which we should if we've designed the experiment well), but somehow the pattern is broken, there becomes strong evidence that at least one trial has been mis-run. (Also, when there is a mis-run, the ANOVA analysis results will often be more flattened out, with significance spread over many interactions and fewer "standout" factors.) By running ANOG, the experimenter might be able to highlight which run or runs seem to violate the overall pattern of goodness. In this sense, ANOG is a useful sanity check on the full experiment.

Design of Experiments for Standard Deviations

Just as we may be interested in knowing the effects of various factors on the mean response of an output variable, we may also want to know whether the standard deviation differs relative to the different levels of input variables. To accomplish this, we can run standard experiment designs, such as a 2^3, with our output variable being the standard deviation of aggregate values which were all run at a specific combination. This will, unfortunately, require rather large sample sizes, because defining a standard deviation precisely is more difficult than determining the mean. We also need to be cautious that we take replicates rather than repeats. Repeats will only provide an estimate of a within-run standard deviation, which could greatly underestimate the true standard deviation at any run combination.

Besides the added complexity of running so many replicates, the other challenge of these types of experiments involves the analysis. Traditional analytic methods involved taking the log of each combination's standard deviation and then analyzing that variable as if it were an unreplicated result. Thus, a 2^3 full factorial with 10 replicates (80 total runs) would be reduced to a single 2^3 involving 8 log(s) results. This analysis method totally ignores how well each of those standard deviations was derived, so that experiments with 3 replicates and 300 replicates are analyzed exactly the same.

Fortunately, there are two alternative analytical methods which do take into account the number of replicates. The first is quite complex, and uses what are called "Maximum Likelihood Estimates" (MLE). These are well-known methods to the statistician, but are generally too difficult for engineers. However, certain computer software programs, such as Minitab, now permit MLE analysis, although caution is quite necessary because the program's default for analyzing standard deviation experiments is the traditional method.

The second method of analysis follows an F-test approach and tests variances. It assumes that the changes in variance due to the different levels of a factor are multiplicative, not additive. In order to compute significance, all the variances at the high level of a factor are pooled, and this value is divided by the pooled variances at the low level of the factor. Given that there are m combinations at each high and low level, and n replicates, this ratio is tested against the F statistic with m(n-1) degrees of freedom in both numerator and denominator. All main effects and all interactions can be tested in this way.

Example 3: A 2^3 full factorial with 24 replicates was run with the three factors A, B and C each at a low and high level. The variance was computed for each treatment combination. The results are as follows:

A	B	C	Variance
-1	-1	-1	0.823
1	-1	-1	1.187
-1	1	-1	3.186
1	1	-1	2.34
-1	-1	1	0.651
1	-1	1	1.477
-1	1	1	2.048
1	1	1	1.516

We now need to figure the F ratio:

$$F_x = \frac{\sum_{k=1}^{4} s_p^2(x_{high})}{\sum_{k=1}^{4} s_p^2(x_{low})}$$

For factor A this would be:

$$F_A = \frac{1.187 + 2.340 + 1.477 + 1.516}{0.823 + 3.186 + 0.651 + 2.048} = \frac{6.520}{6.708} = 0.972$$

The probability value corresponding to F = 0.972 with 92 df in both numerator and denominator is 0.446. Since this is a two sided test, the p-value is twice that, equal to 0.89, and clearly not significant. However, if we work through the calculations for all main effects and interactions, only B would be significant at $\alpha = 0.05$, with a p-value of 0.0002. However, if α had been pre-chosen to be 0.10, then the AB interaction would have been significant with a p-value of 0.061.

If these calculations are going to be run more frequently, it is advisable that one creates a spreadsheet to perform the tedious calculations.

One advantage to the F-test approach is that a sample size can be computed to achieve an appropriate sensitivity of the test. Based on a sample size N being computed for a two-level comparison of standard deviations, and m combinations at each high and low levels of the factors, the number of replicates, n = 1 + (N-1)/m.

Optimizing Multiple Responses

Frequently in experimentation, multiple responses are tracked, with the desire to optimize all of these simultaneously. In many instances these would involve both a principal KPOV and its process standard deviation. At other times, there may be multiple KPOVs that are being tracked (for example, one of these might be the variable tracking the secondary metric), and the experimenter might be trying to find appropriate settings which produce some kind of optimum for each. Of course, it is highly unlikely that the optimum settings for the principal KPOV—let's designate that KPOV as Yp—also correspond to the optimum settings for the other outputs of interest (designate them as Y1, Y2, ...). So some kind of compromise is required.

The most straightforward compromise would involve creating a desirability function, F_D, which would include all the output variables in some way. This is not a trivial task! If one has found the region which optimizes the Yp to a value of Yp(best), one term in F_D might be $k[Yp-Yp(best)]^2$, where k is a weighting constant. Such quadratic terms could be added to F_D for the other output variables using different weighting constants. Thus, an example with one principal KPOV and three other important KPOVs (Y1, Y2 and Y3) might be:

$$F_D = k[Yp-Yp(best)]^2 + k_1[Y1-Y1(best)]^2 + k_2[Y2-Y2(best)]^2 + k_3[Y3-Y3(best)]^2.$$

Choosing the values for the four k coefficients would need to involve financial and practical considerations.

Another approach might be to optimize an F_D involving only two of the KPOVs and setting a goal of allowing only solutions which provide some minimum or maximum acceptable values for the other KPOVs (e.g. cost cannot exceed some maximum value; throughput must exceed some minimum value).

To truly optimize the F_D would require an extensive mapping of the experiment "space." And so it is more likely that this latter approach would be more practical. If one can offset any of these variables (using the principle of robustness), it may be worth the effort. From a financial standpoint, including any type of offset that can be applied into the F_D might be highly beneficial.

Verification and Validation

Prior to any release to users of a transfer function or the institution of specifications of optimized KPIV values is a verification phase. That is, even though experimentation may have uncovered a function or optimum levels, these still were based on information resulting from a limited number of trials—no matter how well they were run. Specific concerns that need to be addressed are:

- Was there a lack of fit that indicates that perhaps other factors strongly influence the KPOV?
- Have you performed a confirmation run?
- Is the solution that the experiments suggest valid for the broader conditions that manufacturing will impose on it?
- Is the solution really practical?

Lack of Fit

If the experiments were run so that there were replicates, there will be a reasonable estimate of the standard deviation due to replication. Some computer macros will divide the RMSE into its two components: the reproducibility element which reflects the normal noise in the experiment and a "Lack of Fit" element, which is all the rest. This latter term, which can be given a statistical significance value, characterizes the effects of all the variables which might have been considered uncontrolled noise, but whose optimization could actually contribute to improving the model—if the experimenter knew what they were. If Lack of Fit is statistically significant, it would be wise for the investigator to look more deeply for other potential factors. Such a search would be greatly facilitated by having kept track of all those noise variables while the experiments were being run.

In some cases the estimates of the R^2 value or the RMSE will themselves indicate that the proposed model is not good. If a transfer function is being generated, it would be prudent to estimate the confidence bounds of predicted values to see if these are adequate for the intended purposes. Recall that with regression, prediction capability involving models with an R^2 less than 0.9 could be inadequate. However, in judging models from experiments the sample space is usually quite narrow, thereby naturally diminishing R^2, and so the RMSE becomes a better value for judging model capability.

Confirmation Run

When running fractional factorial experiments it is possible that a trial which includes the specific combination of factor levels that the investigator thinks are best has not been run. At that point it should be obvious that multiple trials using the best levels of the critical KPIVs should be run to validate those levels. In fact, this activity should be done regardless of whether such trial combinations were run in the experiment. This practice should be completed before any publishing of the results, since there is always the possibility that some trials of the experiment were mis-run, resulting in erroneous conclusions; or it is possible that factors not considered in the experiment but which truly do affect the KPOV could now have changed, providing a result that differs from the expected.

Model Adequacy to a Broader Application

Typically experiments are run in such a way that the sample space has been narrowed. This is done to lower the inherent noise levels, thereby improving the signal-to-noise levels and enhancing sensitivity. There might have only been one machine and tester used; a single technician may have performed the experiments carefully; perhaps only one or two fixtures were used; the experiment was run over a very short period of time. What will happen under true manufacturing conditions? What happens over the ensuing months when all three machines are used on all shifts, run by a dozen operators for whom speed may be as important as quality, and fifty different fixtures are used? And perhaps that close control on the critical KPIVs cannot be maintained to the levels that the experimenter expected.

Usually the experimenter cannot wait for months to determine if the proposed model actually works in practice. But a good BB should anticipate which noise factors might truly influence the final outcome, and perhaps even include them in the experiments.

A Practical Solution

There are always risks when trying to find levels of the critical KPIVs that optimize the KPOV that those levels might not be manufacturable—or the required specifications for some of those variables might turn out to be rather expensive to maintain. Trade-offs in designs must always be considered even as the levels of the critical KPIVs are being decided for the experiments.

There is the very sad story of the first design for a small form-factor disk drive that was being developed by IBM in the late 1970's. One component, the actuator, which is the fixture that holds the heads in place and moves them over the disk surfaces at a very rapid speed, benefits from being made of a very light-weight but rigid material. The designers chose to make these out of magnesium. However, when they tried to machine these magnesium actuators en masse, they found that they were quite impractical to fabricate, experiencing multiple machining problems.

Taguchi Designs

Taguchi Designs are those experiment designs created by the Japanese engineer Genichi Taguchi which had become quite popular in several industries in the 1980's. These are generally 2- and 3-level multiple-factor designs which can become quite fractionated as more and more variables are added to the investigation. They have the advantage of being presented in diagram form, with multiple diagrams (corresponding to different experiment approaches) being available for a given number of factors and their levels.

The more your company knows about statistical methods, the less likely it will be that Taguchi Designs will be useful. First, the proper use of these designs involves already knowing which interactions are likely to occur; these must specifically be included as part of the experiment, with all other interactions presumed to be insignificant. This may work well in industries where experiments are being used for the first time and the primary goal is to investigate main effects and "obvious" interactions. Furthermore, no aliasing tables are presented which would potentially highlight risks of missing and/or confounding interactions. Finally, these designs are typically taught without regard to a concern for an appropriate sample size; yet they are usually tested via ANOVA with an α value of 0.05. And they are generally not run in a sequential manner. These may look like screening experiments, but the results are often interpreted as providing the final settings.

Although Taguchi himself says that confirmation runs must always be made before releasing any type of model, it is quite clear that those processes which have received more scrutiny in the past are much more likely to have some unexplored but important interaction that these designs cannot uncover. This is, of course, much more likely in technology industries. One engineer from Texas Instruments once stated in a general presentation that of all the Taguchi experiments run at TI with which he was familiar, only 10%

of the experiment results were consistent with the confirmation run. This is a pretty poor track record, but serves as strong warning. These designs are probably best used in the early stages of process exploration—and here, again, they rarely have an advantage over the conventional designs.

---

[1] Montgomery, Douglas. "Design and Analysis of Experiments" (1976), John Wiley & Sons, pp. 292-300.

[2] Diamond, William J. "Practical Experiment Designs: for Engineers and Scientists" (2001), John Wiley & Sons.

CHAPTER 14

STATISTICAL PROCESS CONTROL

Having Control Charts does not mean a company has SPC.

Statistical Process Control (SPC) is the oldest of the more popular quality control methods practiced in Manufacturing. It was developed in 1924 by Walter Shewhart, and as a result, the charts that are used are frequently called Shewhart Charts. The method in the early days was also called Statistical *Quality* Control, but the nomenclature was then changed in the 1980's to emphasize that quality should not just be the responsibility of the Quality Department (the size of which at those earlier times typically was quite large), but should primarily rest on those involved in the process—operators, technicians, and process engineers.

At its procedural roots, SPC is more than just control charts. It is a methodology that:

- Evaluates the stability of a process over time.
- Points out the existence of special causes of variation.
- Once these special causes are eliminated, it is then used to monitor the process to maintain expected processing performance despite normal process variation.

Thus, it is an important tool for the phases of Measure (evaluating stability for capability assessment), Analyze (showing sources that affect the

KPOV adversely), and Control (maintaining the improvement in process capability).

Since a typical Black Belt class goes into sufficient detail on how the charts are created, interpreted and implemented, I will avoid repeating most of that information. These charts principally covered are the variables charts $\bar{x}$ & R, $\bar{x}$ & s, and the IR (Individual and Moving Range), and the attribute charts p, np, c, and u. However, there are many topics regarding these charts that are not (or may not be) covered, and which may be important for the BB.

Common Errors

Perhaps the first important point involves the implementation of SPC into a factory. As a statistician at IBM, I was called upon to evaluate SPC at seven of IBM's suppliers. Of these seven (some of whom were major manufacturers), only one was implementing SPC correctly—and that one supplier was literally producing parts in his garage! Most suppliers were producing wallpaper. What were their errors?

- Most were not reacting to an out-of-control condition properly.
- Some charts showed limits that were obviously incorrectly calculated (either being too wide or too narrow).
- Most had too many charts to track and react to on a timely basis.
- Some were using the wrong type of chart or charting method for the variable they were tracking.

Let's now cover these errors in more detail.

First, there are many potential signals that indicate a process is out of control. A chart should not simply be judged on whether a point falls outside the control limits. Instead, it is better to make an out-of-control declaration when the process shows a non-random pattern. There are two sets of eight rules that are available to help engineers discern non-random patterns: the Western Electric rules and the slightly superior rules that appeared in the *Journal of Quality Technology*[1]. It is probably <u>not</u> prudent to implement all of these rules, since the probability of a false alarm increases from about 1 in 370 points (corresponding to reacting to a point outside the control limits) to about 1 in 47 for all eight tests. But these companies I reviewed were failing these rules in such an obvious manner that one didn't have to count how many points were either on one side of the center line, trending, or close to one of the control limits (but, of course, still inside!). Thus, these non-random patterns were blatant, but weren't being reacted to. It is important for proper implementation that every out-of-control signal is reacted to immediately.

IBM in Rochester was not immune from such mistakes. In fact, in its first written application for the Malcolm Baldrige National Quality Award in 1989, a chart was presented that showed a process where all the points were closely hugging the center line far from the control limits. Clearly these limits had not been calculated correctly. But presumably those who included this chart thought that it indicated a high level of quality. That may be, but it also showed that those involved in the process did not understand SPC. My colleague, Dan Rand, and I (from our site's Statistical Competency Center [SCC]) pointed out this mistake (after the application had already been submitted, since we hadn't seen it before). Our site received a visit from the examining committee, but it didn't win.

However, the next year our plant manager again decided to try to win the Award—ostensibly because quality had improved, but perhaps more so because they felt that they were better experienced in dealing with the examiners. Again an application was created which contained a control chart—which, unfortunately (again) was not given to the SCC for review—for it once again showed that our site didn't know what it was doing with regard to SPC! It presented an attribute chart, specifically a u chart showing defects removed per 1000 lines of code, with a lower control limit below zero. The LCL should have been set at zero, since there are no negative defects. [There was possibly another error as well since the limits showed an unlikely constant sample size.] The Quality Award examiners again came to our site and apparently didn't say anything about our erroneous chart. But the Rochester IBM site won the Malcolm Baldrige National Quality Award for large companies that year!

What is the proper way to react to an out-of-control signal? Most suppliers chose to take a follow-up point; if that fell inside the control limits, they concluded the process was fine. But this totally violates the spirit of Statistical Process Control. First, other than the initial investigation of a process, Manufacturing is supposed to set up control charts on that process only after the process has already proven to be stable. Thus, the control chart is operated under the expectation that it will remain stable. And so the usual control limits are set at $\mu \pm 3\sigma_{parameter}$, which corresponds to having the accidental possibility of a random point from that stable process falling outside the limits equal to .0027—which corresponds to one chance in 370 points.

Therefore, the fundamental supposition is that the process will continue to remain stable, until some special cause arises. That is, the process is considered "innocent" until there is strong evidence that it is "guilty," which would be an out-of-control signal. If that signal does occur, a new hypothesis must be created: that the process is unstable and needs to be proven to still be good (indicating a false alarm or perhaps a mis-measurement occurred) in order to continue. To prove this requires standard hypothesis testing methods, with sample sizes that are usually at least four times the original subgroup size (the practitioner needs to actually calculate the proper sample size). Taking just another subgroup sample would provide only a 50% chance of another out-of-control signal if the mean had shifted a full $3\sigma/\sqrt{n}$.

It is often easy to tell when the control limits have been miscalculated. Either the points fall far from the control limits (and usually near the center line) or there are many points that fall outside the control limits. In the first case, process improvement may have occurred but that improvement has not been incorporated into the control chart. Or the limits may have simply been miscalculated through a mathematical error or a table look-up error.

In the latter case of multiple points being out of control, the control chart may now not even be implemented or on display, since it is showing consistent instability. But the process is not necessarily unstable! Instead, if the process is based in any way on batch processing, it is likely that the within-batch variation, upon which the control chart limits are calculated, is smaller than the overall process variation. And so the calculated limits are more narrow than they ought to be. In these cases, the batch-process control chart should be used, which consists of the IR charts where the individuals plotted are actually the means of the subgroups, with an s chart added to monitor within-group variation. Such charts are sometimes labeled "between/within" to distinguish them. The reality is that a very large percentage of processes have some form of batch character, and control charts limits calculated in the normal way are too narrow.

As I indicated before, the charts that many of the companies I visited could be called "wallpaper," since there were so many displayed charts. A company practicing good SPC will put charts only on those critical and important variables for which either control or monitoring is required. For less critical variables, other methods can be used to occasionally check quality. When disk drive manufacturing came to the IBM site at which I was working in the early 1980's, the project manager, who was brought in from Japan, dictated that all variables would be charted. Although this gave my statistician colleagues and me lots of teaching opportunities, I think that the concentration on charts displaced a greater attention to the process that could have been better spent on optimization.

The last of the issues that companies violate is to use the wrong type of chart or charting method for the purpose at hand. I have already indicated the most common case: using $\bar{x}$ standard charts when the process is really dominated by batches. But there are other cases, too. Data from attribute situations also often can be considered to come from batch processes. In these cases, one should use the subgroup proportion (or count) value as an individual value and create an IR chart from them. Often p charts are used for processes that have a very low proportion defective; here the c chart would be more effective. [There is also another type of chart better used when the proportion defective is quite small, which is discussed later as the "Low Occurrence Attribute Chart."] Many companies also lump all their data together (for example, from different machines), and so the biases that result from the different mean levels of each creates an artificial inflation of the within-subgroup standard deviation, thereby incorrectly widening the control limits. Unless the SPC practitioner knows for certain that each machine operates with the same mean and standard deviation, results from different machines need to be tracked separately.

One of the largest misconceptions involves the use of the $\bar{x}$ & R chart. This chart should rarely be used! For sample sizes of 2, both the R and s chart are equivalent. But as sample sizes increase, the $\bar{x}$ & s chart becomes increasingly more precise in the estimates that result for the control chart limits, making a noticeable difference even at subgroup sizes of 5. (This is because the standard deviation is a better estimate of process variation than the range, with the confidence interval thus being wider when calculated from the range.) Realize that the use of the x̄ & R chart really dates back to Shewhart's time, when there was no easy way to calculate a standard deviation. But today, the majority of charts can be created by computer for which that calculation is no more difficult than calculating the range. And even a hand-held calculator can be used to produce a value for standard deviation nearly as quickly as the range can be calculated in the head. Thus, x̄ & R charts should only be used on manually generated charts where operators must make all the necessary calculations. As an additional observation, the control limits are calculated even more precisely when the average variance is used rather than the average standard deviation.

Proper Subgroup Size and Sampling Frequency

Very little is typically presented in Black Belt classes with regard to what subgroup size to use and how often a sample is taken. Usually, a default position is taken, such as a subgroup size of 5 and sampling should be taken once or twice a shift. But more appropriate values for both of these can be calculated with only a small amount of process information.

When it comes to subgroup size it is important to recognize the deep roots of tradition that still pervade when choosing the default level of 5. When Shewhart first created the control chart he understood that operators with minimal mathematical education were likely to be the ones to calculate the subgroup averages. If one wants simplicity, samples of size 5 are easiest. All one does is add up the five numbers, double that sum, and move the decimal point over. For example, if the operator were to have the observations 5.6, 5.8, 6.0, 5.6, and 5.5, the sum is 28.5; double that to 57.0; and move the decimal point; the average is 5.7. [Yes, subgroups of size 10 would be easier, but this size is probably excessive.]

In today's world very few control charts are being generated by hand using minimally educated operators. In fact, most are automatically generated by computers which aren't affected by the complexity of a non-traditional subgroup size or finding a variance or standard deviation so that an s chart can be used instead of an R chart. Thus, the practitioner should choose a subgroup size that truly has meaning for process control. Perhaps the best metric to use for this purpose is the process capability. Since the process is assumed to be stable, one can calculate the amount of material being produced out of specifications. If the process is centered and the mean should shift, more material will be out of spec. The practitioner then needs to predetermine what drop in quality is unacceptable and protect against that shift. This shift, or unacceptable delta, can be converted into a number-of-process-sigmas shift by dividing the unacceptable delta by the process standard deviation.

By posing the problem of subgroup size into one regarding an appropriate sample size using standard hypothesis testing, I was able to create a number of curves (these are really called "operating characteristic curves" in Quality jargon) that show what the power of the subgroup size (1-β risk) is for different sample sizes depending on the process shift, in standard deviation units, that is important for the practitioner. The two charts I created appear on the following two pages, and were first presented to the world in the "One Good Idea" section of *Quality Progress*[2]. These are presented next.

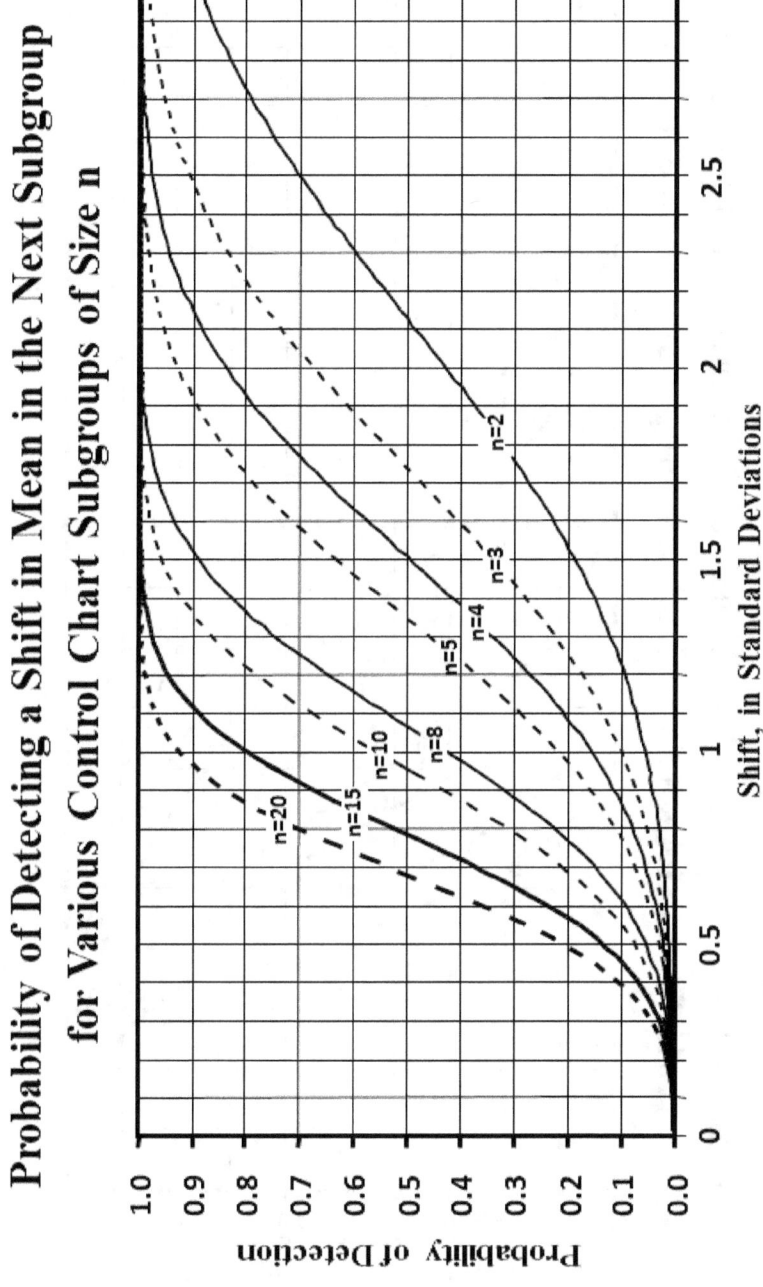

Probability of Detecting a Shift in Mean in the Next 3 Subgroups When Also Using the 2-Points-out-of-3-in-the-Warning-Zone Rule for Various Control Chart Subgroups of Size n

The first diagram provides the power of various subgroup sizes for detecting a shift in mean when only checking to see if the next subgroup's plotted point is outside the 3σ control limits. The second chart indicates the power of various subgroup sizes for detecting a shift in mean in the next three subgroups, assuming that the test for 2-points-out-of-3 beyond 2σ limits is also added to the rule of any single point being outside of the 3σ limits.

For example, if the SPC practitioner has a process standard deviation of 12 mm, and wants to have a 90% chance of detecting a shift in the mean of 18 mm, this corresponds to a shift of 1.5 standard deviation units, and the appropriate subgroup size would be 8 (using the first chart). If, instead, he was content to have the same sureness within the next three subgroups, then a subgroup size of three would suffice. Obviously there is a large degree of subjectivity in choosing both the power of the test and the protection against a shift. But this chart can also be helpful in understanding the risks involved in choosing a subgroup size that might not be appropriate. For example, if one chooses a default subgroup of 5, then there is a 20% chance of missing a shift of 1.7σ in the next subgroup. This might be considered unacceptable from a quality standpoint. As a side note, specific probabilities for specific shifts may not result in an integral subgroup size. One should use the subgroup that is either very close or choose the next size up. And in some cases an interpolation will be required.

Example 1A: Suppose you have a process whose mean is 12.6 mm with a process standard deviation of 0.20 mm. Specifications are at 12.6 ± 0.80 mm = [11.8, 13.4]. The process therefore has Ppk=1.33. You want to guard against a process mean shift with the next subgroup that will produce 3% defective with about 90% confidence. What subgroup size should you use?

First, a process with Ppk = 1.33 has its closest specification 4 process standard deviations away from the mean; that is, Z=4.0. Second, you have to determine what the Z value is for a process with 3% defective. Using tables or the macros that software programs have, this corresponds to Z = 1.88. Therefore, the mean shift that you want to be able to detect with 90% confidence equals 4.0 − 1.88 = 2.12. Looking at the first chart, this corresponds very closely to a subgroup size of 4.

When it comes to determining the frequency of sampling, there are many things to consider. Perhaps the most important of these are:

- How likely is the process to go out of control?
- How much does it cost to sample?
- What does it cost to be running in an out-of-control condition?
- How long does it take to react, and what does this cost?
- What is that chance of detecting a process shift?
- The ease of implementing a sampling plan

By creating a cost model based on these considerations and optimizing that cost based on frequency of sampling, I was able to create an estimating equation for the proper frequency. Since I wanted to eliminate the time element, I based the equation on the number of units made, "n," between appropriate sampling. That equation is:

$$n = \sqrt{\frac{2p(F+T)S}{L(2-p)}}$$

where:
S = Cost of taking and measuring an entire sample
L = Loss per unit (averaged over all units) when operating out of statistical control = (1-Yield) × [Individual part scrap/rework cost]
T = Time lag (in number of units) it takes to react
F = Average number of units between out-of-control conditions if they were found and fixed immediately (i.e. no time lag)
p = Probability of discovering an out-of-control condition with one subgroup
n = Sampling frequency (in number of units produced)

Admittedly, these numbers may not be easy to obtain, especially for a new process. But after a while, reasonable estimates can be made. And since this equation produces an approximation (since there are also many other potential factors that could be involved), a good estimate based on facts is much stronger than a guess.

Example 1B: In the previous example you chose a sample size of 4 to detect with 90% confidence a mean shift that would produce 3% out of specification. Given the following additional information, how often should a subgroup be taken?

- The process runs 2 (8-hour) shifts/day and 5 days/week
- Each shift produces about 400 parts
- A scrapped part represents a loss of $5
- Historically, the process has gone out of statistical control about once every 2 weeks
- It takes about 1 hour to react and fix a process problem
- It costs $.50 to measure a sample unit

From this information, the following important numbers for our equation can be calculated:

S = Cost of sample = 4 × $.50 = $2.00
L = Loss/Unit = $5.00 × 3% = $.15 (we are assuming that the process could shift to the level of producing 3% out of spec)
T = Time Lag = 400 units/shift × 1/8 shift = 50 units
F = Frequency of OOC = 2 weeks × 10 shifts/week × 400 units/shift = 8000 units
p = 0.9

Plugging these numbers into the equation gives:

$$n = \sqrt{\frac{2p(F+T)S}{L(2-p)}} = \sqrt{\frac{2 \cdot (0.9)(8000+50)}{(.15)(2-0.9)}} = 419$$

You should sample every 419 units, but since the process makes 400 per shift, it makes sense to simplify your sampling to once per shift.

Now to return to another issue, which revolves around a proper reaction to an out-of-control signal.

Example 1C: Suppose that after you have implemented the previously suggested subgroup size and frequency, your process has shown the next point outside the control limits on the *high* side. What should you do?

With this out-of-control signal, you should now assume the process has shifted high or has changed in some way. But if the signal is a false alarm, is the process mean still 12.6 mm? You should set up a hypothesis test where

Ho corresponds to a mean of 12.6 mm. But what should your alternative hypothesis look like? Here is where some subjectivity is required. Previously, you had wanted protection against a shift in mean of 2.12 sigmas. But now you should try to be confident that any shift is less than that. This level can be set at a defective level that you would not want your process to be running at long term. With Ppk = 1.33, that defective level had been 0.0064% at most. Perhaps you would guard against the possibility of 0.1% defective. This corresponds to a Z = 3.09, or a shift in mean of 0.91 standard deviation units, or 0.20 × 0.91 = 0.18 mm. Your hypotheses might then be:

Ho: μ = 12.60 mm α = 0.05
Ha: μ = 12.78 mm β = 0.05

You choose conservative values for both Type I and II Errors because you want to have a strong confidence in any decision you make here. Plugging these into computer software looking for Δ/σ = .91 in a one-sided t-test (unless you know for a fact that the standard deviation hasn't changed) gives a sample size equal to 15. As a matter of course, a general rule of thumb to use when taking a second sample is to take a subgroup size about four times bigger than the original subgroup size. This will give you fairly reasonable protection. However, as the defective proportion increases in your stable process, you might want to control process shifts even more tightly.

SPC for Gages

One important activity in the Control Phase is to make sure that the gages which are used to measure the critical KPIVs remain stable. Unfortunately, the methodology to do this is somewhat complicated and is often ignored in Black Belt training. The following is a reasonable approach to maintaining the gages without having to constantly run Gage Studies.

First, the Black Belt really needs to assess the effect of the gage on the value of the KPIV. This also includes the effect on any subgroup mean used in SPC. If σ_{Gage} designates the gage error, then we recognize that the as-measured value of the standard deviation of the KPIV is defined by the relationship:

$$\sigma^2_{Process} = \sigma^2_{True} + \sigma^2_{Gage}$$

also:

$$\mu_{Process} = \mu_{True} + \mu_{Gage}$$

The greater the ratio of $\sigma_{Gage}/\sigma_{True}$, the more the gage needs to be controlled, but only for processes where the Ppk values are more marginal. From this information, the Black Belt can also assess what kind of mean shift and what kind of variance inflation due to the gage will be critical to discover if it happens.

For processes where Ppk is greater than 1.15 and the contribution of the gage is considered fairly small, the use of a single standard measured occasionally and graphed on an IR chart will probably suffice. However, if it is determined that the process quality is fairly sensitive to any gage change, then a different strategy is required. Then one must use the tools of control charts; but they must be used in a different way.

The general method is to own or create a number of standards; call that number "n." These standards can be picked from official standards, or they can be chosen from manufactured parts. In the former case, you can use those known published values. In the latter case, it is necessary to measure each of them multiple times (over a somewhat extended period—perhaps 10 days) to establish "known" values. The known values will be the average of each of the corresponding measurements per part; call these mean values M_1, M_2, ..., M_n. Now when SPC is to be implemented on the gage these different standards will be measured sequentially; call those individual subsequent values $X_1, X_2, ..., X_n$. But what will eventually be charted will not be the X's but the computed differences of these X's from their established values: $\Delta_k = X_k - M_k$. Two sets of charts can now be created moving forward. The first is an I-MR chart of the individual Δ's. The second will involve grouping consecutive Δ's into subgroups. The size of the subgroup, L, can be computed using the methods outlined earlier regarding picking an appropriate subgroup size. From these subgroups $\bar{x}$ & s charts can be created. Now three types of "master parts" need to be considered:

1. Parts or artifacts with known values of the parameter of interest. These parts are expected to be *permanent* under normal handling.

2. Stable parts that need to be measured many times to establish their "known" value. These parts are also expected to be permanent under normal handling.
3. Unstable parts that need to be measured many times to establish their "known" value. These parts are not expected to maintain their "known" value under normal handling over an extended time.

Case 1: Known, Stable Standards
Special case #1: Standards are easy and inexpensive to measure
- May want to sample L (or all) of these all at once, omitting the I-mR chart.

Special Case #2: Number of available standards < L
- May want to put into subgroups of size equal to available number of standards; then "accept" the loss of sensitivity.
- Consecutively re-measure standards until L measurements have been made
  ◦ If there is only one standard, you should group L consecutive values of these.

Note: if the standards are really known, and an exacting gage study has been run, it is possible to immediately implement both sets of charts:
- Historical Mean = 0
- Historical Standard Deviation = σ_{Gage}

Even if σ_{Gage} is not perfectly known, initial set-up of charts can be made with the estimate from the gage studies to start out. Caution needs to be taken for out-of-control indications, since the standard deviation may be somewhat miscalculated.

Case 2: Unknown, Stable Standards
Standards are generally chosen from manufactured parts. (It's usually good to have them be uniformly distributed over the product range.) They can be expected <u>not</u> to change over time.

Procedure
- First, reliable values for the standards must be established. This should involve a minimum of 15 separate measurements on each

standard (taken over at least ten days), and 25 would be better. Make sure these measurements are replicates and not repeats! Designate the letter "g" as the number of replicates per standard. Running an ANOVA on the merged data will provide an RMSE which should estimate well the total gage error. It is probably prudent to run a two-way ANOVA where the second factor will represent the time element (perhaps each set of standards is measured all at one time; or the day of measurement could be used). If the time factor is significant, then there is strong evidence that the gage is not stable. Also, a test for equal variances (Bartlett's) by standard is necessary. If time is not significant, it should be removed from the model, and the RMSE just becomes S_{pooled}.

- Then the general procedure can be followed—adjusting the SPC charts for the added uncertainty in the standards. Since the homemade standards are not known precisely, a guardband that includes the additional error in the mean determination can be applied. This error in the mean can be quantified using a confidence interval:

$$CI_k = M_k \pm \frac{t_{\alpha/2, n(g-1)} S_{pooled}}{\sqrt{g}}$$

- For the I-MR charts, we need to incorporate this additional CI into the control limits. This results in the values of the CLs being:

$$\pm \left[\frac{t_{\alpha/2, n(g-1)} S_{pooled}}{\sqrt{g}} + t_{\alpha/2, n(g-1)} S_{pooled} \right] = \pm \left[1 + \frac{1}{\sqrt{g}} \right] t_{\alpha/2, n(g-1)} S_{pooled}$$

- For the $\bar{x}$ & s chart we just have to include the fact that we are using L standards in each subgroup. Thus the values for the CLs are:

$$CL = \pm \left[\frac{1}{\sqrt{L}} + \frac{1}{\sqrt{gL}} \right] t_{\alpha/2, n(g-1)} S_{pooled}$$

Example 2: Suppose we have pre-chosen 6 parts to be standards (n=6), and we measure each of these 20 times (g=20). Our analysis shows no time dependence nor inequality of variance. Our calculation of s_{pooled} = 2.30. This has been determined with n(g-1) = 6·19 = 114 df. Given that α is to represent normal 3-sigma limits, $t_{\alpha/2,114}$ = 3.067. Then our 99.7% Individual Δ chart control limits will be $\pm [1+1/\sqrt{20}]*3.067*2.30 = \pm 8.63$.

Suppose also that we have chosen a subgroup size of 4 for grouping our data. Comparing the two control limit values (individual and $\bar{x}$), we see the $\bar{x}$ chart CLs are only different from the individuals chart by the factor of $1/\sqrt{L}$. In the present case, this means our CLs are half of the individuals chart, or ±4.32.

Note that in both cases the center line is 0 since we are charting the Δs. Also, our calculations for s_{pooled} and t use all the data, and not just that for the subgroup.

Comments on Case 2:
1. The control limits created in the described manner will be conservative (wide).
   ➢ Accounts for possibilities that means have not been well determined. In practice, this will mean fewer false alarms.
2. Interpretation of the s chart should only involve tests 1 and 5 (1 point outside limits, and 2 out of 3 in Zone A)
   ➢ Sigma is likely to be over-estimated, so runs and trends are possible
3. Control limits should be re-evaluated after 30 and then 50 individual readings to improve the estimates of the means.
4. Individual charts should be done only if you are making single measurements infrequently (e.g. once per day).
   ➢ I-mR charts have too poor of resolution to catch any but the largest of shifts of a given part in the measurement system.
5. If an individual standard is thought to have possibly changed (perhaps it was dropped or mishandled), create an I-mR chart using just the historical data for that part (although using s_{pooled}).

Case 3: Unstable, Homemade Standards
In some cases, standards must be made from delicate parts, and these parts are not expected to maintain their "standard" value over a lengthy period of

time. Nonetheless, they still will have to be measured several times just to create some kind of established value. But g, the number of pre-measurements must be kept fairly low. Also, a set of contingency standards must also be continuously created so that a new standard can be introduced when an old one changes. Obviously, this will become very difficult to implement, and should only be considered when the stability of the gage is suspect.

The method for Case 3 essentially follows that of Case 2 with the following differences:

- Initial charts need to be based on a less-than-optimum set of "g" repeated measurements.
- A set of contingency standards needs to be created, ready to be used as soon as a current standard becomes unsuitable. They should also have "g" measurements done on them.
- Additional individual I-mR charts need to be placed *by part* so that trends can be observed for each current standard. Out-of-control signals for any of these charts would signal that that part should be removed from the standards group and a contingency standard be substituted. Also, a series of "g" measurements should immediately be made on a new contingency standard.

Because the parts are delicate, the fewer measurements made on them the better (from an endurance standpoint). Thus, initial charts will need to be created based on a small set of repeated measurements. I'd recommend 8 measurements taken over at least three days. But if the parts are *very* delicate, you could use 6. However, fewer repeated measurements mean wider control limits, so that changes in the measurement system will not be as readily detected (higher Type II Error).

Again, because the parts are delicate, it is also necessary to monitor each part using I-mR charts on the Δs:

− Monitoring all the Δs on a single chart won't reveal all changes to a single part
− Use the "known" pooled standard deviation; don't rely on the moving range to establish the control limits
− Look for trends or sudden changes

Comments on Case 3:
- When few measurements are made on standards, the sensitivity of the charts is severely compromised.
- More charting is necessary to cover the possibility of broken standards.
- More tracking is necessary to assure contingency standards are available.
- If standards are more robust, recompute s_{pooled} and control limits after 15 repeated measurements on the standards.

Alternative Charting Methods

What has been presented so far has essentially been an expansion of techniques using Shewhart charts. In my experience, regular Shewhart charts work well for stable manufacturing processes in about 50% of the cases, and this percentage increases to 75% when one properly implements the triple-chart method for batch processes. (This assumes that one isn't implementing the charts incorrectly, such as monitoring multiple machines or process lines using a single combined mean.) In the other cases the distribution of the variable under investigation may be highly skewed. Or the data being taken on a subgroup could be highly correlated within itself (this could occur for flatness measurements on a sample, or when there is symmetry occurring in a batch process, such as lapping multiple parts together). Here an analysis of the symmetry might reveal patterns that would allow a non-random choice of positions to be measured, and a regression analysis could be performed that would allow the calculation of a batch's mean and standard deviation that would be better than a random sample. For example, if someone wanted to estimate the thickness of photoresist that has been applied using a spinning motion on a substrate, the thickness should be radially distributed; this information might point to specific radial positions which, when combined with an appropriate algorithm, could predict the mean and standard deviation of the photoresist thickness for the entire substrate based on very few measurements.

There are also situations where the process itself is either very good or very poor. When the process is very good, there are multiple options for monitoring.

Beyond Six Sigma Statistics

Pre-Control

If the variable is not critical, then the simple method of "Pre-control" is applicable. This methodology was developed in the 1950's by a team led by Dorian Shainin. Here no charting or recording of results is performed. Prior to implementation (assuming a stable, in-control process), the regions where the variable value may fall is divided into five sections. Given lower and upper specifications, let Δ = USL – LSL, and the center be the midpoint, C = (LSL + USL)/2. Everything falling within C ± Δ/4 is in the Green Zone. A point falling outside the specifications is in the Red Zone. And any other point is in the Yellow Zone. This is illustrated thusly:

```
    Red  | Yellow |      Green     | Yellow | Red
   ------|--------+--------+-------+--------|------
         LSL              C              USL
```

Samples of two are taken occasionally. If both samples are in the Green Zone or one is in the Green Zone and one is in the Yellow Zone, do nothing. If either point is in the Red Zone or both points are in the same Yellow Zone, stop the process and look for a mean shift. Finally, if the two points fall in opposite Yellow Zones, stop the process and look for a change in variability. If there appears to be continued stability, the method can be revised to sampling parts occasionally one at a time. Then when a point falls in the Red Zone or two in a row are in the same Yellow Zone, stop the process and recenter it. And if two in a row are in opposite Yellow Zones, stop the process and fix the variability. This "stoplight" method should only be done when the process capability is very high (e.g. Ppk > 1.33), or else there will be a substantial exposure to missing important process shifts.

Process Control Charts

When the process has become very good, such as when Ppk > 2.0, there is a temptation to drop the chart altogether. However, if the process variable is still critical, then some kind of monitoring is still advised. Of course, one reasonable approach is to merely drop the subgroup size to 2 or 3 (these would protect against a 3-sigma shift at 90% and 99% respectively according to the subgroup size charts). This has one disadvantage in that there will be times when the charts will produce a false alarm by chance which still requires a response, but for which there is probably no concern of producing material out of spec.

One potential improvement is to create modified control limits which rely as much on the specifications as they do the standard SPC approach. For this reason, I like to call them "Process Control Charts." The principle is simple. For a very good process, it is quite likely that a limited shift in mean, such as $m\sigma$, of the process will not produce unacceptable material. We can incorporate that fact into our control limits by expanding them by that amount. Thus, if we had previously established control limits at LCL and UCL, but feel that we can tolerate an $m\sigma$ shift, our Process Control Chart limits would now be set at LCL - $m\sigma$ and UCL + $m\sigma$.

In reality, the subgroup size and the value of m should probably be established together. This is because that if a bigger shift occurs than $m\sigma$, the engineer probably wants to act more quickly to discover the cause of the shift. The sensitivities to additional shifts can be found from the Subgroup Size charts previously given. For the same process, the larger m is, the larger the subgroup size should be so that the risk of missing any further shift is limited.

Example 3: An engineer has responsibility for a process involving a critical variable, but the current process has a Ppk = 2.33 (a 7σ process). She feels that a process shift of up to 2σ will not be deleterious to part quality and so is considering using Process Control Charts. She has multiple options. If she chooses to put her modified limits at LCL - 2σ and UCL + 2σ, she will want to have a much higher chance of discovering an additional 2σ process shift, which would put her process mean at only 3σ away from the specification (with the very real possibility of producing some parts out of spec). Using the Subgroup Size chart, she might choose to sample 6, which would give her over a 95% chance of discovering that extra 2σ shift.

Alternatively, if samples are somewhat expensive, she could opt to put her modified limits at LCL – 1.3σ and UCL + 1.3σ. Then an additional process shift of 2.7σ would put her process at 3σ away from the specification, and a subgroup size of 3 would give her over a 95% chance of discovering that shift in the next subgroup.

We must be very careful in instituting Process Control Charts, since they do violate the quality principle of being "on target with minimum variation." But if we reference back to the Taguchi Loss Function, we can see that if the specifications really are established with τ in mind, a 7σ process will easily tolerate a one-sigma shift without inflating τ significantly. On the other hand, if in the rare case where brick-wall specifications are appropriate, the Process Control Charts can be quite useful.

Weighted Charts

There exists a family of control charts where the decision that determines if an out-of-control signal has occurred is based not simply on the last subgroup data point. Instead, the most recent data points are combined in particular ways, and it is the trend of these points which determines the process stability. The three main types of charts that are used are the Moving Average (MA), Exponentially Weighted Moving Average (EWMA), and the Cumulative Sum (Cusum) charts. Virtually any Quality text that covers SPC in a reasonably detailed way will demonstrate these charts' use, and it is not my intention to repeat their formulae. Instead, I want to highlight their usefulness, for they can be much more effective at detecting smaller process shifts than standard Shewhart charts while having equal sensitivity to larger shifts.

The best of these methods is the Cusum chart. It depends on applying a template based on the quality requirements called a "V Mask." This V Mask is placed at the last subgroup data point, and the trends present in the previous subgroups will determine if the V Mask covers any of the previous points, thereby indicating a process shift. Cusum charts are extremely awkward to implement manually, and thus should only be used when the data is automatically fed into a computer for analysis. Modifications to the output can easily highlight out-of-control signals without having to actually show the V Mask.

Cusum charts are considerably more powerful in uncovering smaller process shifts, and are the recommended method to use when operating processes with Ppk values less than 0.9 where a small shift can result in significantly more out-of-specification material being produced. Unfortunately, the use of these charts has been very limited in practice, probably for the same reasons that other better approaches have been avoided: traditional Shewhart charts have been around a long time and are relatively simple, and the inertia makes change hard.

Low Occurrence Attribute Chart

Occasionally, a process involving attributes becomes very good, and then the typical p or c charts require such high sample sizes that standard monitoring using Shewhart charts becomes impractical. One approach to this problem, attributable to T.N. Goh[3], involves monitoring the run length between defectives (or defects), and issuing a signal when that length either becomes too short (indicating process deterioration) or too long (indicating process improvement). For stable processes, one can calculate what is called the "Average Run Length" or ARL, which is the average consecutive number of good parts between defect occurrences. ARL = 1/p. Then one needs to establish an α value for monitoring. This α can be the standard 0.0027 usually used for Shewhart charts or something a little higher, depending on how easy it is to react to an out-of-control signal. Then special control limits can be created:

$$LCL = -ARL \cdot \ln(1 - \frac{\alpha}{2})$$
$$CL = 0.6931 \cdot ARL$$
$$UCL = -ARL \cdot \ln(\frac{\alpha}{2})$$

The procedure is to plot the number of consecutive conforming items (between defects found) on semi-log paper, and interpret the charts similarly to standard control charts, reacting both to points outside the control limits, but also to multiple sequential points near the lower boundary.

Example 4: You have a process whose defect level is 400 dppm, or p = 0.0004. ARL = 1/p = 2500. If α is chosen to be 0.01, then the control limits would be:

$$\text{LCL} = -2500 \cdot \ln(0.995) = 12.5$$
$$\text{CL} = 0.6931 \cdot 2500 = 1733$$
$$\text{UCL} = -2500 \cdot \ln(0.005) = 13{,}246$$

Other Charting Methods

The literature is filled with alternative monitoring methods. Many may have a slight advantage in some way over the methods described in this chapter, but the advantages are often offset by other disadvantages. For example, one method called the Run-Sum method just gives integral values to points falling outside of ±1 sigma of the center line, increasing the integer for points getting further way and resetting to zero when the center line is crossed. Thus, no charting actually need be done; only a count is tallied with a reaction given when a criterion count is met or exceeded. Such a method is much simpler, but loses the historical record and is slightly less sensitive to process shifts than standard variables charts.

When the process distribution is clearly non-normal, such that the Central Limit Theorem principle does not guarantee a normal distribution for the means, there are two options. The first is to transform the variable; an appropriate application of the Box-Cox transformation method could easily yield a useful transformation for control charting, although the real-measurement information would be lost. The second option is to use a median chart. Unfortunately, to have any reasonably narrow control limits, the subgroup size should probably be at least 7, and then the CLT may actually be applicable or the transformation be more useful.

Similarly, there are attribute charts which attempt to grade the level of defect (such as a Demerit System). They have their use, but the likely frequency of use does not warrant discussing further in this book.

Sometimes the subgroup size varies for variable charts. This may make it difficult to assess the chart for rules other than one point outside the control limits. However, by employing a transformation, the control limits can be set to a constant value, simplifying the interpretation. For any subgroup mean, $\bar{x}$, of size n, the proper transform is:

$$Z = \frac{(\bar{x} - \mu)}{\sigma_{proc}/\sqrt{n}}$$

Where σ_{proc} is the established process standard deviation and μ is the established process mean (usually $\bar{x}$). The control chart will then have a center line equal to zero with (3-sigma) control limits at ±3. The s chart can also be normalized, but only for one of the two limits. Because the upper limit is usually of interest, the transformation to W can be made:

$$W = s/B_4 c_4 \sigma$$

Where B_4 and c_4 are the standard values from control chart theory and are dependent on the subgroup size. The W chart will have an upper limit of 1, but the lower limit must be ignored.

Finally, there are certain circumstances where the actual time used for manufacturing is very short, and so one may want to evaluate the process as quickly as possible. The family of charts used here fall under the category of "Short Run SPC." Although these charting methods will have limited use, I am including one approach that I developed for short run SPC in the Appendix to this chapter.

Final Thoughts

The literature provides a whole host of other available options, usually depending on special knowledge about the process itself (e.g. sequential points are correlated to each other or points within a subgroup are correlated to each other), or when one wants to combine multiple process variables into a single variable for charting. The engineer really needs to remember that the basic assumptions of randomness, independence and stability should always be verified before establishing any standard control chart and only look for alternatives when they are violated.

The implementation itself also requires an attention to education about chart use, interpretation, and reaction. For when these aren't done properly, the value of the charts can be significantly compromised, perhaps to the point where they are ignored or unnecessarily discarded.

Appendix: Short Run SPC

When the actual time used for manufacturing is very short, such that it is impractical to take 20 or 25 subgroups of size 5, yet one wants to evaluate the process as quickly as possible especially while the process is running in its early stages, the method of Short Run SPC may be useful. Some purposes of Short Run SPC are

- Make a quality product immediately
- Assess the process on the fly
- Maintain the process in control
- Qualify a process's capability

The method described below is based on an article by Yang and Hillier[4]. The method involves the placing of statistically valid control limits on a chart after only five subgroups have been taken, and then recomputing limits after five more and twenty more subgroups have been taken.

To understand how Short Run SPC differs from standard control charting one needs to realize that typical Shewhart charts require 25 subgroups to establish the process mean and standard deviation. In some calculations, these estimates become the estimates for μ and σ, as if the sample were infinite. (Sometimes the calculated standard deviation is adjusted slightly with the c_4 constant to account for the fact that the sample is not infinite.) If we want to establish control limits with a much smaller sample, we will need to adjust for the possibility that the true standard deviation may indeed be much bigger. Fortunately, statistical theory actually allows limits to be calculated for any number of subgroups (beyond two); such limits were presented in the Yang and Hillier paper. When applied appropriately, these limits can be used to determine if a process is running consistently—and by using only a limited number of subgroup samples.

For simplicity, we will assume a subgroup size of 5. Although we will use $\bar{x}$ and s charts, the control limits will be based on the pooled variance, providing a more robust estimate of variation. This standard deviation, ω, and overall average, $\bar{\bar{x}}$, are defined as:

$$\omega = \sqrt{\frac{1}{n}\sum_{j=1}^{n} s_j^2} \quad \text{and} \quad \bar{\bar{x}} = \frac{1}{n}\sum_{j=1}^{n} \bar{x}_j$$

where n is the total number of subgroups from which the control limits are being calculated, s_j is the standard deviation of the jth subgroup, and $\bar{x}_j$ is the average of the jth subgroup. The control limits are then calculated:

Average chart: $\quad$ CL = $\bar{\bar{x}} \pm A\omega$;
Standard deviation chart: $\quad$ LCL = $B_L\omega$
$\quad\quad\quad\quad\quad\quad\quad\quad\quad\quad\quad$ UCL = $B_U\omega$

Where A, B_L and B_U are defined in the table below, depending on how many subgroups have been taken and which observations will be judged.

The basic procedure is as follows:

1. Take five sequential subgroups of size 5. Calculate $\bar{\bar{x}}$ and the standard deviation ω; calculate the control limits using the first line in the table (the limits for only this group are calculated much in the same way as was used for the limits calculated using Analysis of Means [ANOM, in chapter 9]); then graph the $\bar{x}$'s and s's on a chart with these control limits. If all points are inside the control limits, conclude an acceptable degree of process stability and go to the next step.

2. Calculate new control limits using the second line in the table, and plot these on the charts to be applied to the next five subgroups. These limits will <u>not</u> be recalculated as subgroups #6 through #10 are taken. (These limits are different because the set of control limits judging the first five subgroups needs to take in to account that they are not independent of the points they are judging, whereas the second group of five <u>will</u> be independent.)

3. If these next five points are in control, recalculate $\bar{\bar{x}}$ and ω using all ten subgroups. Then new control limits are recomputed for judging the next fifteen subgroups using the third line in the table.

4. If the next fifteen points are in control, recalculate $\bar{\bar{x}}$ and ω using all twenty-five subgroups. Then new control limits are recom-

puted for judging the next 25 subgroups using the fourth line in the table.
5. Finally, if these next 25 points are in control and more data is to be collected, recalculate $\bar{\bar{x}}$ and ω using all 50 subgroups. Then new control limits are recomputed for judging all subsequent subgroups using the fifth (and final) line in the table.

The table to be used for these calculations is as follows:

Instructions	A	B_L	B_U
First 5 subgroups (retroactive)	1.42	.163	1.82
Future points based on first 5 subgroups	1.74	.147	2.66
Future points based on first 10 subgroups	1.55	.149	2.39
Future points based on first 25 subgroups	1.45	.150	2.24
Future points based on first 50 subgroups	1.43	0	2.09

Example 4: This method of Short Run SPC was used in an attempt to qualify a vendor's laser welder, where the consistency of the position was important (it could be re-centered easily to meet specifications). The $\bar{x}$ & s control charting method and charts are produced below based on the summary statistics of the subgroups:

Results After the First 5 Subgroups

$\bar{\bar{x}}$ 235.0
ω 14.8

Limits for First 5 Subgroups
$LCL(x) = \bar{\bar{x}} - A\omega = 235 - (1.42)14.8 = 214.0$
$UCL(x) = \bar{\bar{x}} + A\omega = 235 + (1.42)14.8 = 256.0$
$LCL(s) = B_L\omega = (.163)14.8 = 2.41$
$UCL(s) = B_U\omega = (1.82)14.8 = 26.9$

Limits for Future Subgroups #6 through #10

$$\text{LCL}(x) = \bar{\bar{X}} - A\omega = 235 - (1.74)14.8 = 209.2$$
$$\text{UCL}(x) = \bar{\bar{X}} + A\omega = 235 + (1.74)14.8 = 260.8$$
$$\text{LCL}(s) = B_L\omega = (.147)14.8 = 2.18$$
$$\text{UCL}(s) = B_U\omega = (2.66)14.8 = 39.4$$

Results After the First 10 Subgroups

$\bar{\bar{X}}$ 228.3
ω 15.5

Limits for Future Subgroups #11 through #25

$$\text{LCL}(x) = \bar{\bar{X}} - A\omega = 228.3 - (1.55)15.5 = 204.3$$
$$\text{UCL}(x) = \bar{\bar{X}} + A\omega = 228.3 + (1.55)15.5 = 252.3$$
$$\text{LCL}(s) = B_L\omega = (.149)15.5 = 2.31$$
$$\text{UCL}(s) = B_U\omega = (2.39)15.5 = 37.0$$

The $\bar{x}$ & s control charts through subgroup 17 are shown below:

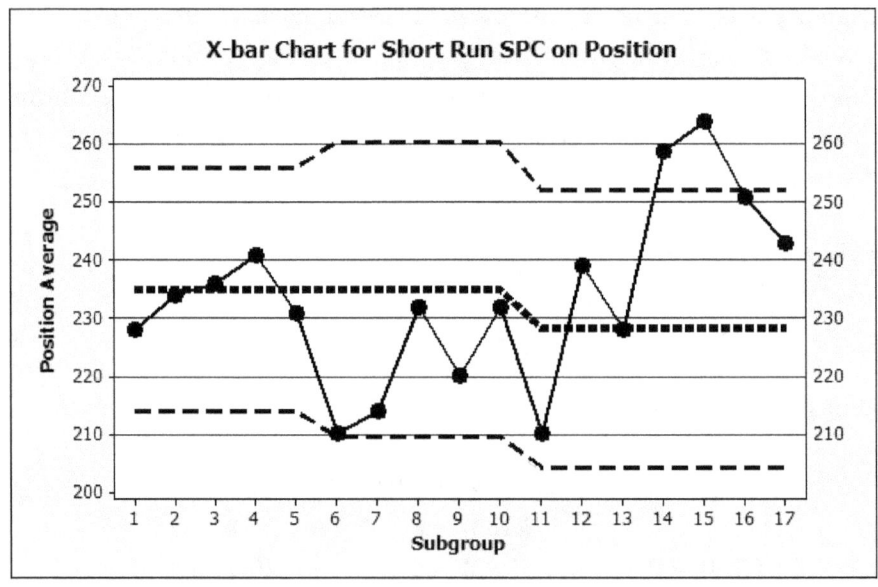

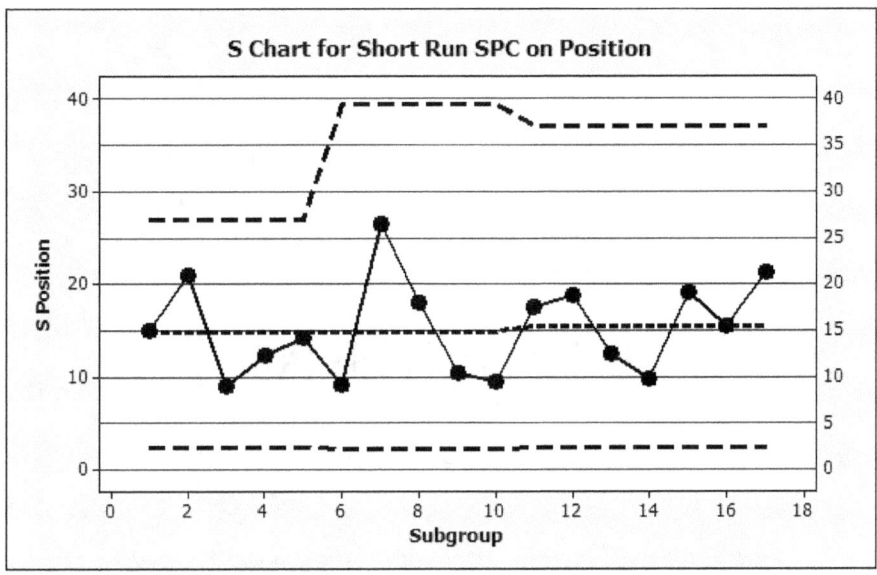

At point #14 the x̄ chart was out of control, and the laser welder was stopped to try to determine the cause of the instability. Note that subgroups beyond #14 were taken because the process was being run continuously, and the measurements and charting took enough time so that three more subgroups were generated. As a postscript, after additional attempts at fixing the laser welder and another round of data taking, the machine still didn't demonstrate stability, and the qualification was delayed.

---

[1]   Nelson, Lloyd S. "The Shewhart Control Chart—Tests for Special Causes. *Journal of Quality Technology* (1984), 16, No. 4.

[2]   Dockendorf, Lyle. "Choosing Appropriate Sample Subgroup Sizes for Control Charts." *Quality Progress*, October, 1992, p.160.

[3]   Goh, T.N. "A Control Chart for Very High Yield Processes." *Quality Assurance*, 13, No. 1, March 1987.

[4]   Yang, Chung-How and Hillier, Frederick S. "Mean and Variance Control Chart Limits Based on a Small Number for Subgroups." *Journal of Quality Technology* (1970), 2, No. 1, pp. 9-16.

CHAPTER 15

CRITICAL THINKING

God, grant me the serenity to accept the things I cannot change,
The courage to change the things I can,
And wisdom to know the difference.

— *Reinhold Niebuhr*

Besides common sense, one of the most useful skills that any Black Belt can possess is the ability to think critically. In the broad scope it entails being able to see the forest *and* the trees, and be able to pick out the trees that are the most important for the purpose at hand. It means letting the facts speak for themselves, but only in the proper context. It involves being able to bring to bear a multiple of viewpoints so that the whole picture can be grasped. It entails having a reasonable sense of suspicion stemming from the knowledge that appearances can be deceiving. And it means suspending judgment because of insufficient evidence.

For the Black Belt, skills in critical thinking both complement and enhance the use of statistical tools. And as applied to a project as a whole critical thinking helps the Black Belt:

- Establish early whether the project addresses a procedural problem or one that will require statistical analysis
- Know when a project is too big or too small

- Apply the proper tool at the appropriate time
- Have the intuition to sense and detect the red herrings
- Know the skills, talents and abilities of potential team members
- Investigate other tools that will be helpful

Now let's put these advantages into more concrete terms.

What type of Project is this?

Adhering to the Six Sigma strategy is essential in the early stages of a project. Measure Phase is all about understanding the process as it exists today. It also means understanding what kind of "defect" the project is trying to reduce. If parts from a smooth continuous distribution are falling outside specifications, then it's likely that statistical methods will ultimately be important in leading to the best solution. If the distribution is not consistent, then it is likely that there is some outside factor that is creating that inconsistency. A deeper look at the process methods may uncover the sources of the variation or the proper statistical methods may also increase the probability of success in discovering a solution. The previously mentioned project by Nick Pontikos is an excellent example of such an approach. He discovered that two of the four shifts were following the SOP while the other two were not; yet most of the defects were being produced by the shifts following the SOP.

Finally, if the defect is actually a flaw of some kind unrelated to a distribution specification, the most efficient approach will be to fully understand the procedures involved to uncover what kind of handling or manufacturing operation could produce that defect. Quite often in Business Process (Transactional) Six Sigma the concern is a specific defect, and Process Maps, Cause & Effect, and Root Cause Analysis (including Current Reality Trees) when used correctly have the highest probability of uncovering the source of the defects. In some cases, some simple hypothesis tests (or less commonly Analysis of Means for proportions or counts) might be required to verify, but the discovery method primarily involves investigating procedures.

In the same category, critical thinking also includes creative thinking. Detecting the source of defects sometimes involves the same skills as creating an effective FMEA. What possibly could/did go wrong? Certainly experience—especially by those who are intimately involved with the process—

can provide significant contributions to the uncovering of the root cause. Yet the team still may need to be able to discard their present paradigms and "think outside the box" to find the best approach to a root cause. Sometimes the negative effects of preconceived notions of variables considered to be unchangeable (such as policies or supplier parts) may be overcome by working towards some kind of win-win solution. And sometimes we don't really know what is "unchangeable" until we try to change it.

Know when a project is too big or too small

Nothing can bog down a team more than a project that is too large. Then the project drags on in time. Team members who thought they were signing up for a limited time find themselves frequently called to meetings and given tasks to perform well after the date they thought their involvement was to be ended; and their response is slowed. As time passes, related processes (or even personnel) can change, which might affect the current project. In the technology industries competition or new discoveries might force radical changes in the product.

Certainly proper project selection and resource allocation are important. But the Black Belt benefits greatly if he can apply some critical thinking to his assignment and appropriately estimate the size of the project. In particular, heeding some of the warning signs of the factors that either make the project too big or will delay the execution will aid his assessment. Some questions to ask are:

- Is this a cross-functional project? Do I have support and access throughout?
- Does the current KPOV have an adequate measurement system? (Developing a better one can take some time.)
- What are some of the likely KPIVs? And more importantly, do these have adequate measurement systems? (Developing better ones can take a great deal of time.)
- Will essential team members be available when needed?
- Does the relevant management and especially the process owner have sufficient knowledge of Six Sigma to be able to accept a solution that gets proposed based on data analysis?

- What project management skills do I have now? Will these be adequate for this project?
- How available is equipment for running experiments? Is there a long lead time?
- If I do come up with a solution, how long will it take to verify its effectiveness?

In the opposite direction, a project that is too small may not be worth the Black Belt's time; that is, it may not provide a reasonable return on investment. We used to call some of these "Nike" projects, because the solution had already been decided upon and it was a matter of "just do it" (the Nike slogan).

Finally, there is a balance as to just how much improvement should be targeted. The basic Six Sigma paradigm is to aim for a 70% improvement. But an analysis of the entitlement might suggest that this target is either too low or too high. Furthermore, it might be more efficacious to achieve a 40% improvement in one month than a 70% improvement in four months.

Apply the proper tool at the appropriate time

In Measure Phase, the tools used are essentially prescriptive. That is, the Black Belt should generally use all of the major tools, and the order in which the tools are used is mostly fixed. However, Analyze Phase (and beyond) presents a greater amount of complexity since it is not always clear which statistical tool is best to use at any given time. For example, a one-way ANOVA is probably a better choice than a 2-sample t-test when multiple levels of a potential KPIV are present. But if homogeneity of variance is not present, the ANOVA approach could yield invalid conclusions.

Sometimes (especially in the technology industries) there is an oversupply of data, and there is a tendency to look at all of it as if each variable is a potential KPIV. Thus, we might see regressions being run using all the KPIVs, with the end result being that some truly insignificant variables have low p-values or there exists so much multicollinearity that the results are invalid. Furthermore, since this is usually observational data, apparent relationships might emerge that are not real. (And don't forget that KPIVs with large measurement error provide erroneous regression results.) Here regression might provide some evidence for screening out variables so as to investigate the survivors with experiments, but there is the strong possibility of missing critical KPIVs as well. Often, experiments provide much greater insight than regression. The results of observational studies should lead to new hypotheses, not conclusions.

With observational data, the quantity might be so much that hypothesis tests run on them will always show statistical significance. But it is important to check that against <u>practical</u> significance. Then, in creating follow-on hypothesis tests it is essential to obtain an appropriate sample size and to take a random and representative sample.

Unfortunately, data is often combined when it should be handled more as coming from a batch process. This is especially true with attribute data. Too often in Control Phase there is a tendency to use the simple $\bar{x}$ and s chart rather than the batch-process control chart (I-mR-R/s). But attribute charts are probably even more prone to being subject to batch-to-batch influence.

Have the intuition to sense and detect the red herrings

When a Black Belt is first becoming familiar with the tools of Six Sigma, the use of and results from these tools can be quite confusing. Of course, this is following the natural course of learning, and as experience increases, the methodology and tools become easier to use.

Because of this inexperience it is easy to uncover false clues that lead the Black Belt down paths of investigation that prove to be fruitless. This is especially true when the team already has a bias toward those KPIVs which seem important just from (what they consider to be) "common sense." However, in most of these cases there also emerges some degree of evidence to either oppose or contradict the likely strong nature of the suspected KPIV. A good Black Belt will eventually develop this extra sensitivity to contradictory information and act on it early in the investigative process so as to minimize the time spent in fruitless research.

Know the skills, talents and abilities of potential team members

Every potential member on a Black Belt's team has particular skills, knowledge and capabilities. Some of these attributes have been learned through standard education; others have been developed from experience. Standard resumes often reveal this important information, although more important information can come through actual familiarity with the individuals or from networking with contacts who know these potential members.

Similarly, the personalities of these people also can become known through the Black Belt's own personal knowledge or that of his contacts. Some people just don't work well in a team environment!

What is usually not appreciated nor investigated involves what kind of project-related activities a potential team member enjoys. For if those people are assigned tasks they enjoy during a project, they will usually excel at them and provide results ahead of schedule. The opposite is usually true. People assigned tasks that they don't like to do often have trouble completing these well and in a timely manner.

To elaborate further, I need to digress into a personal story. Early in my career I became aware of a book that soon changed my life. The book was titled *The Truth About You*[1]. Its basic premise was that everyone has essentially been "pre-programmed" with a single motivating factor in their life. That is, everyone has a particular drive in their life that (internally) demands to be fulfilled. If it can't be satisfied in a job, the person will find another way, such as through a hobby. Within this motivational drive there are also certain circumstances or a milieu through which the person satisfies this drive best. For example, they may wish to act alone, be with one other person, or be in a group. Or they may express it best kinetically rather than theoretically. By investigating one's own life for activities that 1) provided satisfaction and 2) felt good about doing, one can find a pattern that will help reveal that single motivating factor.

This book totally changed my life. I concluded that my motivating force was to "make perfect order out of chaos of abstract things." Yet, as a physicist I was constantly dealing with physical things, and doing a mediocre job of it. I changed careers and became a statistician, successfully applying my physical knowledge with a drive to solve problems using numbers. I loved it, and I had an intrinsic drive to become ever better at it.

The point of this digression is to emphasize that our companies and society do little to understand the deep underlying motivation of its citizens and employees, and often funnel them into positions that usually do not bring out the best in the individual. As a Black Belt assembling a team, the ability to discern that motivation can make a big difference in choosing effective members and assigning them tasks. Certainly there are other personality profile tools that are useful, such as the Myers-Briggs. But truly capturing each person's intrinsic motivation allows an assignment of duties most rewarding to the individuals, and thus brings out the best, both in morale and results.

Investigate other tools that will be helpful

The Black Belt's standard tool kit, when applied appropriately, can be quite powerful in finding the KPIVs in a project. Yet there are many additional tools—some covered in the next chapter—that would enable the Black Belt to do an even better job. Stephen Covey, in his important book *The Seven Habits of Highly Effective People*[2], lists as the last habit "Sharpen the Saw." Analogous to having a dull bladed saw which requires far more effort to cut while a sharp saw makes the work much easier, people who continuously improve their skills will be able to perform tasks much more efficiently and effectively. Perhaps the first act of investigation that a Black Belt should take is to read Covey's book. And there are many other practical books and courses that will smooth out the person-to-person interactions that are essential to working with people in organizations. One such book/course is *Crucial Conversations*[3], which explores the wrong ways people interact and proposes improved techniques in communication.

From a statistics standpoint, new methods are constantly being created, especially as computing power has improved dramatically. For example, because of the higher speed, methods utilizing a "Maximum Likelihood" approach can now provide more precise answers. If the Black Belt is involved in frequent experiments, expanding DOE skills can open up possibilities of more efficient designs—under the right circumstances. Bayesian Statistics is a branch of statistics that allows prior knowledge to be brought to analyses (classical statistics usually assumes nothing is known), possibly allowing smaller sample sizes. When both data and variables are plentiful, the tools of Principle Components, Partial Least Squares and Cluster Analysis can unveil patterns in the data that would otherwise remain hidden. And even Exploratory Data Analysis (EDA) can provide alternative views of data that might better reveal critical KPIVs.

Critical Thinking is actually a developed skill that results, in part, from thinking "a second time." That means that it involves taking the time to look at a problem from multiple directions and with multiple perspectives. A Problem Statement within a Project may succinctly define the what, where, when, and why of a particular defect, but the project itself is much more complex because of the people and circumstances. When these are more fully taken into account, the chances of success—as well as the magnitude of that success—can be greatly enhanced.

---

[1] Miller, Arthur F. and Mattson, Ralph. *The Truth About You.* Fleming H. Revell Company, 1977.

[2] Covey, Stephen, *The Seven Habits of Highly Effective People.* New York: Simon & Schuster Company, 1989.

[3] Patterson, Kerry; Grenny, Joseph; McMillan, Ron; and Switzler, Al. *Crucial Conversations.* McGraw-Hill, 2002.

CHAPTER 16

ADVANCED TOPICS

Never stop learning.

Many of the topics discussed so far have been expansions of the statistical tools already familiar to the Black Belt. However, there are whole other regions of statistical investigation to which most Black Belts have had little or no exposure through their standard training. There are good reasons for this. Most of these topics are fairly complicated, which would require a large amount of time to learn. Secondly, very few of the Black Belts doing projects would have a need to use these particular tools. Thus, teaching these subjects would not be an effective use of time during training.

My intention in this chapter is not to teach these topics in detail, for each topic could actually be a chapter (or book!) in its own right. Instead, I want to provide the reader with an exposure to these tools such that the Black Belt might more easily recognize a project situation for which any of these tools could apply. Then they can either do further study or consult with a Master Black Belt or a statistician for additional information on how best to proceed. In the Advanced Statistics classes I have developed, these topics are dealt with in some detail, but the information was supplemented by Excel spreadsheets (which I created) that provided the engineer with tools to seamlessly perform the important statistical calculations without having to do the complex mathematics himself.

Acceptance Sampling

Often an engineer needs to purchase material or components from a supplier in order to run his process or make his product. Then the quality of the incoming material or components can become an important factor in the quality of the engineer's final product. The question then is how the engineer can be assured of that incoming quality.

Of course, the first (and best) approach is to require that the supplier show their own methods for assuring quality. This is often done through the use of SPC or some other method of process monitoring. The monitoring of these charts is often left to a "Supplier Quality Engineer," but as I've noticed in the past, if this individual does not have a strong knowledge of SPC, there is ample opportunity for poorer quality material being accepted as good. Unfortunately, there are also occasions when the supplier isn't always totally honest; this may happen when the supplier is under time constraints. But even worse, the customer may also be under time constraints (thus the time demand on the supplier), and feel forced to have to use the inferior product. This situation is best avoided by better planning by both the supplier and the customer.

However, there are other times when SPC is either not available or not practical. In these cases, it might be important for the customer to perform an independent check on the supplier's quality. This can be done through a method called "Acceptance Sampling." The principle behind Acceptance Sampling is that a random sample is taken from the supplier's shipment—called a "lot," and either the pass/fail proportion is calculated, or the mean and standard deviation are calculated. Based on the quality requirements of the customer, the lot is "dispositioned," that is, it is either accepted or rejected. Rejected lots should be returned to the supplier, but sometimes receive a 100% inspection. A more detailed coverage of Acceptance Sampling and the material presented below can be found in Acheson Duncan's book *Industrial Statistics and Quality Control*.

For simplicity, I will first discuss the attribute case, even though it usually results in a much larger sample. Typically a specific sampling plan is drawn up. Four numbers are required:

- AQL—"Acceptable Quality Level"—a low proportion defective in a lot that the customer is willing to accept with a high probability.
- α—the probability of rejecting a lot whose quality level is at the AQL.
- RQL—"Rejectable Quality Level"—a higher proportion defective in a lot that the customer is very reluctant to accept. Sometimes called the "Least Quality Level" or the "Lot Tolerance Percent Defective" (LTPD).
- β—the probability of accepting a lot whose quality level is at the RQL.

If this sounds a lot like hypothesis testing, it is. But there is a twist. From these requirements a sampling plan is devised. Often, if the lot is large, both α and/or β are reduced, since the larger the lot the more risk to the manufacturing line if the quality is poor. The sampling plan consists of a sample size, n, and an accept number, c. If the number of defectives found in the sample are less than or equal to c the lot is accepted. If that number is greater than c the lot is rejected. Essentially, this is a hypothesis test where the criterion value is calculated beforehand. One item that usually accompanies such a plan is what is called an "Operating Characteristic" curve, or OC curve. This is a graph that shows the continuous probability of acceptance for any defective level in the lot. Such a plot is shown below:

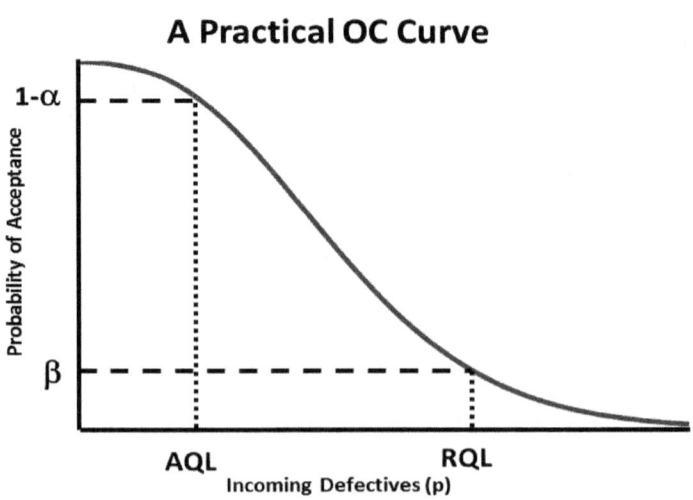

These curves highlight the risks of accepting the lot for any defective proportion, but have their greatest use in comparing several possible sampling plans. Such plans include moving AQL and RQL closer together (requiring a bigger sample size), or implementing either of two other types of alternative acceptance sampling plans.

The first of these alternatives is the Double Sampling plan. In this case a sample of size n1 is taken where n1<n. Two criteria are generated: c1 and c2. If the number of defectives found is less than or equal to c1 the lot is accepted; if the number of defectives found is greater than c2 the lot is rejected. Otherwise a second sample of size n2 is taken, and if the total number of defectives found in both samples equals c2 or less the lot is accepted. Otherwise it is rejected. The advantage to this plan is that when the true lot defective level is either very low or very high the decision can be made with a smaller sample (n1). If instead the quality level hovers between the AQL and RQL, the second sample is usually necessary. Since n1+n2>n, this means more sampling is required. Furthermore, double sampling can require a delay in the dispositioning of the lot, since time may have to be taken in order to process the second sample.

The second alternative to single sampling is the Sequential Sampling plan. Here samples of size 1 are taken one at a time, and the cumulative defective count versus the cumulative sample is graphed on a chart that contains three regions: accept, reject, and continue sampling. As soon as a point falls into either the accept or reject region, sampling stops and the lot is dispositioned; otherwise another part is sampled. A graph illustrating the plan, with results, is shown next:

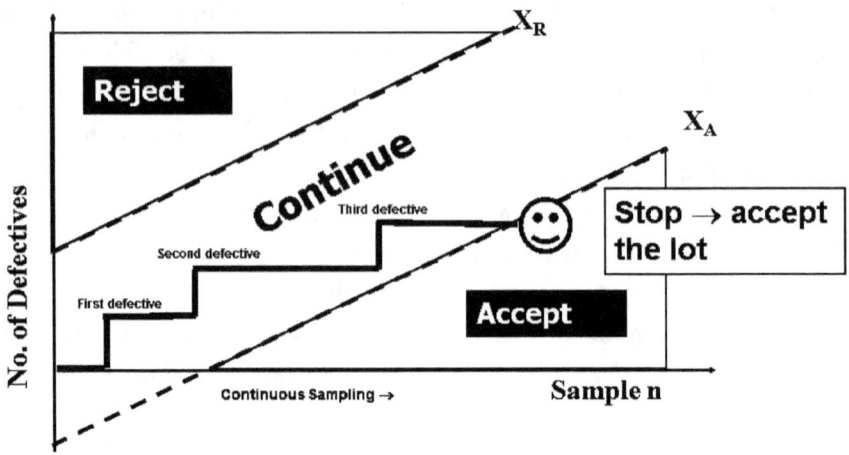

The lines, represented by X_R and X_A delineate the reject and accept regions, and are generated through a statistical technique called the Sequential Probability Ratio Test, or SPRT. Such charts have been used to monitor the quality of disk drives in Seagate's Ongoing Reliability testing. [See Duncan's book for the derivation of the X_R and X_A lines.]

As with Double Sampling, when the true lot defective level is either very low or very high the decision can be made with a smaller sample. Yet if the lot defective is close to halfway between the AQL and RQL, sampling can be limitless! In practice, a stopping point, usually between 2n and 3n is implemented. But if this is done, the change in probabilities should be incorporated into the Sequential Sampling plan.

All the sampling plans described so far assume that the lot is large compared to the overall sample that is taken. The general rule is that n must be no more than 1/10th of the lot size. This is because the assumption is being made that the proportion defective in the lot essentially remains constant as samples are taken, and so the binomial distribution applies to the probabilities. But for a more finite lot, each defective unit discovered actually can lower the probabilities of drawing additional defective units. In such cases, the use of the *Hypergeometric Distribution* becomes essential. If you have this complicated case you may need to consult a statistician. However, plans with limited lot sizes have been formalized—along with the single and double sampling plans—into "Military Standard" (or Mil Std) plans that are generally accessible.

Other types of plans can be drawn up if the customer performs 100% inspection on rejected lots and substitutes good units for the removed defective units. This is called "rectifying inspection." With this activity for virtually any relevant incoming quality, estimates of the "Average Outgoing Quality" (AOQ) can be made for certain plans, since some lots will pass and others will be inspected 100%. For any given inspection plan there is a specific lot proportion which results in a worst case outgoing quality, and the AOQ for this is called the "Average Outgoing Quality Limit" (AOQL). Different inspection plans can be chosen depending on the desired AOQL.

So far the sampling plans discussed have involved a fraction defective, and in practice such plans either have relatively high RQLs or extremely high sample sizes. Such is the nature of the binomial distribution. However, if the engineer can make measurements of a continuous variable on the parts, then an alternative approach, "Sampling by Variables," should be undertaken. (This was covered in Chapter 6 in the section on "statistical specifications," but is worth repeating here for topic completeness; in this section it will have a slightly different look.) Again the basis will be an AQL with an associated α and an RQL with an associated β. But AQL and RQL will be based on the fraction outside a one-sided specification assuming a normal distribution—that is, the area in the tail of the distribution. Ultimately, the fate of the lot will depend on the Cpk calculated from the sample relative to a criterion Cpk*.

To compute the appropriate sample size and criterion, four values derived from the standard normal distribution must first be computed:

- $1 - P(AQL)$: called Z_{AQL}
- $1 - P(RQL)$: called Z_{RQL}
- $1 - \alpha$: called Z_α
- $1 - \beta$: called Z_β

Then the criterion and sample size (for the case where the standard deviation is not known) are:

$$Cpk^* = \frac{1}{3}\left(\frac{Z_\alpha Z_{RQL} + Z_\beta Z_{AQL}}{Z_\alpha + Z_\beta}\right)$$

$$n = \left(1 + \frac{9(Cpk^*)^2}{2}\right)\left(\frac{Z_\alpha + Z_\beta}{Z_{AQL} - Z_{RQL}}\right)^2$$

If Cpk(sample) > Cpk*, then accept the lot.

Example 1: Bond strength of a wire chip bond is extremely important. Normal testing has indicated that less than 1 in a million bonds is below the current specification. What Sampling-by-Variables plan would protect against a failure rate of 1 in ten thousand with a risk of only 10%, while passing lots 95% if they are meeting a 1 in a million failure rate?

The normal distribution values are:

- For $1 - P(AQL) = .999999$, $Z_{AQL} = 4.7534$
- For $1 - P(RQL) = .9999$, $Z_{RQL} = 3.7190$
- For $1 - \alpha = 0.95$, $Z_\alpha = 1.6459$
- For $1 - \beta = 0.90$, $Z_\beta = 1.2186$

Substituting these values into the formulae give a Cpk* = 1.393 and a sample size of 76. Incidentally, if one were sampling only attributes the appropriate sample size would be 21,333.

For Sampling-by-Variables plans there is also a Military Standard that can be followed, Mil Std 414. And if the standard deviation is known, a different formula would apply. Realize that there are many other potential acceptance sampling plans available. But the ones shown here will handle most of the situations the Black Belt is likely to encounter.

Reliability

The statistics of Reliability is a very complex topic, and many statisticians have concentrated their careers on reliability and its applications.

One useful short definition of reliability is that it is the study of product failure in order to make predictions of future failures. How is this done in practice? First, the product must be tested in a way that induces multiple failures—either through extended testing time, extra stress, or both. Based both on the failures and the survivors, a distribution model is conjectured, usually f(time) or f(cycles). Then cumulative failures in a population can be inferred for any future time or number of cycles the product is used. Good estimates of these distribution models are essential for a company in establishing warranties on its products: long warranties produce customer confidence (and hopefully more customers who might even be willing to pay more for a product); but if too many failures occur in the warranty period, the producer will likely lose a good deal of money, multiple customers, and even its reputation.

Obviously, the prediction of the correct distribution is paramount. There are many distributions to choose from! Without going into detail, the most popular are the Exponential (which presumes a constant failure rate, which itself means that the history of a part is irrelevant to its future probability of failure), the Normal (often used in wear-out situations), the Lognormal and the Weibull. These latter two distributions are frequently used to empirically fit the failure data since they are very versatile in this regard. Other less common but occasionally used reliability distributions are the Gamma and Extreme Value distributions, the latter sometimes being used when a failure occurs either when the first of many similarly functioning components fails or all of many similarly functioning parts fail. And there are other, less commonly used distributions.

Often, the engineering experience is that the failure rate distribution follows a "bathtub" curve. A higher number of early failures occur because of manufacturing defects, followed by a period of a nearly constant failure rate, which is followed by a higher rate due to wear-out, corrosion, stress, etc. When this model is used, if there is a burn-in period to eliminate early failures, an estimate can be made of the future failure rate, which can then be translated into a distribution model. From this, the most popularly published number for reliability is usually issued: MTBF, or *mean time between failures* (sometimes also called the MTTF or *mean time to failure*).

Unfortunately, MTBF is one of the most deceptive numbers for the public: it is usually stated as a high time value (e.g. multiple years), but the actual *experienced* failure rate corresponds to something much worse. A simple example would be a reported MTBF of 50 years, or more commonly stated 438,000 hours. The customer naturally thinks his product will never fail while he needs it. However, with that MTBF, approximately 9.5% of those units are projected to fail in the first five years! The honest thing for the producer to provide is the 5-year failure rate, or something similar; not the MTBF. But this doesn't happen since it doesn't sound nearly as good. (Note: MTBF can be computed for any distribution, not just one with a constant failure rate. But except for an underlying distribution that is normal, the MTBF provides an inflated sense of goodness.)

In the testing phase it is almost always impractical to test the units until all or most of them fail. Thus, the test is curtailed at some point in time, some number of cycles, or some number of failed units. In the analysis, units that have not failed are said to have been "censored." It is completely unknown at what point they would have failed. (In some cases, units are removed earlier for reasons unrelated to the failure mode that is being investigated, in which case the analysis must take into account multiple censoring points, further complicating the computations.) A simple illustration would be to presume that failure follows a normal distribution, and ten out of 100 parts have failed after 50,000 on/off cycles. The analyst's job is then to infer what the true mean and standard deviation is for the entire population based on the data of the left tail of that distribution. But from the following diagram the reader should be able to see how hard it would be to estimate the true distribution from the available data (the dotted line is the *estimated* distribution—even if it isn't the correct one).

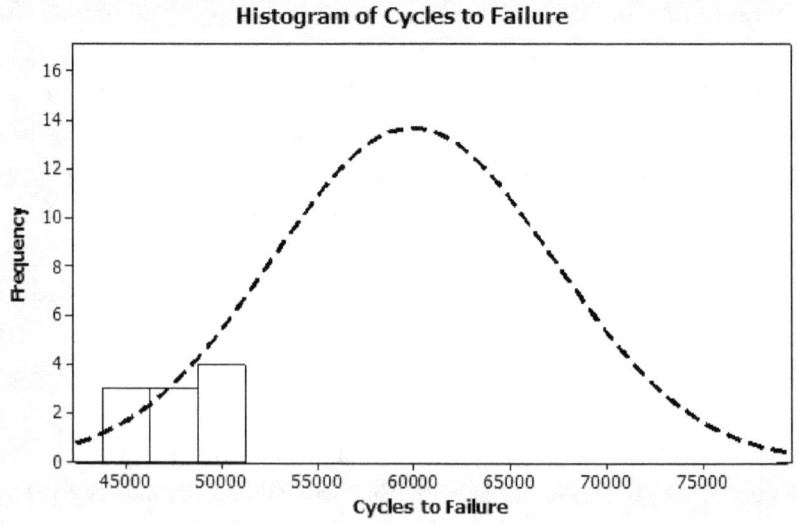

To complicate reliability predictions, failure under normal use might take so much time or so many cycles that it becomes totally impractical to test them. In these cases, "accelerated" testing takes place by performing the testing in an environment where failures are likely to occur faster. Such environments may include higher temperatures, higher operating voltages, corrosion inducing atmosphere (e.g. adding water vapor or SO_2), etc. The task of the analyst is then to estimate just how much these stressed conditions "accelerate" the time or number of cycles to failure. Fortunately, based on experience, there are many good models for estimating the effects of stress—as long as the stress isn't so extreme as to induce other types of failure (imagine, for example, plastic parts deforming because of increased temperature). Under the best of circumstances, these acceleration models have been verified through historical testing of similar product; in many more cases the acceleration model is an educated guess.

As the reader might surmise, reliability is usually a "black art." There are so many assumptions that might only be weakly supported by facts, and the conclusions drawn—even if valid—often have hugely wide confidence bounds. Here are the problems:

1. The identity of the underlying reliability distribution is often based on limited data. My experience and use of simulation has shown that it is usually impossible to tell, with confidence, what that distribution is without having many more failures than what can be had by practical testing. Here, having a history of failure of similar products greatly facilitates the choice of distribution.

2. Even if the reliability distribution is correctly identified (e.g. Weilbull or lognormal), the estimates of the parameters that define the shape and spread have wide confidence bounds on them. Furthermore, the fit to that data has its own random variability. All these result in significantly wide confidence bounds on the estimates of the left-most tail. In practice, some shape parameters are often defined to be integral, more for convenience than for theoretical reasons.

3. If doing accelerated testing, the accelerating function also needs to be estimated, which further adds to the widths of the confidence

bounds. And if the function might be incorrect, there is no way to factor in its deleterious effect on the estimates.
4. Point estimates are often created for the reliability at some predetermined time or number of cycles, but the confidence bounds seem never to be reported. In rare cases, the <u>best-case</u> confidence limit may be reported.

But even with all its faults, reliability estimation should be usually viewed as the "only game in town." That is, there are seldom better alternatives. Often, producers will conduct "ongoing reliability testing" or ORT. That is, they take a fairly large sample and test it for an extended period, such as a month to three months. As these reach their termination time (without failing), they are replaced with new units. This is often the best proof that can be offered to customers. However, some large customers demand even more stringent proof of reliability, even though quality is excellent. This can result in poor relationships and finger pointing, rather than discussing the facts regarding the limitations of testing.

Along with the reliability testing, an extremely important ancillary activity is failure analysis. When a unit fails, it behooves the producer to find out why. For the failure mode could be a manufacturing defect rather than a genuine reliability failure. Unfortunately, many units which may fail in the field and are returned seem to work fine when tested in the lab. There is no trouble found ("NTF"). This, of course, does not make estimating reliability any easier!

Finally, with reliability testing usually being too extreme, one alternative has arisen that can help make better estimates. This involves removing test units and measuring parameters that can predict failure. For example, by measuring the amount of wear after a certain time being used, an extrapolated failure time could be estimated. Companies with high-reliability products are now researching the failure modes to see what predictive parameters might exist for their product.

The Black Belt needs to recognize that the statistics of reliability is only one aspect that is important to making a reliable product. Good engineering should anticipate what can go wrong via a tool like FMEA. If, for example, contamination shortens life, then a reduction in that contamination using better filters or making the product more resistant to corrosion could result in longer life. In short, a good understanding of the physics involved in the failure can result in a better product far more effectively than performing better testing.

Binary Logistic Regression

In standard regression analysis, continuous and occasionally attribute variables are used to create a model that predicts the results of a continuous variable. With Binary Logistic Regression, a similarly constructed model predicts a continuously increasing or decreasing probability of a binary outcome. What is starkly different from standard regression is that the "y" variable for each individual observation is either just a "0" or a "1."

A couple simple examples should illustrate the principles. Suppose you are shooting a basketball toward the hoop ten times each from various distances. From 3 feet away you shoot all 10 shots into the hoop for a 100% performance. You move back 3 feet and shoot 10 more shots, but this time you miss one for a 90% success rate. You continue moving back 3 more feet and shooting 10 shots until you are at 51 feet and haven't made a basket in your last 40 shots (since being 39 feet away). From this data you could construct a model that predicts the probability of making a basket from any distance. This final function is S shaped, and is called either a *logistic* or *logit* function. This logit function restricts the probability values to be between 0 and 1 inclusive.

In the previous example, a fraction successful was generated for each distance, but Binary Logistic Regression doesn't require such summarized data. Instead, you as the shooter could have taken a first shot at 3 feet, but then moved back 2 inches for each successive shot, recording whether you were successful in making a basket or not. Binary Logistic Regression would still provide a model that predicts the probability of making a basket from any distance.

For more complicated cases involving multiple predictor variables a good analogy would be that the ordinary least squares regression model would predict an intermediate continuous variable; call it "W." Then W is related to the continuous binomial probability function in a way similar to that of the distance from the hoop relating to the probability of making a basket. The resulting logit function would look like the following:

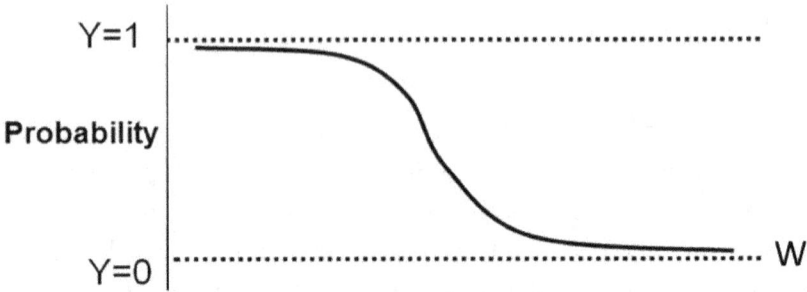

Software modeling allows for the creation of appropriate models. But just as with standard regression, there is uncertainty in the prediction coefficients, and it is considerably less clear how that uncertainty affects estimates of probability for any given set of observations. There is a whole set of different types of diagnostics and measures of goodness, which makes Logistic Regression a subject all to itself. It should be noted that since the predicted variable used in the analysis is binary, significantly less information results from a single data point compared to the continuous case. Thus, good models require a very large number of observations

What has been discussed has involved only the case of a binary output variable. But extensions of this tool can be used for cases where multiple discrete outcomes are possible.

Monte Carlo Simulation

Monte Carlo Simulation involves generating random numbers that belong to specific pre-chosen parent distributions. Then these numbers are usually combined using an estimated transfer function to see what the possible outcomes might be. By generating a very large number of random observations, it is hoped that the parent distributions, as well as all their possible combinations with other parent distributions are well represented. This simulation is usually performed when the final outcomes from the combination of the parent distributions cannot reasonably be estimated using statistical theory.

Of course, to be most effective, the researcher will need to have a basic idea of the equation that relates the input variable to the output variable. And with the choice of the input observations coming from the "known" distributions of the input variables, the investigator will be able to see what the possible distribution would be for the output variable.

A simple example would be to simulate the toss of two dice to see what their sum would be. (Of course, running through all combinations mathematically would be more accurate.) In a more complicated example, I might have a function $y = x1 + x2$, and both x1 and x2 follow relatively complicated distributions like the Chi-Square. In a practical case, I might want to know the upper 95% confidence bound of that sum for my known input distributions. By running 10,000 simulated pairs of x1 and x2, a reasonable estimate for that CI would involve sorting the resultant y values from lowest to highest, and observe what y value corresponds to the 9501th sum. Although there is some uncertainty in the CI, it would still be a pretty good estimate that would not be available using statistical theory. (One could also try to fit an empirical distribution to all the resultant data. If a good fit is found it would probably provide an even better estimate of the confidence bound.)

The technique itself is relatively easy, since most good statistical software is able to generate hundreds of thousands of random observations from a pre-chosen distribution. And even if there is limited data on the input variable(s) so that the distributions are not known, one can randomly choose from the actual (input) observations and mix them together. This technique is sometimes called the "bootstrap" method. Again, the usual hard part is having a good idea of what the transfer function is.

The proper use of Monte Carlo Simulation can help the Black Belt in two ways. First, it can provide an estimate of likely outcomes for a *conjectured* solution to a real problem. For example, the BB might suspect that certain KPIVs affect the KPOV. A simulation might provide evidence that the proposed model is incorrect based on real outputs. In this sense, the BB would be looking at a "what-if" scenario. Thus, if the BB wanted to test out the validity of orthogonal regression, he could artificially generate two data sets from "measurement systems" which measure the same parts with error. Then he can verify that the orthogonal regression method provides a better value for the relationship of correlation than ordinary least squares.

Second, it can provide a means to help determine appropriate specifications. The engineer can take the derived transfer function and use random values generated from the known manufacturing distributions of the KPIVs to see what kind of distribution will result for the KPOV. A modification of the specification limits for any of the KPIVs will result in a different KPOV distribution. From this, the engineer may be able to determine the most cost-effective approach to either the control of the KPIVs, or if it would be less expensive, to screen the KPOV.

A superior approach would be to use the Taguchi Loss Function Cost Ratio (τ), described in Chapter 6. Suppose there are n different KPIVs. It is not unreasonable to assume that good values for the target of each of the KPIVs, T1, T2, ... Tn, is known (if not, these can be adjusted later). The required sigmas, $\sigma1, \sigma2, ... \sigma n$, to reach an overall τ_{KPOV} equal to 1.00 still need to be established. Each KPIV will have its own τ value, $\tau_1, \tau_2, ... \tau_n$, which now can be weighted to achieve the overall τ_{KPOV} value:

$$\tau_{KPOV} = \overline{\tau} = \frac{W_1\tau_1 + W_2\tau_2 + ... + W_n\tau_n}{W_1 + W_2 + ... W_n}$$

Initial estimates will be based on known distributions and equal weighting. But through simulation, other scenarios can be generated, changing the present standard deviations to what will be required (σk) to achieve τ_{KPOV} equal to 1.00. Similarly, the weighting functions should be adjusted to reflect the actual impact any given KPIV may have on the KPOV. This procedure is not easy, but often it is far easier to try things out *in theory* than to make multiple physical test runs which might only yield partially useful results.

I have performed hundreds of Monte Carlo simulations to test out new theories, validate approaches, or estimate possible outcomes. But one problem I've often run into is that related to randomness! Any simulated distribution has its own probability of being very representative or not. When one takes smaller samples for simulation purposes, that probability of being non-representative increases, and often the expected result from theory does not agree well with any given simulation run. As a result, if a set of small sample size needs to be run (for example, to reflect what Manufacturing or Development is likely to provide), it is important to run hundreds, if not thousands of these sets before one arrives at any valid conclusion.

Time Series Analysis

The basic idea behind time series analysis is that if a process variable shows a repeated pattern (with variation) over time, it should be possible to mathematically extrapolate that pattern to future times. In its simplest form this technique differs from regression in that the finite pattern is overlaid on an increasing or decreasing line and repeated. The minimum requirement for analysis is to have data that represents at least two full cycles.

The most common application for time series analysis is in forecasting, and an obvious use might seem to involve weather forecasting assuming global warming: the summer and winter cycles would be overlaid on an ever increasing temperature line. For most Black Belts, however, there is rarely any process which is cyclic that also involves another variable which gradually raises or lowers the overall pattern.

During my teaching years there were three prospective Black Belts in my classes whose proposed projects involved the improvement of financial forecasting. During the initial project reviews of the first two I first considered the possibility that their projects might benefit from time series analysis, and I suggested that they retrieve past data to determine if any kind of pattern could be discerned. When they returned for the next project review, what they provided was nothing resembling a repeated pattern.

The fundamental problem with financial forecasting is that the past cannot predict the future over any longer periods of time. There are too many uncontrolled variables! Competition, terrorist attacks, recessions, sector bubbles, and rumors all can have major impacts on the finances of any given company, and they are not predictable. These two Black Belts continued on with their projects, and although I never saw their end results, I am sure that future forecasting wasn't substantially improved. When the third prospective Black Belt presented his initial project definition, I simple urged him to immediately find another project.

In twenty five years of statistical consulting in technology companies, I never encountered a problem where time series analysis could be used effectively. Realize that even if one has two decent cycles, there is still tremendous error in the extrapolation. And just as with regression where an excellent fit is required to obtain useful *interpolated* predictions, time series analysis rarely provides anything resembling an excellent fit, much less confidence that the pattern can be extrapolated. This is a tool that virtually every Black Belt should avoid.

As a side note, time series analysis doesn't seem to be working well for global warming predictions either. At this writing, virtually every eminent model has failed to accurately predict the temperatures we're presently experiencing.

Other Advanced Methods

Statistics provides even more methods that could be useful to a Black Belt under certain circumstances. Perhaps the broadest and most rewarding falls under the general name of "Data Mining." These techniques involve looking at and dissecting larger data sets to see what they may reveal. When looked at with the right tools, patterns will often emerge. These tools range from Exploratory Data Analysis (EDA) to Cluster Analysis and beyond. Many often involve complex computer algorithms which can search in billions of directions. The recent literature is filled with many new techniques and esoteric approaches. Unfortunately, these generally are more complicated and have less general use than what has been covered in this chapter.

The Black Belt should realize that most problems have multiple approaches. However, finding the absolute best solution may not be the optimal *practical* solution, for there are usually time and cost considerations which should affect how the BB arrives at a solution. Often, an improvement of 65% arrived at quickly is more cost effective than one of 85% that takes many months and deprives the BB of time to spend on other projects. But with an awareness of these advanced techniques, especially when learned and practiced, some Black Belts can achieve these higher levels of improvement without sacrificing significant project time.

REFERENCES

Bissel, A. F. (1990). "How Reliable is your Capability Index?" *Applied Statistics,* 39, #3.

Carr, W. E. (1985). "An Exciting Alternative to Fisher's Exact Test for Two Proportions." *Journal of Quality Technology,* 17, pp. 128-133.

Casagrande, J. T.; Pike, M. C.; and Smith, P. G. (1978). "An Improved Approximate Formula for Calculating Sample Sizes for Comparing Two Binomial Distributions." *Biometrics* 34, pp. 483-486.

Covey, Stephen, *The Seven Habits of Highly Effective People.* New York: Simon & Schuster Company, 1989.

Diamond, William J. *Practical Experiment Designs: for Engineers and Scientists.* John Wiley & Sons, 2001.

Dockendorf, Lyle (1992). "Choosing Appropriate Sample Subgroup Sizes for Control Charts." *Quality Progress,* 25, #10.

Duncan, A. J. (1986). *Quality Control and Industrial Statistics (Fifth Edition).* Homewood, Illinois, 1986.

Deming, W. E. *Statistical Adjustment of Data.* Dover Publications, 1943.

Goh, T.N. (1987). "A Control Chart for Very High Yield Processes." *Quality Assurance,* 13, #1.

Hahn, Gerald J. and Shapiro, Samuel S. *Statistical Models in Engineering.* John Wiley & Sons, 1967.

Mandel, John. "Fitting Straight Lines When Both Variables are Subject to Error." *Journal of Quality Technology*, 16, #1, 1984.

McLeod, A. I.; and Bellhouse, D. R. (1983). "A Convenient Algorithm for Drawing a Simple Random Sample." *Applied Statistics*, 32, #2.

Miller, Arthur F. and Mattson, Ralph. *The Truth About You.* Fleming H. Revell Company, 1977.

Montgomery, Douglas. *Design and Analysis of Experiments.* John Wiley & Sons, 1976.

Nelson, L. S. (1987). "Comparison of Poisson Means: the General Case." *Journal of Quality Technology*, 19.

Nelson, Lloyd S. (1984) "The Shewhart Control Chart—Tests for Special Causes." *Journal of Quality Technology.* 16, No. 4.

Newcombe, R. E. (1998). "Interval Estimation for the Difference between Independent Proportions: Comparison of Eleven Methods." *Statistics in Medicine* 17.

Patterson, Kerry; Grenny, Joseph; McMillan, Ron; and Switzler, Al. *Crucial Conversations.* McGraw-Hill Inc., 2002.

Ross, Phillip J. *Taguchi Techniques for Quality Engineering.* McGraw-Hill Inc., 1988.

Yang, Chung-How and Hillier, Frederick S. "Mean and Variance Control Chart Limits Based on a Small Number for Subgroups." *Journal of Quality Technology* (1970), 2, No. 1, pp. 9-16.

INDEX

Note: references to methods or procedures that are part of the standard Six Sigma body of knowledge are not listed in this Index. They can be found on pages 7-12.

α (alpha), see Risks, Type I and Type II
Acceptance sampling, see Sampling, acceptance
Accuracy, in MSA, 32
Aliasing (in DOE), 163
Analysis of Goodness (ANOG), 174ff
Analysis of means (ANOM), 38, 116ff, 132, 210
Analysis of variance (ANOVA), 36, 38ff
  for means, 111ff
  in experiments, 160, 174, 182
  in MSA, 38ff, 58ff
  in SPC, 199
Average outgoing quality (AOQ), 227
Average outgoing quality limit (AOQL), 227

β (beta), see Risks, Type I and Type II
Backwards elimination, 144

Bartlett's test, 117, 199
Batches
  considerations in experiments, 164ff
  considerations in SPC, 187ff, 202
  process analyses, 123ff, 218
Bayes Theorem, 93ff
Best subsets, 144ff
Binary logistic regression, 233ff
Binned Regression, 139ff
Binomial distribution, 104ff, 119, 2226, 233
Bissel, A.F., 104
Block designs, incomplete, 60ff

Carr, Wendell, 107
χ^2 (chi-square) distribution, 102, 107, 117ff, 235
Chi-square goodness of fit test, 117ff, 159ff
Cluster analysis, 221, 238

241

Collinearity, 145ff
Components of variance, see Variance components
Comprehensive gage study, 35ff, 59, 139
Confidence interval
   for Cpk, 103ff
   for means, 101
   for standard deviations, 34
      for gage standard deviations, 33, 37, 49, 56ff
Confirmation run, 180
Contingency standards, 201ff
Contingency table, 118
Control charts, 184ff
   for gages, 196ff
   batch-process, 187ff
   contrast R and s charts, 188
   Cusum, 205
   low occurrence attributes, 206
   normalized, 207
   Process, 203ff
   short run, 209ff
Cook's distance, 143
Correlation, 32
   coefficient, 63, 145
   tester, 40ff
   using in part dependent systematic measurement error, 53ff
   using orthogonal regression, 136ff
   versus regression, 46
Correlation, in MSA, 32, 40ff
Cost, 18, 68, 71, 101, 238
   Expected Values, 91
   metric, see Taguchi Loss Function cost metric
   sampling considerations, 189ff
   using Taguchi Loss Function, 76ff
Counts (see Rates)
C-p (Cp or Mallow's Cp), 143ff
Cpk, 68, 103ff
   and Tau, 85ff
   effect on misclassification, 49ff
Cpm, 87ff
Critical difference, see Difference, Critical
Critical thinking, 214ff
Crucial Conversations, 220
CTx, 18
Cumulative Sum charts (Cusum), 205

Data, 19ff
   observational, 136, 217
Defect definition, 16ff
Degrees of freedom
   for Poisson sample size, 107ff
   for standard deviations, 65
      in MSA, 29, 33ff, 47
      in ANOVA, 56ff, 60
      in chi-square test, 117ff
      in Experiments, 163, 169, 177
      in Means testing, 124ff
Deming, W.E., 41
Design of Experiments, 160ff
   for standard deviations, 176ff
Desirability function, 179
Destructive testing MSA, 55ff
Difference, Critical in means, 98ff, 126ff, 162

Difference, Critical in proportions, 105
Difference, Significant, 113, 118
Distribution, 20ff, 54, 207
   Binomial, 104, 226
   χ^2, 102, 107, 117ff
   F, 102
   Hypergeometric, 226
   identification, 20ff
   moments of, 21
   Non-central t, 103
   Non-normal, 70ff, 101
   Normal, 27, 227, 230
   of Means, 124
   outliers, 25ff, 83
   Poisson, 104, 107
   Reliability, 228ff
   t, 124
   uniform in MSA parts, 34
Distribution-free analysis, 76ff
Dot plot, 26
Double sampling, 225ff

Effects
   Fixed, 113
   Lack-of-fit, 137ff, 154
   Random, 117
Error
   Composite, 62ff
   Measurement, 29ff, 135ff, 150, 153ff
      Measurement, Part-Dependent Systematic, 51ff
   Repeatability, 37, 56ff
   Reproducibility, 37, 57ff
   Residual, 36, 37, 58ff, 113ff

EWMA charts, 205
Expected Values, 89, 91ff, 115, 120ff

F distribution, 102
F ratio, 177
F test for sigma experiments, 177ff
Factorial experiments, 59, 160ff
Family error rates, 112, 116
FET (see Fisher's exact test)
Fisher's exact test, 105
Fixed factors, 38, 58, 113ff
Forward selection, 144
Frequency, sampling for SPC, 189ff

Gage error (see also Measurement Systems Analysis), 29ff, 43, 52ff, 62ff, 136, 171, 196, 199
   Composite, 62ff
Gage studies (see Measurement Systems Analysis)
Gage study, comprehensive, 35ff, 59ff, 139
General linear models, 39, 114ff
GLM (see General linear models)
Goodness of fit test, 117ff, 158ff
Graeco-Latin square, 167ff

Hat matrix diagonal, 148
Homogeneity of variances, 135, 158, 217
Hypergeometric distribution, 226
Hyper-Graeco-Latin square, 168
Hypothesis testing

1- and 2-sample proportions and rates, 104ff
1- and 2-sample testing, 98ff
3 or more populations, 110ff
in Acceptance sampling, 224
in experiments, 162ff
in SPC, 187, 190ff
on Orthogonal regression slopes, 43ff
with batch processes, 124ff, 131ff
with statistical specifications, 72ff

Improvement targets, 69
Incomplete block designs, 60ff
Interval, confidence, see Confidence interval

Latin square, 166ff
Least squares means, 114, 169
Let's Make a Deal problem, 89
Levene's test, 101, 117
Linear regression, 141, 156
Linearity (in gages), 32, 34, 50ff, 56
Log(arithm) transformation, 152
Low-occurrence attribute charts, 206ff

Malcolm Baldrige Award, 186
Mallow's Cp, (or C-p), 143ff
Mandel, John, 42
Maximum likelihood estimation, 115, 177, 220
Mean time between failures (MTBF), 229
Means criteria, 74ff

Measurement error (see Error, Measurement)
Measurement Systems Analysis, 29ff (see also Gage error)
metrics, 33ff
misclassification, 36, 47ff
repeatability, 30ff, 37ff, 56ff, 169
reproducibility, 30ff, 35ff, 57ff, 169
Median, 23, 158
Median chart, 207
Mixed models in ANOVA, 115
Monte Carlo simulation, 57, 122, 234ff
Motivation, 219ff
MSA (see Measurement Systems Analysis)
MTBF, 229
Multicollinearity, 145ff, 157, 217
Multiple responses, optimizing, 178
Multiple variable regression, 140ff

No trouble found, (NTF), 232
Non-linear regression, 155
Non-normal distribution, 70ff, 101
Non-parametric statistics, 101, 117, 158ff
Normal approximation for Binomial, 106ff, 119
Normal approximation for Poisson, 108
Normal distribution, 20, 27, 70, 227, 230
censored reliability example, 230
in outlier tests, 27ff

Normal distribution probabilities by sigma, 27ff
Normality assumptions, 102, 112, 117, 135, 147, 158
Normalizing variables, 115, 146

Observed counts, 119ff
Ongoing reliability tests (ORT), 226, 232
Operating characteristic curve, 190, 224
Orthogonal regression, 41ff, 136ff
  in MSA studies, 51ff, 62
  use when error in predictors, 153ff
Outliers, 21, 25ff, 61, 83, 137, 147, 168
  using Tau, 83ff

Pareto analysis, 17
Parsimony, 143ff
Part-dependent systematic measurement error, 51ff
Partial least squares, 221
Plackett-Burman designs, 165ff
Poisson distribution, 104, 107
Power of test (see also Risks, Type II), 117, 118, 159, 190ff, 205
Precision, in MSA, 32
Pre-control charts, 203ff
PRESS statistic, 149
Principle components, 42, 221
Probability, 16, 18, 27, 63, 88ff, 104ff, 178, 233
Process control charts, 203ff

Project selection, 14ff
Proportions, 98, 103ff, 117ff, 132ff, 164, 188, 223
Proportions, Tests, 98, 103ff, 117ff, 160
P-values, 97, 99, 104, 112ff, 131, 145, 159, 178

Quadratic (behavior), 40, 141

R^2, 41ff, 136ff, 180
R^2-adj, 136ff
Random factors, 38, 113
Random numbers, 109ff 234
Rates, testing, 98, 103ff, 118, 164
Regression, 134ff
  Best subsets, 144
  Binned, 139ff
  error in predictor variables, 136ff, 153ff
  metrics 142ff
  Non-linear, 141, 155ff
  normalizing variables, 146
  Ordinary least squares, 40, 134, 141, 233, 235
  Orthogonal, see Orthogonal regression
  parsimony, 143
Reliability, 228ff
Repeatability, (see also MSA repeatability), 168
Repeats, 164, 176, 199
Replicates, 51, 116, 143, 163, 164, 176ff, 199

Representative (sample), 19ff, 38, 47, 98, 108, 217
Reproducibility, (see also MSA reproducibility), 169, 180
Residual analysis, 39, 50, 112, 135, 147ff, 152, 157
Residuals, standardized, 147
Residuals, studentized, 147
Risks, Type I and Type II, 72, 98
   in Acceptance Sampling, 224
   with batch processes, 127ff
   SPC, 190ff
RMSE (see Root mean square error)
Robustness, design for, 172
Rolled throughput yield (RTY), 25
Root mean square error, 136, 141ff, 170, 179ff

Sample (see Sampling, etc.)
Sample Size (see Sampling, etc. by topic)
Sample, random, 20, 34, 108ff, 223
Sample, stratified, 109
Sampling, 20ff, 101ff
   Acceptance, 72, 223ff
      double, 225
      sequential, 225
   by variables, 72ff, 227ff
   double, 225ff
   for batch means, 124ff
   for counts or rates, 107ff, 122
   for Experiments, 162, 176, 178, 182
   for means, 99, 102, 115
   for proportions, 105ff, 122
   for SPC, 187ff

for standard deviations, 102, 117
for hypothesis testing, 97ff
for regression, 44ff
frequency for SPC, 189, 194
risks, see Risks
rules of thumb, 23
unknown lot size, 108
Sequential probability ratio test, 226
Sequential sampling plan, 225
Shift, 1.5 sigma, 68ff
Short-run SPC, 209ff
Sign test (nonparametric), 159
Significance, practical, 161, 218
Significance, statistical, 39, 62, 111ff, 145, 166, 177, 180, 218
Sister parts, 55
Six Sigma, Operational, 8ff
Slope, effect on using OLS, 40ff, 136ff
Slope, orthogonal regression, 43
Slope, testing using orthogonal regression, 43ff
SPC (see Statistical process control)
SPC for gages, 196ff
SPC, short-run, 209ff
Specifications, problems with, 16ff, 34, 41, 47ff, 67ff, 77, 84
Specifications, statistical, 71ff
Stability, in gages, 33, 61ff, 201
Stability, process, 184, 203, 205, 210
Standard deviation testing, 24, 97ff, 101ff, 116, 176ff
Standard error, 124
   effect of multicollinearity, 145ff
   on Orthogonal regression slope, 44

Statistical process control (or SPC), 68, 116, 184ff
Statistical specifications, 69ff
Stepwise selection, 144
Subgroup size (in SPC), 189ff

t distribution, 124
Taguchi (experiment) designs, 182ff
Taguchi loss function, 75
Taguchi loss function cost ratio, 77ff, 205, 236
Tails criteria, 72ff
Team (members), 36, 215ff
Tests
   Proportions, 98, 104ff, 118ff, 164
   Rates, 98, 104ff, 119ff, 164

Standard deviations, 2, 98ff, 101ff, 117, 176ff
Time series analysis, 236ff
TLFCR (see Taguchi loss function cost ratio)
Tolerance intervals, 103ff
Transfer function, 140, 172, 179, 234
Transformations, 70, 152ff, 155, 207ff

Variance components, 37ff, 54, 61, 131, 169
Variance inflation factor, 145
Variance, analysis of, (see Analysis of variance)

Z score, 71, 83

www.ingramcontent.com/pod-product-compliance
Lightning Source LLC
LaVergne TN
LVHW010314070526
838199LV00065B/5557